Transition Year in Action

Gerry Jeffers

The Liffey Press

Published by
The Liffey Press Ltd
Raheny Shopping Centre, Second Floor
Raheny, Dublin 5, Ireland
www.theliffeypress.com

A catalogue record of this book is
available from the British Library.

ISBN 978-1-908308-76-4

For cover photographs, thanks to TY students in Firhouse
Community College, Dublin, in particular Jan Sanchez, Martha
Knight, Kimolo Ndee and Niamh Kedney, as well as to Principal
Mark McDonald and teacher Carmel Boyle.

Printed in Ireland by SprintPrint.

CONTENTS

Acknowlededements

The inspiration and co-operation of many people made this book possible. Firstly, to the students, teachers, co-ordinators, principals, parents, researchers and others who agreed to be interviewed or who contributed otherwise to this book, a sincere thank you. Thanks also to my students over many years whose engagement, responses, comments and questions shaped – and continue to shape – much of my educational thinking.

I have also been blessed through working with some wonderful colleagues. Teachers in Firhouse Community College in the 1980s, under Michael Geaney's leadership, took many educationally courageous decisions and it was my good fortune to be part of that team. In the 1990s, being part of the support services leading the mainstreaming of Transition Year brought me into contact with many creative colleagues including, Chris Connolly, Jim Byrne, Séamus Cannon, Bridie Corkery, Eileen Doyle, Mary Anne Halton, Phil Halpin. Eilis Humphreys, Mary Keane, Denise Kelly, Rachel Keogh, Ruth Marshall, Alec McAlister, Geraldine Mooney-Simmie, Karl O'Connell, Michael O'Leary, Lynda O'Toole, Billy Reidy, Dermot Quish, Patsy Sweeney, Margaret Wainwright, P.J. White, Maura Clancy and many others. That work also opened many doors into schools where principals, co-ordinators, teachers and students generously shared their experiences of TY. In Maynooth University's Education Department I was fortunate to work with imaginative colleagues in an atmosphere of enquiry and scholarship under the leadership of John Coolahan, Pádraig Hogan, Tom Collins, Aidan Mulkeen and, more recently, Rose Dolan and Sha-

vii

ron Todd. The critical support of Jim Gleeson of the University of Limerick has also been of immense value.

Margaret Cavanagh and Eilis Humphreys contributed many constructive comments to an earlier draft of the text and David Givens of The Liffey Press was at all times quietly efficient and affirming. Finally, thanks to my wife Winifred. I greatly value her incisive ability to balance challenge and encouragement, and for continuing to be a wonderful critical and supportive friend.

Gerry Jeffers
September 2015

Dedication

To Úna and Patrick

Abbreviations Used in Text

AFL – Assessment for Learning

ASD – Autism Spectrum Disorder

CAD – Computer Aided Design

CAO – Central Applications Office

CBS – Christian Brothers School

CEB – Curriculum and Exminations Board

CDPC – Combat Diseases of Poverty Consortium

CPD – Continuing Professional Development

CSPE – Civic, Social and Political Education

DE – Department of Education (1921–1997)

DEIS – Delivering Equality of Opportunity in Schools

DES – Department of Education and Science (1997–2010)
         Department of Education and Skills (from 2010)

EPA – Environmental Protection Agency

ERC – Education Research Centre

ESRI – Economic and Social Research Institute

FAI – Football Association of Ireland

GAA – Gaelic Athletic Association

GCSE – General Certificate of Secondary Education

ICT – Information and Communications Technology

IDEA – Irish Development Education Association

IRFU – Irish Rugby Football Union

ISSU – Irish Second-level Students Union

JC – Junior Cycle

JCSP – Junior Certificate School Programme

LC – Leaving Certificate (established)

LCA – Leaving Certificate Applied

LCVP – Leaving Certificate Vocational Programme

MDGs – Millennium Development Goals

NCAD – National College of Art and Design

NCCA – National Council for Curriculum and Assessment

NPCpp – National Parents Council, post-primary

NUIM – National University of Ireland Maynooth (now Maynooth University)

NYCI – National Youth Council of Ireland

PDST – Professional Development Service for Teachers

PISA – Programme for International Student Assessment

PME – Professional Masters of Education

RIAI – Royal Institute of the Architects of Ireland

SARI – Sport Against Racism Ireland

SDGs – Sustainable Development Goals

SDPI – School Development Planning Initiative

SEAI – Sustainable Energy Authority of Ireland

TUI – Teachers Union of Ireland

TY – Transition Year

TYP – Transition Year Programme

UCAS – Universities and Colleges Admissions Service

UCD – University College Dublin

UNCRC – United Nations Convention on the Rights of the Child

WSE – Whole School Evaluation

WWGS – WorldWise Global Schools

YSE – Young Scientist Exhibition

YSI – Young Social Innovators

INTRODUCTION

'You know, it will never catch on, this Transition Year thing.' The occasion was a workshop for more than 60 teachers in the school where they worked. It was the mid-1990s and the speaker, a teacher, looked approvingly at his colleagues as they nodded in support. 'Why do you think that?' asked my co-facilitator, Eilis Humphreys, gently. 'It's far too idealistic,' shot back the reply. 'And parents won't buy it,' he added confidently.

There were many occasions during the mainstreaming phase of the TY programme when members of the Transition Year Support Service – 14 seconded teachers – faced similar scepticism. And the sceptics had evidence on their side. Twenty years earlier, when the Minister for Education, Richard Burke, had first suggested TY, most schools politely ignored the idea. Initially, the media showed little enthusiasm for TY. An early Martyn Turner cartoon in *The Education Times* (1974) poked fun at the Minister's proposal. TY students mixing with workers on a building site were imagined adopting different philosophical positions. Characters saying, 'I dig Socrates' and 'I dig Plato' are juxtaposed with those saying, 'I dig holes in the ground' and 'I mix concrete therefore I am.' There is also a student saying, 'Sometimes I sits and thinks ... sometimes I just sits.' These jokey references capture well some of the ambition of the TY programme as well as legitimate concerns. Among the questions posed were, how can out-of-school learning be combined with serious reflections on life? And if students are given freedom to reflect, might they just waste the time?

1

Within the Department of Education, especially after Burke became a European Commissioner, there was little evidence of encouragement for schools to take up TY. For example, a *White Paper on Educational Development* in 1980 devoted a whole chapter to curriculum development without making any direct reference to the programme (DE, 1980).

TY *is* an idealistic project. From the outset it has been a fragile plant in the educational garden. It lives in continual danger of being colonised by more pragmatic values and impulses. At the same time, the TY story is one of a bright idea that, despite a hesitant start, has taken root in the system. In its 2004 *Brief Description of the Irish Education System*, the Department of Education and Science declared:

> Transition Year, which has been one of the major innovations in Irish education, is an option which is now firmly embedded in the system (DES, 2004).

TY aims, unashamedly, at providing 'a broad educational experience with a view to the attainment of increased maturity' (DE, 1993). It recognises that young people aged 15 to 16 need time, space and opportunities to move from a highly structured environment to one where they take greater responsibility for their own learning and decision-making.

The TY mission is stated as:

> To promote the personal, social, educational and vocational development of pupils and to prepare them for their role as autonomous, participative, and responsible members of society (ibid., p 4).

The 1993 *Guidelines*, updating those issued in 1986, proceed to articulate three interrelated aims that should permeate every TY programme:

> Education for maturity with the emphasis on personal development including social awareness and increased social competence.

The promotion of general, technical and academic skills with an emphasis on interdisciplinary and self-directed learning.

Education through experience of adult and working life as a basis for personal development and maturity (ibid., p 4).

Within this framework, each school is invited and empowered to shape its own TY programme. As the *Guidelines* state, 'Curriculum content is a matter for selection and adaptation by the individual school having regard to these guidelines, the requirements of pupils and the views of parents' (ibid, p. 5).

Perhaps most radically of all, the official guidelines, having set out this clear mission and aims for TY, proceed to state that, 'The aims and philosophy of Transition Year should permeate the entire school' (ibid, p. 4).

From the outset TY has been the site of continual struggle, between the mainstream and the margins, between pragmatism and idealism, between what's already established and innovation, between conformity and originality. Of course, every school needs routines, a certain compliance even; however, a persistent danger is that teachers, students and parents become socialised into comfort zones that ensure safety in tried and tested methods and mantras. TY challenges all that. It invites risk-taking. It eschews coasting. It values process over product. Part of TY's appeal is that it is counter-cultural. Young people often remark that, in TY, it is as if the script that operated in Junior Cycle has been torn up. They talk about teachers being liberated in TY.

At the heart of discussions, debates and arguments about TY lie important questions about adolescent development, about learning, about teaching and about schooling itself.

Practice

Perhaps inevitably in a media-driven, sound-bite culture, the parts of TY that attract public attention are often once-off, novel activities with various levels of educational relevance. Journalists' imaginations are fired by students from Ashton School in Cork travelling to Dublin with their garden for the Bloom Festival, or preparations in Belvedere College for an urban, roof top horti-cultural farm, both attractive examples of original thinking in TY. Popular culture is less good at capturing the nuances of changing educational practices within schools that nurture maturity.

TY creates spaces for young people to pursue interests, to immerse themselves in projects, to engage in new activities. Sometimes this results in spectacular achievements and at times uncomfortable questions for the wider society as young citizens become truly active. One case in point are the winners of the 2015 Young Scientist competition. Ian O'Sullivan and Eimear Murphy, TY students at Coláiste Treasa in Kanturk, County Cork, won the award with a project entitled 'Alcohol Consumption: Does the apple fall far from the tree?' They wanted to find out if teenagers' drinking habits were affected by their parents' alcohol consump-tion so they surveyed around 900 fifth and sixth year students in the Kanturk-Mallow area. They also surveyed the parents of 360 students, who agreed to reveal details about their own drinking habits and attitudes to alcohol. The judges recognised the value of the TY students' work for Irish society, including the shaping of family alcohol behaviour in a positive way.

Every school aspires to become the best possible for its cur-rent students. One purpose of this book is to capture glimpses of schools at their best, engaging in aspects of TY that realise the programme's idealistic vision. It aims to tell stories from the view-points of practitioners, in particular teachers and students, about how TY works in practice. The intention is that the contents will inform, even inspire, others to continue to devise and implement creative TY programmes that contribute to young people's holistic development. It also attempts to confront some of the issues facing the TY programme.

TY is not unlike a diamond: different facets sparkle in differ-ent ways. Subjects, modules, activities and informants have been selected in arbitrary, at times opportunistic, ways. In some cases I had first-hand experience of excellent practice, in other cases I de-pended on recommendations from trusted friends, colleagues and former students. I suspect that I could have approached dozens of different schools and got as many variations on the TY theme.

Indeed, there is such rich practice up and down the country that a second book could be filled with engaging accounts of facets of TY.

In the bigger picture of school change, TY often feels the squeeze, sandwiched as it is between the Junior Cycle and the Leaving Certificate programmes. However, while TY may be marginal it can, for individual teachers, represent real engagement with innovation, change and professional development and give them confidence, courage and greater competence to be creative in JC and LC classrooms. TY also fosters warmer and more mutually respectful relationships between students and their teachers, as well as among students themselves.

A central theme to emerge from this book is of teachers inventing, manufacturing, orchestrating and curating learning experiences – of teachers being good teachers.

Their inventiveness is often theatrical, designed to engage young people's imagination. The evidence also shows the value of cultures of co-operation where students' suggestions drive teachers to take risks. This harnessing of adolescent energies contrasts with cultures of control, compliance and conformity. The best practices in TY can be seen as examples of living out the spirit of the United Nations Convention on the Rights of the Child (UNCRC), where schools are sites where young people's rights, especially their rights to participation, are realised.

The challenge to re-imagine schools for the twenty-first century is daunting. TY can be seen as a step in that direction. Much school work can be driven by external motivation. Developing intrinsic motivation, assisting young people to discover the joys of learning, nurturing autonomy, mastery and purposefulness can be very demanding. TY offers an exciting case study of how much of this can be put into action.

Realising the potential of TY, or other innovative educational practices, requires imaginative leadership, at the centre and across the school. As Keith Leithwood and colleagues (2004) noted, successful leaders engage in three sets of core practices:

1. Setting directions – shared vision and group goals, high performance expectations

2. Developing people – individual support, intellectual/emotional stimulation, modelling

3. Redesigning the organisation – collaborative cultures and structures, building productive relations with parents and the community.

This book presents many concrete examples of such leadership in action by principals, TY co-ordinators, teachers and students.

One way of looking at this book is to liken it to an album of photographs. A series of snapshots of TY in action is presented. Some give a bird's-eye view, long shots if you like. Others are close-ups where the lens zooms in on individual classrooms. Sometimes a chapter looks like a collage, juxtaposing contrasting images. It does not claim to be a comprehensive account of over 600 TY programmes currently operating. Like photos from a memorable holiday, the images reveal key moments, but the reader needs to recognise that significant events may be absent. However, the overall intention, and one hopes, effect, is to illuminate the broad dimensions of TY programmes with a view to enriching practice.

SECOND-LEVEL STUDENTS' PERSPECTIVES

This conversation took place in Liberty Hall, Dublin where the headquarters of the Irish Second-level Students Union (ISSU) is based. Rob McDonnell is ISSU President and a sixth year student, Joanna Siewierska is Deputy President and also a sixth year student, Craig McHugh, a fifth year student is immediate Past President and Alexander Fogarty is a TY student. The interview took place on 18 June 2015, the day after both Rob and Joanna completed the Leaving Certification examination (in Communication and Design Graphics and Polish respectively). This is an edited version of the conversation.

Gerry: The ISSU conducted some research into Transition Year. What was the purpose of this research?

Rob: The Department (of Education and Skills) commissioned the report about TY in schools and they wanted student input and the ISSU was seen as the best group when we tendered for it. The Government wanted to reform a lot of things in the education system at the time. It was a review of TY. Some see it as a 'doss' year.

Craig: There was some controversy about TY at the time. There was even talk that Ruairí Quinn (Minister for Education and Skills, 2011-2014) was going to take it out completely.

Alexander: Actually, my school was invited to one of the reviews and I remember being at it. Some of the senior students were saying maybe TY is not so good but we, the younger ones, wanted to keep it, to experience it. Yes, there was controversy.

Gerry: So how did you go about it?

Rob: There was a survey and four regional events, one in Cork, one in Galway and two in Dublin, one for the city and one for Leinster. Each school's Student Council was asked to send two people to the event. So, we explored TY: What it it? What does it mean to you? What would you like to get from it?

Gerry: OK, what were the big findings?

Craig: It was very obvious that TY is massively underfunded. It's expensive for those who take it on. It's informal education and there is inequality of access. Those with the money can afford to do TY, they can afford an extra year in school. Those who can't afford it miss out. So that was a big finding, the expense and the knock-on effect that has.

Joanna: The research also showed that TY isn't the same as the Junior Cycle. There is much less structure. But they almost found it too loose. The fact that you can walk in to a classroom and the teacher says, 'What do you want to do?' is hard because, at that age, you don't know. At the beginning it is something exciting and new, especially if there is a trip or a musical coming up. But then you could have three months to do a project and you might do it the night before, so it can turn into wasted time.

Gerry: Was that a strong message from the research?

Joanna: Definitely and I was surprised that young people were given this great freedom and they asked for some structure. I think maybe we need some more structure, not for assessment, but as a better introduction to senior level, maybe more deadlines, more goals.

Craig: We also found that there is great variation in TY. So, in a town you might have one school here and down the road another school and two totally different TYs. It seems that, depending on what school you went to, or even which TY co-ordinator you had, dictated what kind of TY experience you got. It's more inequality in education; what happens in TY has a massive effect on the next two years, even the rest of your life.

Gerry: Should they be all the same?

Craig: No, I don't think they should be all the same but maybe more structure so there is a minimum standard of what's done in TY and what you get out of it.

Rob: On the inequality issue, TY is about trying out new things but some things are only offered to a certain number. Take the four of us. TY gave us the opportunity to get involved in the students' union so we love TY but that's just us. Other people like TY because they had the time to start new things, new interests, new hobbies and things and they discovered themselves and that's all great. But the majority of people at the session I facilitated were unhappy at how little their school offered them.

Joanna: It's not just what the school offers, it's also what the time allows you to do.

Alexander: So it comes down to the individual person. When I compare myself to my group of friends I was always doing something, maybe to do with ISSU or NYCI or these different organisations I got involved in, but not everyone was like that. I think it's to do with mindset, how you perceive TY. Some people go in and say, yes, I'm going to get the most out of this year. Others go in and say, ah sure it'll be grand, the teachers will sort me out.

Gerry: Can you tell me more about the events? Were you all at them?

Rob: No. A lot of the ISSU people from that time have gone on to college. I was at two of them.

Gerry: Were there noticeable regional variations?

Rob: I don't think the urban-rural difference was as obvious as the money one. In particular there was a big difference between south-side Dublin and inner city Dublin schools. The contrast there was 'we went on a skiing trip,' but others were doing nothing like that.

Alexander: I can relate to that. My cousin did TY in a private school on the south side of Dublin and I go to a public school outside Dublin. I would have loved to have done her TY. It was amazing. Her school set up an exchange in France or Spain for any students who weren't enjoying the year, so she managed to go to Spain for three months, a great opportunity, for half the price of going through an agency.

Gerry: But it sounds like you had a good TY?

Alexander: I had a great TY. I think it was me personally. I'm that kind of person who would always embrace things, make the most of opportunities, make the best of things. I'm told I'm quite a well spoken young person. I don't want to be cocky about it but I'm able to have a full-on discussion with a teacher, have the banter at the same time, have good craic. I also think you develop that better relationship with teachers in TY. That comes from the free flow, the conversations. It's not them saying, 'Here, learn this, learn that.' There's more talk.

Gerry: So, I'm hearing about inequality of costs and unevenness of programmes. But was the message from this research that TY is a good thing that might need a bit of tweaking or was the message something different?

Joanna: I think a majority would like to keep TY optional. A lot agreed it was beneficial but that not everyone wants to do it. There was also the point made earlier for more structure so that it's not all over the place. That would sort out some of the inequality.

Gerry: What about the argument that the people who might benefit most from TY don't realise that when they are 15, and don't choose it?

Joanna: I'm not sure if that came up in our report but I do think there is a need for a transition year after sixth year, before college, maybe a bit more than there is at 15. But that's another story.

Craig: Well, I think the idea of a year between junior cycle and senior cycle is about growing up. Part of growing up is about realising your potential, becoming a person who is proactive, can take initiative. Alex is a good example of that. He saw the free space and said, 'I'm going to use the space to do something.' But that comes down to the person. So, from my personal point of view, what needs to be put into the TY system is a structure that encourages proactivism. We need to make developing proactive students an integral part of the education system.

Gerry: Some people reading this might say, 'But we have a structure for TY.'

Craig: Structure isn't necessarily just subjects. It's also goals and achievements. It's not only about putting 22 people in a classroom and teaching them to be proactive; it's about putting them in situations where they have to be proactive. I think we need to take a lot of things from non-formal education and put them into classrooms. That's what we are missing out on in the other three and two years: aspects of non-formal education.

Rob: I know there is a timetable in TY with every subject under the sun and that's your base and on top of that you are let out of class to do other things. The people who love TY are those who love being out of class, not because they are dossers, but because they want to learn new things. But think about the ones who are stuck in a Physics or Chemistry classroom, with no intention of doing these subjects for Leaving Cert, and not doing what they thought they would be doing in TY. That's not good for motivation and motivation is important. To come back to something you asked earlier: work experience is something most schools do and (at the events) a lot of people in the countryside said how limited work experience is, especially if you are in a small town. You might be able to go to a factory if you are lucky, or a co-op, but in Dublin you hear about people going to Google or Microsoft. They are jobs for the future whereas in the town where I am people are getting work experience in supermarkets. Work experience is really important; you're talking with people and developing a lot of skills. That's another inequality.

Gerry: You say work experience is important. What other positives are there?

Craig: I think there are programmes out there, like mini-company, like YSI that promote exactly what you need to get out of TY but in many cases they are not taken up. You often have a choice like mini-company *or* YSI. We need more programmes like them. There's also the Formula One in schools, Young Scientist that sort of thing.

Rob: Junk Kouture.

Alexander: In my school it was a bit different. When we went in to the first science class in September, we were told, 'OK, we're all doing the Young Scientist. You all have to come up with an idea. You have to do it.' It was good because if they had said, 'Does anyone want to do it?' nobody would have done anything. Everybody would have said, 'No, I don't want to to that.' I think we got four really good projects out of the 70 of us.

Joanna: In my school we tried out the YSI programme and maybe because it's a smaller school or the teacher wasn't trained enough but that completely fell through. It turned out in the end that the musical was what really made the year for most students. We also did projects like Junk Kouture, Fighting Words and a few others. I like what you are saying about structure and being given a broader option of things, maximising a school's resources. I think it's good to put a bit of pressure on to try things. We found it very discouraging when our YSI project didn't work out.

Gerry: One of the dilemmas that arises relates to what we might call continuity subjects. Did that continuity dimension, what happens in TY and what happens in fifth and sixth year come up in the discussions?

Craig: Well, maybe if I make a comparable point. I experienced French in Junior Cycle, in TY and in fifth year now. The difference between Junior Cycle French and Leaving Cert is massive. I found the bridge didn't really exist in TY. It was a massive jump. In TY I enjoyed watching French movies and doing French projects but I didn't feel prepared for the big jump. Now I know that in the absence of TY you still have a big jump. Does TY have a role to play in building a bridge, connecting the two sides, or is it a separate thing altogether?

Joanna: Exactly. That did come up. OK there are some taster sessions for subjects and that's good but there are not adequate preparations for core subjects. For example, we were doing Project Maths for the Leaving Cert but we hadn't done it for the Junior Cert. TY was the perfect opportunity to introduce us to basic concepts for Project Maths. It didn't happen. So we went into fifth year not confident about Maths and we struggled. That could have been eased by a bridge.

Alexander: I had a great Maths teacher in TY. She said, from the get-go, look, we're not meant to start the (Leaving Cert) course but I'm going to get you ready for it.

Gerry: Were the people at the conversations mainly TY students?

Rob: Mainly senior cycle students. There were a few TY students and a few younger ones because we wanted to hear what they had to say before they did TY.

Gerry: Previous research has found people very enthusiastic at the end of TY but sometimes as the Leaving Cert pressure mounts wondering about the balance in the programme. It can be a bit contradictory. Did that come up?

Rob: Well, there's always going to be criticisms of the Leaving Cert.

Craig: This whole idea that they have 'wasted' a year, that they could have been out of school a year earlier, is a bit contradictory. Let's face it, in some cases they just dossed around for the year and then you have to ask, 'Did they doss around?' Maybe they actually learned something important. It's not just about educational maturity. It's about personal maturity. You grow up in TY.

Joanna: There were aspects of my TY that weren't successful, but there were some that were, like my involvement with ISSU. I continued my involvement with some organisations into fifth year. Some said, we're now in fifth year, the fun is over, put all that away. But I said that involvement with ISSU or SpunOut or politicians was among what I enjoyed most in TY. That motivated me to study because if I want to pursue a career in that direction, I am going to need high points (in the LC). But I didn't want to lose the motivation so I kept up activities that I began in TY. Yes, it did take some time away from my studies this year, organising things for the ISSU at weekends instead of doing Project Maths. Maybe it wasn't the smartest choice but I managed to keep a balance. Without TY I wouldn't have had that balance. I could have been killing myself with stress this year. But I didn't. I finished my exams yesterday and I'm okay. Up to Easter I was still balancing things, doing a little bit of this and a little bit of that. Since Easter I just focused on my studies.

Alexander: I'd say if you met any of us, say, in five years time, maybe when we had finished college or whatever, we'd say TY was the best decision we made because it helps through college and through life. At the same time, if you ask someone who didn't do TY, they are probably going to say, 'Maybe I should have done TY.' I can see friends now even in third year and they are saying, 'Wow, I wish I was going into TY' because they know it's straight into fifth year, straight into the same mode they are in now and they are not going to get that break. Okay, they will have the summer but they won't have that year to do what they want to experience.

Rob: On that, a lot of people I was with found it hard to get back into fifth year after TY. There was some resentment, 'Aw, why did I do that TY?' But it's coming back to what Joanna said there, people gain habits in TY, they develop interests but they are discouraged from keeping those up. TY is a great time for socialising, going out, making new friends. You can't do that as much in fifth year and, of course, TY gets the blame when asked, 'Why are you not doing well?' What the ISSU report found in 2013 was a lot of people saying, 'I enjoyed it but it ruined my study pattern, my ability to study.' So TY gets a lot of the blame as well. I don't think that's always fair. It's life. You have to learn from experience.

Craig: Alex talked there about a break. That's exactly what people need, away from the stress of exams and an opportunity to explore.

Gerry: I hear those issues relating to fifth year. I have heard teachers say that when teaching a class with a combination of students who have done TY and those who haven't, the TY ones are more focused, more mature.

Alexander: They have the motivation and they are a year older.

Joanna: It can be that, but it can also be that the very studious ones are the ones who do TY.

Gerry: As we come towards a close, I'd like to put a question: some people who might read this and ask, 'How typical are those four students from ISSU?' So, you have probably met this question before. How do you respond?

Craig: Yes, you can't criticise that question. Everyone who is involved in school student activism has this urge to change things. Maybe that's not typical of every 15, 16, 17 or 18 year old. But if I look back on my own TY, I did doss around but I also did get up and do stuff, some things which really changed my experiences of the world. Perhaps not every student gets to do that. Perhaps not every student wants that. I think we are four relatively proactive people, maybe not typical, but I do think there is a sense of proactivism by the end of TY.

Rob: We've also tried not just to give our own views but what came out of the research.

Gerry: To go back to the start: you were strong about inequality, about unevenness between schools and within schools, some mixed messages about structure. Is that a tension?

Alexander: It's not a tension. If a structure is not there, you're going to doss; if it is too much you will say, 'I don't want this.' Like, I had it just right. I had a good TY. I had an English teacher that gave me the right amount of freedom and the right amount of strictness as well. We were given projects on movies. We read a book that we all thought was terrible and we looked at the film and he let us do a project on it. We actually had to make a movie trailer for it. The balance was there.

Craig: Yes, and the inequality is not just about money, it's about educational inequality as well. To go back to those who don't do TY and to maybe fixing the bridge between junior cycle and senior cycle, those who do TY are better prepared for the Leaving Cert. You are creating this inequality. Maybe those who do it can afford it and come from backgrounds that encourage taking up TY.

Gerry: Joanna said, early on, that she thinks TY should be optional. Are you saying, Craig, that compulsory might be more desirable?

Craig: From my personal perspective, it would be a lot fairer to make it available to everyone. It's not necessarily that people don't choose to do TY, it's that they can't afford it.

Alexander: If the idea of the bridge was clearer maybe more would do it.

Joanna:Yes, it's money and it's basic insecurity as well. I was talking to someone who said, 'I don't want to do TY. I don't think you get enough lifeskills and I don't want to spend a year doing a musical.' She didn't feel she was going to gain enough from it. So, maybe bridging the academic a little bit better would be good, but not by doing exams. I also think it's important to address the issues brought up by students, and to give better choices within TY and, perhaps, more training up of the teachers.

Alexander: But you do nothing *but* lifeskills in TY.

Craig: What lifeskills do you get in first to third year, or in fifth and sixth year? You get to learn what it's like to work in the real world through work experience, through non-formal educational experiences. I'd also like to say I've done some international work on behalf of ISSU. TY is massively respected across the world. I heard that when there was talk about the Department of Education scrapping TY there was massive reaction against it across organisations and institutions. They were saying, essentially, 'TY is our baby. This is the kind of education that we need.' Compared to other countries, Irish education may seem very regressive. We have this massive contrast: five years of studying to a test that really doesn't exist anywhere else, and then TY, very radical to some, but I think it keeps us level with other education systems. Outside of TY, the education system in Ireland is simply not fair and it is stacked against students as well.

Gerry: Maybe we will leave it there. Thank you very much.

2

DEVELOPMENT EDUCATION
– CHANGING THE WORLD IN
TRANSITION YEAR

In April 2015, at 'The World We Want' gathering of 300 teenage campaigners in Dublin, Seán Sherlock, Minister for Development and Trade, presented the first ever Global Passport Awards to more than twenty schools. 'The Global Passport is a way to both document development education projects happening in schools, and acknowledge the quality of the work that is taking place on these issues in Irish classrooms,' according to Mary McCarthy of WorldWise Global Schools (WWGS). WWGS, an Irish Aid initiative, is a 'one-stop-shop' for all post-primary schools that want to engage in development education. Three schools achieved the Special Global Passport award for exceptional level of engagement with development education: two of them, coincidentally, named Coláiste Bhríde, one in Carnew, County Wicklow, the other in Clondalkin, Dublin. The third school was St Mary's Academy in Carlow.

A strong history

For more than a decade Coláiste Bhríde, Carnew, which serves south Wicklow, north Wexford and parts of County Carlow, has been at the cutting edge of development education initiatives. Teacher Eleanor Lee is pivotal to this, though she is keen to emphasise a 'whole school' approach and the various partnerships the school has built up. 'The simple answer to how we achieved our Special Global Passport is "partnership", says Eleanor. 'Some of these partnership journeys of collaboration have been incredible. And we couldn't have achieved this without the ongoing support of staff, students, parents, Linda our principal, and other key partners, she insists.

Three strong visual reminders of the school's global perspective greet the visitor. A Green Flag, the school's sixth – the theme is global citizenship – flutters proudly outside the entrance. Going through the front door one is struck by a large map of Africa, packed with photographs. This tells many stories about the school's involvement with a myriad of projects. Looking upwards, the visitor sees the flags of more than twenty countries. 'They represent the diversity of our inclusive school community, says Eleanor,

Principal Linda Dunne sees education for citizenship, global and local, as central to young people's school experience. 'TY is a great space for enabling young people discover their interests, possibilities and passions, says Linda. 'It's important to keep the programme fresh so we encourage teachers to innovate. Every year we try to add something new. We keep an eye on balancing academic and other initiatives, she adds. The conversation is peppered with references to Junk Kouture, Build a Bank, SAGE, coding, mini-company and work experience, but projects related to development education are a consistent strand in the school's TY experience. Like Eleanor, Linda also emphasises various partnerships with Coláiste Bhríde.

Wide range

To illustrate the range of 'dev ed'-related activities, Eleanor Lee offers a commentary on a colourful array of photographs. One is of students at the Climate Change Challenge weekend run by Trócaire. Another of a Fair Trade project. There are shots of a Student Council-run X Factor-type event at Christmas which raises funds for many of the projects. There are images of Carnew teachers who volunteered to work in developing countries, pictures of students and teachers in Uganda, in Kenya's Rift Valley, in Tanzania. 'That's the group who devised a charter as part of a gender equality project and presented it to some members of Dáil Éireann, adds

Eleanor pointing to another group. 'That initiative opened up a lot of avenues,' she adds. There are also some celebrity-type shots: with UN Secretary General Ban Ki-moon, with President Mary McAleese and with a variety of Irish politicians.

It is clear that Eleanor seizes every opportunity for her students to engage in serious conversations about their research with policymakers. The list of images continues: Concern debates, an organ donation project, a visit to a mosque, the aftermath of the Haiti earthquake, Young Scientist entries, Green schools, the National Youth Council consultation of Post 2015 priorities. 'Yes, a long history of dev-ed activities brought us to where we are today,' says Eleanor.

IDEA

The Irish Development Education Association (IDEA) uses a slogan that attempts to encapsulate how it sees development education: 'It's about solidarity, not pity. It's about development as a shared responsibility.' IDEA sees development education as:

> ... an educational process aimed at increasing awareness and understanding of the rapidly changing, interdependent and unequal world in which we live. It seeks to engage people in analysis, reflection and action for local and global citizenship and participation. It is about supporting people in understanding, and in acting to transform the social, cultural, political and economic structures which affect their lives and others at personal, community, national and international levels.[1]

'Development education,' according to *One World, One Future, Ireland's Policy for International Development* (2013), 'aims to deepen understanding, and encourage people towards taking action for a more just and equal world. It provides a unique opportunity for people in Ireland to reflect on their roles and responsibilities as global citizens.' This translates into practical support from Irish Aid for groups like IDEA, WorldWise Global Schools and the Ubuntu Network. Non-governmental organisations like

[1] The IDEA website is at www.ideaonline.ie.

Trócaire, Concern and others also co-operate with schools and teacher education institutions in providing development education.

Research on development education in Irish schools is limited, but consistently points to a strong sense of solidarity with people in poorer countries among teachers and students, although there are some striking ambiguities. For example, in *Development Education in Irish Post-primary Schools: Knowledge, Attitudes and Activism*, a team of researchers led by Jim Gleeson of the University of Limerick found 61 per cent of respondents stating that 'development education was either very important or as important as other subjects in the life of the school.' At the same time, '36 per cent did not identify development education as having any particular place in the life of the school.' The report (Gleeson et al , 2007) also found that over three-quarters of the school representatives felt that students should have exposure to development education issues at some stage during their second-level education. Almost half of them felt that development education should be a mandatory part of the students' experience right up to and including Leaving Certificate.

That research also concluded that the enthusiasm for dev-ed is often 'due to the voluntary efforts of individual proponents of the values of development education, rather than officially adopted school policies.' While Eleanor Lee in Coláiste Bhríde can undoubtedly be described as a 'dev-ed champion', she and Linda Dunne have worked hard to integrate dev-ed into school policies and practices. They return to the partnership idea, pointing to a recent CPD event for 18 teachers from five schools (Coláiste Bhríde, Creagh College, Gorey and three Carlow schools, St Mary's Academy, St Leo's and Presentation College).

Self-Help Africa

Eleanor explains how the school's engagement with development education grew from its relationship with Self-Help Africa (which merged with Gorta in 2014). 'A teacher in our school was related to one of the founders of the NGO,' she says. 'This led to staff and students travelling on study visits to African countries. When they got back they reported to staff and students. The focus was on awareness raising and understanding rather than on fundraising. Then, fortunately, Coláiste Bhríde was invited by St. Mary's Academy, Carlow to become involved in the "Development Issues Project" which organised workshops for students from other schools who were using the new resource and this really was a turning point,' explains Eleanor. 'Between 2007 and 2012 we must have participated in four or five workshops each year and they were incredibly useful,' she says. 'The course and project was initially developed by Joseph Clowry, St. Mary's Academy Carlow, Katrina Foley, St. Mary's CBS, Portlaoise and Patsy Toland of Self Help Africa. The NCCA validated resource *Development Issues, A Course for Transition Year* is of great practical benefit in the classroom. It had ready-made class plans and is full of good ideas. It was updated in 2015 and is available at the developmenteducation.ie website,' she adds. It is worth noting that Eleanor, Linda and Joe all identify those workshops as crucial in growing the 'dev-ed' culture that pervades Coláiste Bhríde.

Maynooth University

'Another very productive partnership has been with Maynooth University,' Eleanor continues. 'That began through the Combat Diseases of Poverty Consortium (CDPC). Joe Clowry, with whom we had worked previously, became Education Officer with CDPC in 2008. He led a brilliant outreach arm of that project and, over the following four years brought eleven different researchers from East Africa into our classrooms. That was very empowering. Then, as "dev-ed" spread throughout the school, students from Coláiste Bhríde were invited to play a role in the Development Education Week run in Maynooth for student teachers. We now work closely with Angela Rickard and her colleagues there. This is a great experience for our TY students, facilitating workshops on active learning for PME and Science Ed student teachers,' she says. 'The school's engagement with Maynooth has also led our students to demonstrating ICT applications for learning to student teachers.'

YSI

On the road to the Global Passport Award, there have been many milestone events. Eleanor remembers vividly when a student suggested a poverty week. 'The teenagers were very enthusiastic. They wanted to live in poverty for a week. At first they suggested pitching tents outside the Engineering room, washing in the river and so on,' she says. She listened and they talked about doing the week but living in their own homes and coming to school every day. She says that the students reported it as a powerful experience, so powerful that they developed a resource that any other school interested in engaging in a poverty week can use. The students had a keen awareness that they live in a world where millions live on scraps and go to sleep hungry most nights. 'Feeling hungry, dirty and lost was an effective way of learning about poverty and having your morale lowered,' said one. Another, Trudie, is quoted on the resource as saying: 'Tonight, I'll go to bed hungry, and I'll think about those who go to bed hungry every night of their lives, and tomorrow I'll do something to change that.'

That impulse to action is central to development education and Eleanor says that the Young Social Innovators (YSI) project provided her with a great structure with which to build dev-ed projects. 'I love the focus on student-led, action-based projects,' she says. Her students collaborated with their counterparts in St Peter's College, Dunboyne, County Meath and undertook a joint project on poverty. As well as the poverty week resource, the students produced a book *Twenty Fifteen: Thoughts and reflections on the first Millennium Development Goal – to eradicate poverty and hunger.* Contributions from Seamus Heaney, Anne Enright, Pauline McLynn, Hugo Hamilton, Sebastian Barry, Bernard McLaverty and Joseph O'Connor sit alongside those of the students. The students from the two schools were named 'Young Social Innovators of the Year 2009' for their joint project on poverty, 'The Butterfly Effect.'

The overall intention of YSI is that the young participants work in teams to effect change in relation to their chosen social issue at local, national or international community levels. They identify a

problem, carry out associated research meet with relevant people and organisations and come up with an innovative response.
The key elements of the programme include professional education and development of teachers, the provision of educational
resources, student project work and public presentations by students at Speak Out fora, culminating for many participants in a
Showcase and celebration of the young peoples' projects.

According to Rachel Collier, a co-founder of Young Social Innovators, YSI encourages, motivates and creates new opportunities for young people to actively participate in the world around
them. 'We try to engage young people wherever they are – in
schools, communities, youth organisations, in families, in or out of
work – and prepare them to fully take part in civic action whether
through volunteerism, community service, service-learning, citizenship education, social entrepreneurship and innovation,' she
adds. 'It's about changing the world for good. The YSI focus is on
empowering young people to use their own talents to be social
innovators. Through this they experience and develop their innate
sense of justice, responsibility and capacity to create a fairer, more
caring and equal society.'

Action focused

Eleanor's passion for dev-ed has been enabled and nurtured
through TY in particular. 'Most of my projects are hooked to the
MDGs (Millennium Development Goals). I find YSI is very visual.
The speak-outs are very vocal. Students from other schools get to
see what we are doing. All the time students are learning empathy,
responsibility, sustainability, citizenship. It's real education, exer-
cising our responsibility to look at injustices in the world with critical eyes and to realise that each person has a responsibility to address some of these issues.' She fondly recalls a comment made by
a student during the filming of *Development Education: A Chance
for Change.*[2] In the face of global injustices, he said, 'I'm not going
to sit around until I'm 50, like Bono, to do something about it.'

---

[2] This film can be viewed at www.ubuntu.ie under Teaching Resources,
Generic DE Resources.

Eleanor suggests that at ages 15 to 16, TY time, young people are not only very open to ideas about global citizenship but also to active learning methodologies. 'It's not about copy and biro,' she adds. 'We do walking debates, short or extended ones, and they are lovely platforms to show respect for other people's viewpoints and opinions.' With many projects she begins by engaging the students in drawing up a charter of good practice within the group. 'It empowers students to find their voice,' she says. 'I also try to carry this through in small things, for example getting a student to contact an NGO inviting them to our school. They experience being trusted. I also find that asking students for their opinions on topics like gender, conflict, climate change, HIV and Aids, organ transplants, food security, MDGs and fair trade is helpful.' She also talks enthusiastically about using photopacks.

Evolving projects

With a fixed curriculum one of the great occupational hazards is that when something works reasonably well, the temptation is to keep repeating it. TY is not immune to this danger. Each year Eleanor deliberately changes the focus of her development education work. 'Every year there are different projects,' she adds. She cites the example of a food security project that led students to create a vegetable garden. 'That year many students came from agricultural backgrounds so they thought it was an appealing idea,' expands Eleanor. 'So we got a piece of land, got the parents on board and in with the tractor. Then the snow came. It was on the ground for a week. We couldn't dig a spade into the frozen ground for a month. This sparked good discussions about many topics including climate justice, hunger and supermarkets. It also prompted us to be creative. We developed a courtyard space into an allotment-type garden. There was also a glasshouse. It became a fabulous oasis within the school. We called it the Garden of Eden with its lettuces, cabbages, carrots and other vegetables.'

Cross-curricular work

This project and many other examples in Carnew illustrate how development education can be cross-curricular. Eleanor recalls students being interviewed *as Gaeilge* about their project by TG4. The scientific dimensions were also strong. 'I remember marvelling one day at Dr Julie, a gynaecologist and paediatrician, quizzing the two project managers. Julie was from East Africa and was in Ireland researching with the Combat Diseases of Poverty Consotrium. These two 16 year olds engaged in a long discussion with her about project management and food security. I am sure it was a very positive experience for all concerned,' comments Eleanor. She adds that a recent survey of subject departments, conducted by students, provides further evidence of global citizenship as a cross-curricular theme in Coláiste Bhríde.

Whole school approach

Eleanor returns frequently to the idea of a whole school approach, imagining the school as a 'dev ed' school the way others might see themselves as rugby schools or music schools. She emphasises how, over the past few years, active methods have been integrated into many teachers' classroom practices She mentions 'Think, pair, share,' Round Robin, Wait time, placemats, graphic organisers. She describes the Super Hero game where students identify their own talents in groups. Then, on a poster page, they design a superhero character and give the character a name. Powerfully, the drawing and artwork has to illustrate the talents of each student from the group, like Captain Planet, who is going to save the planet with his dancing shoes or whatever. 'You tap into their energies and interests,' she continues. 'I often pose the question, "OK guys, how are we going to change the world?" Now, they don't have a great level of self-confidence starting off, but they do have the skills and talents that they can bring to the group, and to see them move on from this is very nurturing.'

'Then, a few years ago, I went on a study trip to New Zealand and came back with more fresh ideas,' continues Eleanor. 'Now our classrooms are very much based on co-operative learning principles. Technology, especially iPads in classrooms, has been transformative. The virtual learning environment is great for scaffolding students and for developing our flipped classrooms.'

More recent partnerships

'Creating our Carlow/Carnew dev-ed network with four other schools has been very enriching for all of us,' says Eleanor of the initiative she took with Aileen Tennant and Joe Clowry. 'So has establishing the Ireland and Tanzania Secondary School Network, in partnership with Young Scientist Tanzania, and the Climate Justice Schools Programme. Through those programmes there are teacher exchanges between Irish teachers and our counterparts in Tanzania. That is a really strong form of CPD,' she says. 'I think all these partnerships have been very positive. It ensures we don't get complacent in our own little bubble.'

Looking back and forward

As a teacher of Home Economics in this school with over 850 students, Eleanor Lee says that facilitating development education has been a most rewarding experience. Eleanor is Programme Co-ordinator for TY and Leaving Certificate Applied. A core activity for Eleanor is the development education modules that are time-tabled for double class periods as an integral part of TY. She states: 'It's such a privilege to work with young people. They sometimes look at me suspiciously when I start by saying we are going to change the world. Later they realise, "wow, we actually have done something to make a difference". It gives me more enthusiasm and energy for teaching than I had when at started at 22 years of age, back in the last century.'

'Now that we are recognised as a Dev-Ed School, with our Special Global Passport, we have new responsibilities. There are many ways we can add metaphorical stamps to the passport which we have achieved,' she says. 'The emergence of the Sustainable Development Goals (SDGs) gives us all new challenges but also a framework for further action.' Eleanor leaves the final words to Anne-Marie, a TY student on the Dev-Ed committee: 'We didn't get a passport just to leave it on the shelf. We got it so we can go places. We love the quote from Anne Frank: How wonderful it is that nobody need wait a single moment before starting to improve the world. That's our goal and we will get there, one step at a time.'

3

Learning by Doing –
The Business of Mini-companies

'We wanted a simple idea, to produce something that was not too difficult to make,' says Transition Year student Tiernan, handing over a neatly crafted piece of oak that functions as an ingenious wine bottle holder. The base is cut precisely at a 45° angle and there is a small opening close to the top of the holder. Insert a bottle of wine and it remains in a horizontal position with the holder at 45°. These holders retail in shops in West Cork at €12.00 each.

Tiernan and TY classmates J.P. and Paddy, from Mount St Michael Secondary School, Rosscarbery, County Cork, might have called their creation 'balance and poise' but instead named their mini-company Fionnadhmaid. 'A mini-company is a simulation activity that mirrors setting up and operating a business,' explains Caroline McHale of the Professional Development Service for Teachers (PDST) and an enthusiastic advocate of enterprise education. 'Mini-company encourages students to use their initiative and creative talents to design, produce and market goods or services. In doing so, students gain insights into work environments, meeting deadlines, teamwork, resolving conflicts, enterprise and the commercial world,' she says.

'Mini-company' appears in a variety of ways on TY timetables and every year students come up with an impressive array of products and services. Occasionally, there are truly original ideas and, frequently, projects that include distinctly local features. For example, the Fionnadhmaid team imprints a range of customised markings on the oak, including placenames and an attractive

28

fuchsia image, echoing a popular sight on the summer hedgerows of West Cork. When we spoke the team had just received a fresh order for 100 holders from West Cork Distillery.

Their mini-company teacher, Sheila Jennings, is also the TY co-ordinator in Mount St Michael where TY is compulsory. 'Out of 78 students, 43 opted for mini-company this year,' explains Sheila. 'Initially, I present the background context for mini-companies – a world that values people who are adaptable, self-motivated, people with ideas as well as people skills, who can work as part of a team and can communicate what's important to them. We are fortunate in West Cork as there is a Leader enterprise competition for schools from Crosshaven to Castletownbere. We tell the students about it and also about the "Get up and Go" competition run by the PDST.' Mini-company takes place on Tuesday afternoons in the Rosscarbery school with a triple class of 120 minutes. 'At Christmas we run a trade fair in the school which TY students, teachers and others attend. Local entrepreneurs judge the trade fair and four mini-companies are selected to represent the school in the two competitions,' she adds.

In her experience of mini-company, Sheila says, 'the hardest part for the students is to come up with a good idea. I emphasise that it has to be their idea. I prompt them with questions. What are your interests? What problems associated with your sporting activities could you tackle? What in your life is expensive? What do you see when you look around the kitchen? What about the subjects you are studying? What would you like to get as a present? Did you see any smart ideas on your holidays? and so on.'

Tiernan says that the Fionnadhmaid idea was prompted by seeing something similar when abroad. As he explains their project, the interdisciplinary nature of many mini-companies becomes clearer. Fionnadhmaid involved the team applying skills they had learned in Mathematics, Business, Material Technology – Wood as well as in Art, Craft and Design.

Sheila Jennings prefers, initially, to let the students select a team that includes a balance of skills. 'Of course, I make sure that no one gets left out. From the outset students are learning about compromise, distribution of workload, acceptance of others.' She laughs, 'You know there's nearly always a falling out. I try not to interfere immediately. They have to learn to resolve difficulties. I remind them they have to be friends at the end of the year. No falling out!' Experience has taught Sheila, who is also a teacher of History and Geography, of the value of giving classroom time to practising making phone calls and checking on the contents of letters and e-mails. 'Getting money at the start is another issue,' she adds. 'These students have negotiated a loan from the school principal. They learn about who gets paid back first. They have also run pizza sales, cake sales,' she says. Elsewhere, other mini-companies issue shares to raise finance.

Sheila Jennings notices that when students get interested in a mini-company idea, 'they often put in a lot of extra time outside the three scheduled class periods. The Fionnadhmaid group, for example, did a lot of the work, including calling to local shops, all in their own time. As their interest grew, they became very absorbed in the project.' She pauses. 'They are very competitive as well,' she adds.

Educationally, mini-company is a superb example of 'learning by doing.' David Kolb (1984) sees experiential learning as a four component cyclical learning process. The process integrates experience, perception, cognition and behaviour. In TY activities like mini-company, work experience and other forms of active learning, reflecting on the action taken is key to the learning. Many young people respond very positively to the 'doing' phase of mini-company activity. Some shift naturally to the 'observing' stage when they reflect on things not going quite as planned or expected. Teachers often play an important role in getting students to the 'thinking' stage where more abstract conceptualisation takes place. Hence, in a mini-company context, students learn to make generalisations based on their specific experiences about, for example, raw materials, production processes, innovation, teamwork, deadlines and failure. Fourthly, the cycle moves to the 'planning' stage where a different reality is imagined. Some mini-company teachers say that the 'Do-observe-think-plan' cycle becomes a valuable life-skill perspective for their students.

In linking experience and education, mini-company also embodies a key idea in the thinking of John Dewey (1916). Dewey, frequently regarded as the pre-eminent educational theorist of the twentieth century, emphasised the need for schools and teachers to become intimately acquainted with the conditions of the local community. He believed that teachers should utilise physical, historical, economic, occupational and other features in the community as learning resources. Mini-company provides a great link between social situations outside the school and classroom realities. For some students, mini-company learning can make school more relevant and purposeful and strengthen their motivation for learning generally.

Star cooking

Clare Conneely's students in Ghairmscoil Mhuire, Athenry, County Galway are keen to emphasise the inclusion dimension of their mini-company project, Réalta le Chéile. 'It's not just a business,' explains TY student Clara, 'it's also about autism and trying to understand more about autism.' Clare, a teacher of business subjects who now heads up the dedicated autism unit in the school, says that as part of the social skills module in TY, small groups of students visit the unit. 'It's a form of reverse integration,' says Clare. 'One group of TY students, Sarah, Darren, Aine and Clara got on particularly well with the students in the unit, especially Aran who later took on the role of secretary in the mini-company team.' Clara continues, 'We wrote to friends and well known people asking them for recipes, then put them together in this book,' handing over the colourful book *Recipes from the Stars*. 'It contains recipes from over 50 stars in aid of autism.' Photographs of TV stars Graham Norton and Dáithí Ó Sé, chef Darina Allen, Miss World Rosanna Davidson and sports commentator Micheál O Muircheartaigh grace the cover. Inside, the recipes from these five are complemented by 45 tasty others. 'We were surprised and delighted that most of the people we contacted sent us a recipe,' remarks Clara.

Micheál O Muircheartaigh launched the book in the school in 2015, and proceeds go to the Galway Autism Partnership, the Irish Society for Autism and Autism Ireland. 'It was a good mini-company experience because the students got so involved,' comments Claire Coneely. 'As well as working in the timetabled classes, they stayed back after school. They set deadlines, they developed great self-belief as the project grew. They did so much work themselves. I was impressed with the confident way they were able to approach contributors, then go to the printers in Galway, negotiate with bookshops. I could see them becoming more decisive. They made the case for a room in the school and it became the nerve centre of their operations. Along the way, these students learned so much about autism through meeting their counterparts in the ASD unit and then the charities, all in a very natural way,' she adds.

According to Claire, 'I think mini-companies are a great feature of the TY programme. They demonstrate how learning by doing really works. In this project there was also a lot of fun and I think we underestimate the importance of fun in learning,' adding, 'Over the years I've also seen disagreements and rows and there can be great learning from that.'

Teacher, facilitator, prompter, adviser, observer

It is estimated that about 40 per cent of teachers who facilitate mini-companies are teachers of Business, many others having a background in practical subjects. The comprehensive TY mini-company pack, produced by the SLSS in 2004 (Ryan et al., 2004), sets out five roles for the teacher: teacher, facilitator, prompter, adviser and silent observer. Teacher Tara O'Loughlin in St Caimin's Community School, Shannon, County Clare, says that, from her experience, the mini-company teacher's goal should be to be on the lookout for 'the potential of all students to flourish.' 'You can never predict how personalities in a group will mix,' says Tara. 'Sometimes I wonder whether I should intervene but, generally, I try to let the groups sort out their difficulties. When you trust them, they usually come up with their own ideas, their own solutions,' she adds. Tara illustrates this through the example of Ace Devices, a mini-company that saw her students establishing a fully functioning e-commerce website, which they coded and built themselves. Mini-company HR manager Evan explains that their project arose from the realisation that about 70 per cent of mobile phone chargers break, sometimes after a few months, mainly just above where the cable joins the plug to the phone. 'We developed a simple protective device to protect the cable,' continues his classmate and mini-company managing director Aoibhe. 'It's simple and it works,' she says.

Tara remarks: 'Aoibhe's team of Evan, Cian, Cormac and another Cian had a strong background from the Junior Cycle in design, in technical knowledge, in business as well as in academic achievement. That was a very solid foundation.' The group paid detailed attention to designing their invention, built on their knowledge of 3D printing from Technical Graphics, and also sought legal advice on intellectual copyright. 'Yes, "patent pending" applies to our devices,' comments Aoibhe. 'That's important as we are now selling them worldwide through our website www.acedevices.ie.

Tara O'Loughlin has been facilitating TY enterprise education for more than a decade. 'Young people learn so much through mini-companies, from group dynamics to how enterprise works in practice,' she says. 'Mini-companies are great for building confidence, especially when students attend trade fairs and have to present themselves, be interviewed, answer questions about their product or service, in short, to really communicate.' Tara recalls that the Ace Devices group took lots of initiatives on their own, whereas with other groups, 'I might have to do a lot of the leading.' This observation underlines her point about knowing when to pitch in and when to hold back.

Caroline McHale values the 'can do' attitude that mini-companies engender. In her work supporting teachers and schools, she is keen to nurture an entrepreneurial culture across Irish classrooms. 'Entrepreneurship is more than just starting a business,' says Caroline. 'I believe that everyone has the ability to be innovative and I agree with Einstein who contended that imagination and creativity must be matched by the capacity to turn ideas into reality. Caroline sees mini-company in TY as a versatile vehicle to channel young people's creativity, passion and drive. It would appear that a TY programme without a mini-company might be missing some great learning experiences.

4

ENGAGING THROUGH COMMUNITY CARE

Located just south of Tallaght, to the west of exit 12 on the M50 motorway and beneath the notorious Hell Fire Club on Montpelier Hill, Firhouse Community College has been offering Transition Year since 1986. The school's 'community care' module illustrates how innovative and exciting learning opportunities can develop by linking with community organisations.

Each TY student spends a week on placement in a crèche, a hospital, a special school, a care home or other form of community service. Year-head Carmel Boyle recognises that some placements can be quite challenging. 'We try to prepare them beforehand. We have also discovered that often the real learning only emerges when they have an opportunity to reflect on their experiences in a structured de-briefing programme. We ask them to write about the experience and also make an oral presentation to their class-mates about it.'

Student views

A group of TY students volunteer to share some of their experiences. 'I was in a nursing home, and I didn't like it,' begins Jessica, frankly and forthrightly. 'My main task was to talk to the residents, twenty women with different needs and wants. This was difficult because some had physical and mental disabilities. Some thought they were children. Others thought I was one of their children. I have great admiration for the people who work there. I think you have to be a very strong person to do that kind of work. You also need a good sense of humour. The people working there always had a smile on their face while I was trying to hold back the tears. I like talking to my own grandparents but this was different. I hadn't met this level of disability before. In Transition Year you find out what your strengths are and I don't think mine is with older people. But I think it was a good experience for me, an eye-opener.'

Her classmate Alex was on placement in a training centre with teenagers who had intellectual disabilities. 'At first it was a bit awkward. I found some of them hard to understand. But after a day or two you'd be flying. It was all about communicating. Say you were doing gardening or cleaning up we'd all work together as a team, working well together, communicating,' he says. 'One of the things I learned was that, like everyone else, they have their own personalities, interests and hobbies. They just need more help because of their disabilities. We are all different anyway. We should see the person, not the disability.'

Another TY student, Jan, spent his placement in a special school for children with physical and learning disabilities. 'Many couldn't walk and most were in wheelchairs,' he remembers clearly. 'Communicating was hard. Few could talk properly. You had a sheet of pictures and you would ask them to choose "yes" or "no". We also learned how to use sign language,' he adds, then qualifying his statement, 'well, a bit of sign language.' He recognises that it was an unfamiliar environment and not getting verbal responses to simple questions was off-putting at first. 'But I liked it,' he insists, 'I learned that communication is not just about words. I am not sure if I would want to work in such an atmosphere, but it opened my eyes. It was tough seeing people who found it hard to walk, going to physiotherapy each day, wanting to walk in the park, but not being able to.' Jan also believes that 'Community Care changes you.' He states it like this: 'To be honest, beforehand I was wondering will I get paid. By the second day I didn't care about getting paid because I just wanted to talk to these guys. I'd like to meet and talk with them every week, to work there and to care for them. I just forgot about the money. Better to care for people then yourself. Happiness is found in others.'

Jan says that, in his opinion, community care placements may not suit everybody. 'Some people are not so comfortable with other people. They might prefer retail work or gaming. I think they are used to people helping them. Helping others is something different.' His classmate Van agrees. 'I even heard that some people skipped out for a half day because they didn't like it,' he says. 'I think that just looking at the career side is a bit narrow. These placements teach us a lot about the bigger society in which we live. They also help you become more independent,' he adds.

'My placement was with children up to 18 years of age who have profound mental disabilities,' explains Martha, also a TY student. 'You would go in and talk to them, read books to them, have conversations, even though most of them couldn't speak. They could make choices between two things by looking at them. Some could say yes or no. You could understand them even though it took a bit of time. Sometimes you'd have lunch with them and you would give them drinks and feed them. Afterwards they'd watch films or TV. They loved Barney and children's TV. Other days you'd go on walks with them. They were trying to get one of the girls to eat because she'd been having seizures. We went to a cafe. I got her to eat on the Friday. That was nice. We went to a garden centre. They love the garden centre, the colours, the atmosphere.' How difficult was this placement? Martha says she really liked it even though she accepts not everyone might enjoy a week there. Martha already had some experience of disability as she coaches a basketball team of children with special needs. 'On placement, these children had more severe disabilities but I could still communicate and I got to know them as real people,' she adds.

Van took his guitar on placement. He was in a hospital that provides on-going and respite care and rehabilitation to adults. 'The people there ranged from about 35 up to over 90 years of age,' he says. 'We did a lot of practical things. We helped them do exercise stretching, with checking blood pressure, with trips to the toilet, with dressing, with going to church, walks and, of course, at mealtimes. There was also a lot of fun, playing games like Bingo and Boxty. One 96 year old was brilliant at crosswords. We also sang for them. They loved the old songs from their time.

Some cried. Yes, I brought the guitar. I liked it and they liked it.'
Van agrees with his classmates that communication is central to
community care placements. 'The people in the hospital liked to
tell stories, especially about their childhood. It is really interesting
how different their lives were compared to ours today. One person
was afraid to use a shower,' he recalls. Van, whose parents came to
Ireland from the Philippines, also says that a placement in a hospital shows a good range of careers: doctor, nurse, care worker. 'In
each case you need a lot of patience,' he observes.

Teacher perspectives

A distinct module on community care arose from teachers' observations about work experience placements. During de-briefing
sessions, they noticed that many students responded particularly
well to workplaces that had a community service dimension. So,
they decided that all students should have an opportunity to engage
in a community care placement as well as a work experience one.
Chaplain Anne Daly has played a central role in the development
of a distinct community care module in Firhouse Community College for over a decade. 'Eileen Murphy, who was TY co-ordinator
for many years, established very good relationships between the
school and a range of providers. I think what has worked well for
us is that when students are on placement we visit them to monitor what is going on. That means we know the people in the various places. If a difficulty arises they get in touch. This was built up
by going around during the placements weeks and talking with the
providers. I think it helps that they know I act as community care
co-ordinator so it's not a vague thing like we better contact the
school,' explains Anne. She also adds that it is important that the
school personnel be confident about the providers and how they
respect the people who avail of their services.

The school has also learned that, for the module to work well,
careful planning starts in June before TY has even begun. Students
are asked to indicate broad preferences for placements – work with
older people, with children, with people with disabilities. 'When
they have some input into the placement, I think they are more
committed to it,' suggests Anne. The TY cohort of 103 students is

divided into three groups. Everyone does one week of community care and two weeks of work experience. The students arrange their own work experience placements while the school manages the community care placements with about 25 different providers. As chaplain, Anne has a timetable flexibility that enables her to visit the community care providers. 'It's also about personality,' interjects Carmel Boyle. 'Anne is very well suited to both relating to the providers but also to preparing the students in advance of the placement and then in de-briefing afterwards. I don't think it's a job everyone could do.'

'As the year goes on and we get to know their personalities we are more confident about matching particular students to particular placements,' Carmel continues. 'For example, there are different challenges working in a nursing home compared to being in a special school,' and she adds, 'maturity can be an issue and we have to be fair to the people in the various placement locations as well as to the students.'

'You ask what we are trying to achieve? In the module I think we succeed in giving all students a unique experience that they are unlikely to get otherwise,' explains Anne. 'They meet people whom very few would normally encounter in everyday life. In some cases they see people with severe levels of disability and hardship up close. From what we have seen over the years this has a profound effect on TY students. For example, many say they no longer see the disability, they see the person. Perhaps most of all I think they develop empathy. They see things more from the other person's point of view. They also see things from the provider's perspective. In the de-briefing we ask them how they would feel about working where they have been on placement. While a few say yes, those who say no usually add that they still value the experience. Then during fifth and sixth year when students talk about TY, community care is frequently referenced, invariably as an experience they greatly appreciate.'

'Some providers are quite smart in how they use the Firhouse TY students on placement, for example in taking people on trips away from the institution,' adds Carmel. 'The students realise this and it underlines the two-way, give and take aspect of community care. We don't see very much of that with work experience.'

Listening to the students and teachers in Firhouse Community College discussing 'community care' resonates with the work of Nel Noddings, of Stanford University who writes persuasively about *The Challenge to Care in Schools, An Alternative Approach to Education* (Noddings, 2005). Noddings, a former high school Maths teacher, influenced particularly by the work of John Dewey, believes that the traditional organisation of schooling is intellectually and morally inadequate for contemporary society. She argues that education should be organised around themes of care rather than the traditional disciplines:

> All students should be engaged in a general education that guides them in caring for self, intimate others, global others, plants, animals and the environment, the human-made world, and ideas. Moral life so defined should be frankly embraced as the main goal of education. Such an aim does not work against intellectual development or academic achievement. On the contrary, it supplies a firm foundation for both (ibid. p. 173).

In big picture terms, a community care module in TY can be a step towards realising Noddings' vision.

At the practical level, both Carmel and Anne highlight preparation beforehand and de-briefing afterwards as key ingredients of the community care module. 'Some of the language associated with many aspects of community care is outside what they are used to,' observes Carmel. 'Some of it is laden with particular meanings and connotations. There are a lot of emotions involved. Students often say they are not sure of the appropriate terminology to use. Through the module they become more sensitive to how we talk about people. It's good at sensitising them to diversity,' she says. Allocating time and a safe space for students to talk about what they experienced reinforces the importance of language, sensitivity and empathy. 'I also think it underlines how seriously the school regards this part of TY,' says Carmel.

Prior to the placements, Anne speaks to the students about the spirit of volunteering. From the student interviews, it was clear that this was quite memorable. 'I begin by explaining that they won't be paid in cash for their community care work but that they will be re-paid a hundredfold. I also tell them about volunteering in my own life, what I have got from working for little or no money. I also talk about being able to volunteer anywhere in the world. I give examples of organisations that need volunteers. I emphasise how much of an opportunity it is to go on a community care placement, how important it is for them to be open to new experiences and that they may be surprised by what they will learn.'

If TY as an innovation which questions traditional conceptualisations of schooling is challenging, it is especially evident in a module like community care. 'Eileen Murphy and myself have often discussed and reflected on this part of TY,' remarks Anne. 'Some students find it very difficult and without a support structure are unlikely to engage. Initially, some are even reluctant to travel out of the local area. So, we work on getting a balance between invitation, push and support. Sometimes after the first day, some come to us saying they don't want to continue. We encourage them to hang in there. There are times when we have to explain the purpose of the placement to parents. Because a community care placement was not part of their own school experience, some parents don't immediately value it. We have to build trust. This takes time,' says Anne.

Carmel also notes that, 'What we also see is that two students can go to the same placement location and have very different experiences. I had a conversation with a student last week about going to a Women's Refuge. I think much of the significance of it went over her head. Yet, another student who was there talked about it with very differently It had been a very enriching experience for her. So, we guide their reflection to assist them to probe the experiences, to ask questions about the placements and about themselves. We also take that approach to de-briefing in work experience. It is very effective.'

'For a school starting out I would say the first thing to recognise is that this is not easy,' says Anne. 'You have to look around and see what's available nearby and how far you can reasonably ask students to travel. Then you have to work on building relationships with providers, explaining what you are trying to do and listening to their concerns. This is best done face-to-face. You also have to work closely with the students, encouraging the shy, nervous and reluctant ones. It is also important that on the first day someone sits down with the student and gives them a proper introduction to the placement – purposes, procedures, rules, safety issues, practical suggestions, what to do in an emergency and so on. We've also learned that a block placement of a week is preferable to the one-day-a-week model. I remember one of the staff in a facility telling me very clearly how limited this can be. For example, if a student goes there every Tuesday, the way these services are organised, they will be doing the same thing – maybe crafts, or gardening, of whatever – every Tuesday. But in the course of a week they get to experience the full range of activities. I also think the students get more out of the block, moving from initial awkwardness to immersion to real engagement. We notice that quite a few of them continue to volunteer in these centres after the placement and that's a very encouraging sign,' she concludes.

The original vision for TY

In 1974, the education minister who introduced TY, Richard Burke TD, summed up the kernel of his innovation as follows:

> Because of the growing pressures on students for high grades and competitive success, educational systems are becoming, increasingly, academic tread-mills. Increasingly, too, because of these pressures the school is losing contact with life outside and the student has little or no opportunity 'to stand and stare', to discover the kind of person he (sic) is, the kind of society he will be living in and, in due course, contributing to, its shortcomings and its good points. The suggestion was made that perhaps somewhere in the middle of the course we might stop the treadmill and release the students from the educational pressures for one year so that they could devote time to personal development and community service (Burke, 1974).

Despite its centrality to the original conceptualisation of TY and the presentation of work experience and community service in the official guidelines for schools, not all schools offer a specific community care type module in their TY programme. Many argue that community engagement takes place through work experience, particular when students go on placement to locations such as hospitals, crèches, community centres and care homes. 'In Firhouse Community College we find that making it clear that work experience and community care placements are different and distinct sends an important message to the students,' says Carmel Boyle. The community care module reminds students that not all work is driven by a profit motive. It can give them fresh insights into the needs of society's more vulnerable people. In a co-educational context, it highlights an important value, that care-givng and empathy are important for both boys and girls. Community focused placements can sometimes confirm a person's inclination to study subjects at third-level that don't have an immediate connection with specific school subjects. These include sociology, politics, anthropology, childcare, education, physiotherapy, psychology and applied social studies. Engaging in community care at school can also open possibilities for volunteering in adult life. 'As well as making a positive contribution to the community, volunteering can also enrich the individual's life,' adds Carmel. She says the school is keen to let young people know that while jobs are important, it would be a great mistake to define people by their occupations. 'A life is much more than a career,' she adds.

Nel Noddings is especially eloquent on how care in education is best nurtured through relationships. She writes:

> There is no recipe-like method for establishing relations of trust and care. Those who would care must attend to the other, must feel that surge of energy flowing towards the other's needs and projects. Caring is a capacity (or set of capacities) that requires cultivation. It requires time (Noddings, 2005. p 114).

5

Personal and Social Development through Work Experience

Principal John O'Connor reckons that Coláiste na Sceilge must be one of the most geographically isolated second-level schools in Ireland. Now part of Kerry ETB, the school in Cahirciveen emerged from the amalgamation in the 1990s of four schools on the Iveragh peninsula. 'Getting work experience placements for more than 60 Transition Year students every year is a big challenge,' says John. However, through a combination of imagination, ingenuity and tapping into a wide network, all get placements. 'It might be through an aunt in Galway or an uncle in Dublin but everyone is accommodated,' explains John. 'We try to get meaningful placements, ones where the students learn something new that they might not get at school.' John himself has a particular interest in employment related to the tourist industry. 'We have to offer more options than emigration,' he says. 'I like to think of our past-students maybe going away from Kerry for some years, developing skills that can be applied to local tourism and then re-settling here. Work experience placements can begin to open up those conversations,' he says.

Programme co-ordinator in Coláiste na Sceilge Bríd Collison adds, 'Work experience gives a real chance to try things out. Will they still want to be a Veterinary Nurse once they have finished? Physiotherapy, they discover, is mainly about working with older people and not a football star in sight. Then, of course, there are those who hit the jackpot and would love to manage a small business like Skellig Chocolates.' Bríd continues, 'In work experience, all the things that we stress in school are on show: courtesy, assertiveness, punctuality and empathy. They have a say, meet new people who have no pre-conceptions about them and most will have an opportunity to work as part of a team. Invariably they love it.'

On the eastern side of the country, in one of the capital's burgeoning suburbs, Michael Stanley co-ordinates TY in Castleknock Community College. He's also year head to 120 TY students. 'Work experience takes place on two different weeks, one in November the other in March. But the process begins long before that,' explains Michael. 'Each of the four groups is timetabled for a weekly work preparation class so that orientation and de-briefing get careful attention. I would also talk about it at TY assemblies,' he says. The guidance counsellors also play a role in assisting students identify personal strengths and weaknesses. Students are encouraged to find their own placements. This works well and we like it when employers interview students for a placement. We know that sometimes parents make the arrangements. If that helps the important conversations between students and their parents about work, careers, further study and so on, that's good,' he adds. Michael notes that some students enquire about work experience dates as early as January in third year and start making arrangements. 'Most are very enthusiastic about this aspect of TY,' he says.

The weekly classes take the students through topics such as what's expected from an employee, workplace law, relationships with fellow-workers, superiors and the general public. 'When they go on placement, we give each student a pack that includes a letter from the school, insurance details and an employer assessment form,' says Michael. The form for employers invites them to rate the students as 'excellent,' 'good' or 'fair' under headings such as attendance, punctuality, dress code, relationships with other employees, dealings with the public, quality of work done, use of equipment, attention to health and safety issues. 'Importantly, we also leave room for a written comment,' he says.

When the TY students are on placement Michael makes contact with about one third of the employers each time by a combination of on-site visits and phone calls. 'That's an important relationship. Employers appreciate the contact and if there any issues we get to hear about them,' he says.

As in most schools, some students struggle to find placements. 'In such cases we have a fallback list of employers who have facilitated the school in the past. But we don't advertise this. I prefer students to find their own placements,' says Michael. Generally, he is satisfied that most students get 'worthwhile' placements. 'They tend to range over a broad canvas of careers and locations, from hospitals to Baldonnell Aerodrome, from RTÉ to veterinary surgeons, from newspapers to laboratories.'

Michael Stanley and his colleagues in Castleknock emphasise the importance of de-briefing and reflection in order to maximise the learning from placements. 'Within the wider TY context each student is given a booklet at the start of the year. They record and reflect on various experiences there. Every single document has to be signed by a parent. This encourages parents to discuss TY, especially work and careers, with their children,' he says.

Many purposes

Most schools present work experience as having multiple purposes. These include exposing young people to different environments with a view to enhancing career guidance, personal and social development, social awareness and developing specific skills related to job seeking. The TY guidelines situate placements in an even bigger educational context: learning outside the classroom. They state:

> It is intended that the Transition Year should create opportunities to vary the learning environment and to dispel the notion that learning is something that happens only, or even most effectively, within the classroom. One of the ways of doing this, and of providing an orientation towards the world of work, is to include a component of actual work experience (DE, 1993).

Research findings

Young people frequently identify a work experience placement as a highlight of their TY journey. In *The Transition Year Programme: An Assessment*, Emer Smyth, Delma Byrne and Carmel Hannan observed that while preparation for the world of work is an explicit part of the TY mission, schools vary in their provision of career guidance:

> Work experience represents the main instrument for increasing career awareness with students taking part in work experience placements in almost all of the schools which provide Transition Year (Smyth et al, 2004, p. 224).

These researchers from the ESRI noted variation in duration, timing and structure. They draw attention to a distinction between placements involving 'career sampling' (students trying out job areas they might like to enter in the future) and those involving 'jobs' (where the placements resembled, or even overlapped with, part-time paid jobs outside school hours). They recommend that schools should encourage 'career sampling' and, critically, 'locate the work experience placement within a broader structured programme of preparation and evaluation' (ibid, p. 244).

Aidan Clerkin (2012) observes that early TY programme developers took the view that a practical taste of working life was necessary to allow students to contextualise and put into practice what they were learning in class, quoting the work of John Harris, former principal of Newpark Comprehensive School in Dublin, the first school in Ireland to make TY compulsory. Clerkin, a researcher based in the Educational Research Centre, Drumcondra, Dublin, also quotes Wyn (2009, p. 52) who comments, 'students preparing for life and work could do no better than to have the opportunity of working, within the structure of school, as a precursor to other world-based structures, such as they will later experience.'

'Putting this into practice,' Clerkin continues, 'the work experience component of Transition Year is intended to provide students with an understanding of the world of work, opportunities to take on responsibility, experience of working with adults, generalisable and self-management skills (e.g., time management), and social skills and awareness.' He quotes Kellaghan and Lewis (1991) who noted that the opportunity to be treated as a responsible adult is valued by students, with the social interactions of the workplace often regarded as more important than learning any particular job-specific skills. Students are encouraged to explore and test their assumptions about the job market as they gain a taste of the day-to-day tasks of a particular occupation, and for many students it is their first taste of the workplace.

Clerkin also states, 'nonetheless, traditional gender- and social class-based expectations are evident in the variety of workplaces chosen by students (Jeffers, 2012) with, for example, boys being more inclined to seek experience in the automotive industry and girls more likely to work in hair and beauty.' This study looked at questionnaire responses of 853 young people (359 boys and 494 girls) in 13 different schools who had engaged in work experience placements during the 2010-11 school year – 54 per cent were TY students, 30 per cent were following LCVP and 16 per cent LCA. A total of 90 per cent reported their placements as either 'beneficial' or 'very beneficial.' Among other notable findings were: (1) a bias towards traditional occupations; (2) relatively few placements in pharmaceutical companies or Information Technology-related industries; (3) strong differences along gender lines; (4) students in the one school in the study that charges fees were more inclined to get placements with professionals and to travel away from home, sometimes abroad, for a placement. These findings suggest a need for schools to be more 'interventionist' when it comes to work experience, especially schools with sizeable numbers of educationally disadvantaged children.

Joe Moynihan, a former guidance counsellor and school principal, completed doctoral research in University College Cork in 2013. His focus was on the influence work experience has on subsequent subjects choices made by students along with the effects of that experience on the students' identities and emerging vocational identities. Joe says that 'the findings from the research show that work experience makes a significant contribution to the students' sense of agency in their own lives.' He adds that 'it facilitates the otherwise complex process of subject choice, motivates students to work harder in senior cycle, introduces them to the concepts of active, experience-based and self-directed learning, while boosting their self-confidence and nurturing the emergence of their personal and vocational identities.'

Joe Moynihan also looked at work experience from the perspectives of employers. In his study he found them to be co-operative and very willing to provide the schools with feedback on completion of the placement. He sets out 12 potential benefits to employers who provide placements. These include: influencing the quality of future employees by showcasing their field of work and increasing students' interest in such careers; facilitating the growth of a young person's aspirations and achievements; cost-neutral staff development including supervisory and management skills; recruitment of temporary or seasonal workers; raising an employer's profile in the community; reinforcing good health and safety practices among young people; gaining insights in young people and current educational practices; altruism – giving something back to the community.

In 2013, researchers Annelies Kamp at Dublin City University's School of Education Studies and Dorothy Black of the University of Ulster's School of Education completed a study looking at work experience in schools in the Republic of Ireland and in Northern Ireland. A particular interest was in how workplace learning by students was conceptualised by teachers. This study highlights a number of challenges. In the Republic of Ireland, teachers generally spoke about TY as the 'home' of workplace learning. Despite it being a component of the various LC programmes, interviews became a conversation about TY. There was a sense that this was 'the' opportunity where the benefits of workplace learning could be harnessed. Because of this, it was suggested that students in the Republic of Ireland were likely to be exposed to workplace learning initiatives at a younger age than their Northern Ireland counterparts.

The impact of the recent recession where many part-time jobs had evaporated heightened the importance of workplace learning provided by schools – for some students, this would be the only workplace experience they could indicate to a prospective employer. For those young people not intending – through choice or necessity – to progress to further or higher education this is especially important.

Kamp and Black's study also identified particular gaps between what teachers see as desirable and what happens in practice. For example, Annelies says:

> While many Transition Year co-ordinators and guidance counsellors were committed to the benefits of work experience and understood the complexity of appropriate preparation at all levels – teachers, students, parents, employers – we found that classroom teachers at times had not, or could not, imagine how they might connect the learning that happened in the classroom (by them or by their students) with what happened on a work experience placement.

The study quotes one respondent who, in answer to a question as to whether the kinds of insights gained by students in workplace learning informed other aspects of school, noted:

> It could have, but it didn't. The reality is ... they don't have much experience themselves in a workplace other than teaching and they are so focused on, 'what has that got to do with me? I am here to teach maths. So what? Johnny is in my maths class, he did his work experience. Good for him. But I am here to teach him maths. And I have a curriculum that has to be covered. I have papers that have to be corrected. There is an exam coming up in x amount of days. I'd love to hear about his work experience' is probably what they would say, 'however I just don't have time because if I am listening to Johnny's story I have thirty others who want me to listen to their story and there won't be one sum done in the room.' ... The syllabus and the curriculum is just crammed and there is so much stuff to get through and teachers are so focused on that. So in theory it would be brilliant if that feedback got back to everybody but the reality is that it doesn't. And the reality is that as TY coordinator I didn't have time to even ask teachers would they like to have got it because to get the amount done for TY

itself is a struggle (RoI interview) (Kamp and Black, 2013, p. 22).

Two other quotes further highlight the challenge of integrating work experience into regular classroom learning.

> The greatest limitation/barrier to workplace learning is the lack [of] understand[ing] of its importance. Some employers and educationalists feel workplace learning is some add on or bolt when in fact it is an essential part of the curriculum and the benefits it can bring to all are immense (NI survey) (Kamp and Black, 2013, p. 22).

> Some staff think that the week the pupils are out on work placement that all the knowledge they have gained in their subject area will drain out their ears and their grades will fall so sometimes you have to convince colleagues of the value of a placement (NI interview) (Kamp and Black, 2013, p. 23).

Annelies adds: 'One of our conclusions was that more capacity building at pre-service teacher education as well as continuing professional development should take place.'

Significantly, the Kamp and Black research also illustrates how austerity measures have impacted on practice. Annelies explains: 'The recession has resulted in less teachers, less time and less funding. Combine this with the persistence of narrow measure of school "success" and you get a limiting of possibilities.' For example, responsibilities for maximising the opportunities offered by work experience falls to particular individuals within school settings – usually TY coordinators, guidance counsellors or careers advisors. But in each case, their workloads have expanded. The research offered many insights into how even these expert practitioners were at times now limited to working with employers they'd always worked with who 'knew the ropes', with management and co-ordination being handled by letters, forms, reports and phone calls – 82.5 per cent of respondents indicated that 'lack of time to work with employers' was the biggest barrier to quality work experience. The authors argue that these are not the conditions for collaborative knowledge creation that would foster innovative educational practices to the benefit of students, schools and employers.

Evolving practices

As TY continues to develop, so do practices related to work experience placements. Some schools opt for a one day per week model. Anecdotal evidence suggests that this makes fewer demands on the school timetable but that students miss out on the focused, intense, concentrated experience of a full week in a different environment.

Many schools have developed very good protocols and documentation for work experience placements. Some make these available on their websites, occasionally accompanied by informative videos. Two of many sites worth visiting are Portmarnock Community School in County Dublin and Ashbourne Community School, County Meath.

Employers, sometimes in response to numerous and random requests, devise their own work placements schemes for TY students. For example, Intel in Leixlip, County Kildare, Annadale Technologies in Kerry, Microsoft, the Abbey Theatre, the Law Library (barristers), the Department of Foreign Affairs in Dublin and the Cork Electronics Industry Association have all developed TY-specific placement programmes. TY placements are also part of the 'Smart Futures' initiative to encourage careers related to STEM subjects.

Many hospitals also offered well-designed placements. For example, a goal of the programme offered to TY students by St Patrick's Mental Health Services in Dublin is 'that participants will return to their schools as ambassadors for mental wellbeing with enhanced awareness of mental health issues and how to facilitate help seeking behaviour.' The Royal College of Surgeons offer a 'MiniMed' programme for those considering careers in medicine. Universities are also increasingly offering week-long placements, especially in STEM subject departments, where students get to work alongside researchers and academics. Engineering Your Future, to cite one example, is a week long programme offered by the

Institutes of Technology in Cork, Dublin, Carlow, Tallaght, Waterford as well as UCD.

Of course, dedicated work experience placements offered on a particular week does not always fit in with a school's TY calendar. 'It can be a delicate balancing act,' admits Michael Stanley. 'Flexibility is a hallmark of TY but if you are out of school specialising in one activity you may be missing other important aspects of TY. We look at requests on an individual basis.'

Evolving practices like these also raise questions about who gets in and who gets left out. Some schemes operate a lottery. Some reserve places for TY students in DEIS schools.

Key questions

Ideally, a work experience placement should be part of a special, privileged process for each TY student when new horizons and opportunities are opened up, when expectations are challenged and interrupted and when the student's self-image and motivation is seriously re-configured. For this to happen, schools need to support students in finding appropriate placements, orientate them for their time out of the classroom, monitor the placements carefully and, critically engage in reflective de-briefing to maximise the learning. Schools also need to work in a more structured way with workplace supervisors, especially regarding de-briefing. Furthermore, relating TY work experience to the wider TY experiences inside and outside the classroom emerges as challenging.

Finally, John Dewey provides a sobering thought for all, especially TY co-ordinators, guidance counsellors and work experience organisers. He wrote:

> The belief that all genuine education comes about through experience does not mean that all experiences are genuinely or equally educative. Experience and education cannot be directly equated to each other. For some experiences are mis-educative. Any experience is mis-educative that has the effect of arresting or distorting the growth of further experience (Dewey, 1938).

6

HOW WILL THIS BE GOOD
FOR MY CHILD?

'My daughter went through Transition Year three years ago and I think she got great value from the year,' says Don Myers, President of the National Parent Council post-primary (NPCpp). 'The maturity and confidence she gained has made a huge difference to her future. We saw her grow in confidence and become better at expressing her views. Most striking was the development of an open communication style that had a positive impact on everyone around her,' he says.

Don believes TY 'prepares them well for life,' but also thinks that it 'most unfortunate that not all students who would like to participate in a TY programme can avail of it.' Don's comments echo many of the themes that have emerged from research into parents' views of TY. For example, Ian Murphy who worked in the Inspectorate of the Department of Education and Science in the later 1990s, following a long career in European Schools, conducted a survey of TY in 18 schools. Regarding parents, he wrote:

> Parents' attitudes to the Programme seem to undergo a significant transformation in the course of the year during which their children are doing TYP. Many of them are quite sceptical about the TYP before the year begins. By the end of the year they tend to be much more positive about its benefits. The change in traditional homework patterns and the perception of parents that the school's role should be exclusively academic are two of the factors contributing to some parents' prejudiced view of the TYP. The experi-

ence of seeing their children mature through their TYP experiences does much to alter their original perceptions. Needless to say, if pupils do not commit themselves to the TYP, and a number don't, their parents are quite justified in questioning its value for their children (Murphy, 1999).

Some years later, research commissioned by the DES that looked at TY in six schools, noted that:

Interviews with parents in Maple School and Oak School revealed that, while relatively comfortable when talking about their own sons' and daughters' experiences of TY, they seemed reluctant to venture far beyond this. In each school, parents identified TY very closely with the co-ordinator, speaking in warm, appreciative terms about these two teachers in particular. Parents highlighted the variety of learning situations outside the classroom – trips, musicals, fund-raising projects etc. – as valuable opportunities that enabled their children to relate to each other and to their teachers in more varied ways than within conventional classrooms.

That report went on to contrast parents' views with those of teachers:

Parents frequently stated that their knowledge of TY was limited. They would welcome opportunities to hear more about it. Parents' stated desire for more knowledge about TY contrasts with teachers' perceptions, as a majority of teachers believe that parents are well informed about TY.

Two particular concerns emerged:

While generally positive about TY's contribution to their children's development, parents voiced concern about two possible negative outcomes. Firstly, there was apprehension that TY could drift from 'an academic focus.' Secondly, some parents expressed concern that, having undertaken a TY, a student might leave school before completing the LC. In Oak School, parents expressed some frustration, contrasting what they saw as a most worthwhile TY for their daughters with ones of a poorer quality for their sons (Jeffers, 2007, p. 5).

Subsequent to that study, I commented in the *Irish Independent* (2008):

> Parents' understanding of schooling is shaped strongly by their own schooldays. For many, Transition Year is something new. One finding from research that I undertook for the Department of Education and Science, published last year, is that many parents tend to be open to the idea but need to know more about it.

Parents want schools to inform them and to engage with them about Transition Year: the programme; the thinking behind the various modules; the relationship with the Leaving Certificate.

Furthermore, at parents' meetings it is often presentations by young people recounting their experiences of Transition Year that really help parents understand the programme's aims.

The evidence also points to many parents becoming convinced of the value of Transition Year when they see its effects on their own sons and daughters. Parents warm to their children's new found confidence, fresh excitement in learning, the discovery of hidden talents, enthusiastic responses to new opportunities. They also appreciate what terms like 'independent-learner', 'decision-making skills' and 'more democratic classrooms' mean in practice. (Jeffers, 2008b)

That *Irish Independent* article concluded by suggesting that schools might 'be more forthright in talking with parents about Transition Year, its rationale, its ambition, and about the purposes of schooling.'

National Parents Council, post-primary

As Don Myers sees it, 'the recognition of TY programmes by parents over the last number of years has grown immensely. Parents now appreciate that TY helps students to develop and prepare them for the ever modernising world and that the experience and knowledge gained through this will stand positively in their favour.'

He points to the National Parents Council, post-primary (NPCpp), draft policy on TY, which states that the year 'should be considered as an excellent chance for young people to develop further on the path to maturity.' It notes that 'activities such as work experience, mountain climbing and mini-company work encourage growth and teamwork within the student body.' The NPCpp also believes that 'TY helps build students' self-confidence' and also 'provides serious input into students' understanding of their role in society.'

However, the NPPpp is keenly aware that devolving autonomy to schools to shape their individual programmes can lead to uneven consequences. Don Myers says: 'The quality of TY varies from school to school. A lot is down to the coordinator, school budgets and personnel. Some schools are in a position to offer more places than others but the disappointment is for those who are not successful in acquiring a position in TY.'

'This year, more parents have spoken up and have shown their frustration and annoyance at this. Taking calls from parents who get very emotionally upset because their son or daughter has not been selected is uncomfortable. The process of selection should include consultation with parents and also there should be an appeals process with transparency for those who have been unsuccessful,' says Don.

Paul Beddy, an NPCpp director, continues: 'What we hear from parents is that TY is a cause of conflict and division in some schools. The issue is a limited number of places. Many schools, it seems, have only one or maybe two class groups for TY and more children trying to get places than there are places available.' Like Don, Paul is also acutely aware of trying to support frustrated parents who contact the NPCpp. 'We get phone calls and messages complaining about the way schools select students for TY, often from disappointed parents. There are cases of parents removing their children from a school when their child can't get a place in TY, placing them in another school for the year, and then returning to the first school for fifth year,' says Paul. 'In the NPCpp we think that the selection for TY should include consultation with parents; after all, they are best placed to judge how mature their children are to move straight from third year to fifth year,' he adds. 'It's also our policy that the selection process should include a means of appeal for parents in situations where a child is rejected from TY.' The NPCpp acknowledges that many schools' predicament is that they can't offer TY to all who might want it for reasons of 'space.'

Paul Beddy, as well as being a parent, is also the managing director of a midlands clothing company. He says: 'My own personal view is that TY should be compulsory but that the curriculum should be reviewed. I would like to see more attention to life skills. For example, TY is an ideal time for students to begin a course on driving. Then there is the tax system. That's a real mind-boggler for most of the population.' Paul refers to businessman Fergal Quinn when he says that he thinks young people are not especially skilled in using and interacting on the telephone. He also expresses concern about how some students adjust to fifth year. 'Fifth year hits them like a bomb and many find it difficult to cope,' he contends, 'finding it hard to get back into study routine having been on minimum study for a year.'

Paul also questions the current structures for the appointment and reward of co-ordinators. 'I can fully appreciate that there are agreed systems for appointments in schools but if the current system has an element of seniority over suitability then I don't think this is necessarily best practice in a modern education system,' he says. 'This is not to denigrate the work of TY co-ordinators, it is simply a question to open up debate and what we think should be best practice,' he adds.

Here Paul is referring to in-school management allowances which can range from €3,230 to €8,520. However, the situation regarding TY co-ordination varies greatly from school to school, particularly since the introduction of a moratorium on filling posts of responsibility in 2009; in some schools TY co-ordination is tied to a post with a significant allowance, in others it is independent of the post system. There is ample evidence throughout this book that TY co-ordination makes heavy demands on time, emotions, energy, logistics and imagination. At the same time, a key feature of TY is devolving power to individual schools to manage their own TY programmes with a minimum of outside interference.

Don Myers concludes by saying that 'TY should be a compulsory element of the post primary curriculum as its advantages and qualities have so much potential to enhance the future of our youth. I believe parents should have an active involvement to bring out the best TY programme for their school. The experience of parents should be harvested and utilised to harmonise the best for all concerned.'

A new energising force

As parents with an interest in TY, Edwin and Amanda Landzaad became seriously involved in the project when they set up the Transition Year Ireland website (www.tyireland.com). 'We migrated from South Africa to Ireland with our two children and we are very committed to education,' explains Amanda. 'The idea of TY was mindblowing. It seemed like a great idea but, increasingly, we wondered whether students were getting the most from the opportunities,' continues Edwin. 'Hence, the concept of a freely available information resource for students, parents, schools and providers of TY services was born,' he says. 'Frankly, we were both shocked, and continue to be shocked, when we ask parents about their child's TY experience and are met with a shrug of resignation. It's symptomatic of missed opportunities,' continues Edwin.

'As parents, we could see a wealth of opportunities for young people to involve themselves in numerous TY-related activities, programmes and initiatives. Sometimes it seems that the children or their parents, even the school authorities, are not aware of all that's available,' remarks Amanda. A key viewpoint of the Landzaads is that even if a school has a poor TY programme, all students should not be condemned to a poor year. Would this focus on the individual student – rather than on a school's programme – not lead to chaos in schools? 'Not necessarily,' argues Edwin, 'although there might be occasional clashes between an individual following particular activities and the school's formal timetable, involvement in extra-school activities usually improves motivation and learning.' As seen in the chapter on work experience, schools already struggle with this tension.

'We would like to see parents being more pro-active about their children's TY experience. Put bluntly, a lot of parents are too passive about TY,' says Amanda. The TY *Guidelines* mention parents no fewer than 11 times. Under 'goals and objectives,' parents are identified as educational partners who should be involved 'in all aspects of the programme.' This is subsequently repeated specifically in relation to curriculum content, work experience and community service, assessment and evaluation. Furthermore, under the heading 'Whole-School Approach,' the *Guidelines* state:

> Where parents are already actively involved in school activities, the programme will benefit enormously by continuing and strengthening these links. In other cases, Transition Year can be a catalyst for developing real partnership with parents and the local community.

So, are the Landzaad's pioneering a new dimension of TY with their greater focus on individual options and choices? 'Hits' on the Transition Year Ireland website, as well as their imaginative use of social media such as Facebook and Twitter, point to a new energising force within the TY project. Edwin acknowledges, from his experience teaching architecture in higher education, that monitoring learning 'outside the classroom' and through projects is much more labour intensive than traditional teaching. He suggests that parents could take some sort of motivational and mentoring role, in partnership with schools. Amanda shares this view, adding, 'Ireland's Education Department has come up with this brilliant idea for teenage growth and development but more time should be allocated for the critical job of co-ordination.'

7

MUSIC, DRAMA AND ART ON SHOW

Ballincollig, County Cork is home to one of the largest second-level schools in Ireland. With more than 1,000 students in Coláiste Choilm and just under 400 in the Irish medium Gaelcholáiste Choilm, the vibrant campus throbs with life. 'Since its foundation in the 1980s, the Arts have been integral to the school experience,' states the principal, Michelle Sliney.

'Our school without the Arts would be unimaginable,' she continues. 'They have enriched our celebrations, inspired courage and made our tragedies bearable. They have also been a unique source of enjoyment and pleasure. For all these reasons the Arts are an inseparable part of our students' journey through school.'

Not surprisingly, music, drama and art are central to the school's TY programme. 'Each year, the musical is a major highlight of TY,' remarks Michelle. Indeed, for more than 25 years, from *Evita* to *My Fair Lady*, from *Les Miserables* to *Hairspray*, TY students have entertained and enthralled audiences. These shows are characterised by very high professional standards and are legendary within the school community and beyond.

Unlike many schools where the musical is seen is an extra-curricular or co-curricular activity, in Coláiste Choilm it is integrated into the timetable. Each Wednesday morning from September to Christmas, five 40-minute periods are ring-fenced for 'the musical.' 'The process starts with auditions and interviews,' explains Michelle. 'Each of the 200 TY students selects the area of production in which they wish to participate. Students choose from performance, production, set design and construction, lighting, make-up, costumes and stage management.'

When selected, the cast, which is usually about 100 strong, rehearse in the local GAA pavilion. A further 30 students engage in public relations, sponsorship and the show's printed programme through a mini-company structure. Until November, the remainder pursue a PE programme on Wednesdays. Then, in the run-up to the show at Christmas, they engage with the specific roles.

'Learning through the show takes place at multiple levels,' according to Michelle. 'Great credit is due to the show's directors, Catherine Frost, Belinda Hutchinson and Ronan Holohan, all teachers on the staff. I think they have exceptional abilities to encourage, persuade, nurture and get the best out of students. Obviously, those with particular vocal, acting and dance talents are both supported and challenged, but there are so many opportunities for other talents to flourish,' comments Michelle. She cites the make-up artists, the carpenters, the set designers, the production assistants, the people in the mini-company and the bouncers as examples. 'There are also great opportunities for peer leadership. We see that all the time. And the overall project is a great exercise in teamwork so learning to work together, often under pressure, is very valuable,' she adds. Through participation in the TY show, Michelle believes that students see new potential in themselves and grow in confidence. 'Even though its success depends on enormous additional commitment by teachers, the show in TY leads to great experiences of excellence, immeasurable personal growth and a host of magnificent memories,' concludes Michelle.

The pervasiveness of the Arts in Coláiste Choilm is evident on the school's website. (www.colaistechoilm.org). Unlike schools where the show in TY may be the only opportunity to appear on stage, no fewer that six plays were in rehearsal in March 2015, with involvement from first to sixth year.

TY students took one of the plays, Tom Murphy's *Whistle in the Dark*, about five brothers who emigrate from Ireland to Coventry around 1960, to Coventry where they have a link with the Blue Coat school in that city. Later, in the same term, their Coventry counterparts visited Ballincollig with a multimedia display they had developed about the Irish living in Coventry.

Multiple benefits

Throughout north Kildare and south Meath, the best known feature of the TY programme in Maynooth Post-Primary School is the musical. It is legendary. From *Oliver* in 1995 to *Jesus Christ Superstar* in 2015, each year's production has been spectacular. Parents and visitors comment on the professionalism of these productions. Past students recall their involvement fondly, whether it was *Oklahoma!*, *Grease*, *South Pacific*, *Joseph and his Amazing Technicolour Dreamcoat*, *Guys and Dolls*, *Les Miserables*, *Pirates of Penzance*, *Hairspray*, *West Side Story*, *The Wizard of Oz* or one of the many others. 'Students are involved at every stage of the process,' emphasises Johnny Nevin, principal of the 1,000+ school. 'There are numerous learning opportunities from singing and acting to backstage, even backpacking in supermarkets to raise funds,' he adds.

'It has evolved over two decades to become a defining feature of the school,' explains music teacher Johnny Hanlon. 'Yes, of course, it is very time consuming. In the run-up to the shows in February teachers put in a massive number of hours. There's great commitment,' he adds. For any school considering staging a musical or play as part of its TY programme, funding brings additional headaches. In Maynooth Post-Primary School, partnership with the Parent Teacher Association has worked well. In recent years, the PTA has funded the cost of the tiered seating for the show and also organised the sponsors' reception on the opening night and the after show party for the cast and crew.

An initiative with Maynooth Post-Primary's TY that provides valuable data on students' experience of the musical is the Student Learning Team. Following a competitive process, 13 TY students were invited to join the team. 'The aim is to provide a voice for students, to open communication between students and teachers about teaching and learning,' explains Deputy Principal Clare Garrihy. The team devised a simple questionnaire and processed the results. They then compiled a number of short films on particular benefits.

'Making friends' and ' feeling more comfortable with the year group' emerged as particularly important benefits of involvement with the musical. So did 'learning to work as a team', 'being committed to a task' and 'gaining self-confidence.' Not far behind in importance was 'building stronger relationships/trust with teachers', 'learning how a show is run', 'learning about producing a show' and 'being punctual and organised.' Learning stage directions, learning about the life of Jesus Christ (the survey took place in 2015 after the school had staged *Jesus Christ Superstar)*, and 'building a set' were more likely to be rated 'unimportant' than 'important.' The students surveyed by the team identified 30 other benefits on the musical module in Maynooth Post Primary School.

Why the arts?

Elliot Eisner, a long-time champion in the USA of arts education, has put together an intriguing list of ten lessons which young people can learn through engaging with the arts. Eisner believed that each school has to develop its own unique identity, environment and what he called 'ecology' to support the growth of all participants in the school community, not just the children.

His first assertion is that the arts teach children to make good judgments about qualitative relationships. Unlike much of the curriculum in which 'right' answers and rules dominate, in the arts, it is judgment rather than rules that prevail.

Eisner's second point is that the arts teach us that problems can have more than one solution and that questions can have more than one answer.

Thirdly, the arts celebrate multiple perspectives, underlining that there are many ways to see and to interpret the world.

Eisner's fourth point is that the arts teach young people how the resolution of complex problems can change with circumstance and opportunity. This can develop an ability to be open to the unanticipated possibilities of a work as it unfolds.

Fifthly, Eisner realises how the arts takes us beyond basic literacy and numeracy; neither words in their literal form nor number exhaust what we can know. The limits of our language do not define the limits of our cognition.

His sixth point concerns subtleties. Nuance matters. The arts traffic in subtleties and show us how small differences can have large effects.

Next, Eisner emphasises how all art forms involve translating image into some material reality, helping us learn how to think through and within a material.

His eighth point is that the arts help young people articulate what is difficult to voice. For example, when invited to respond with their feelings to a work of art, they have to delve deep into their poetic capacities to find the words.

His ninth point is that the arts enable us to have experiences we can have from no other source and through such experience to discover the range and variety of what we are capable of feeling.

Finally, Eisner concludes with the powerful point that the position of the arts in school programmes symbolises to young people what adults believe to be important.

As Maxine Greene has remarked: 'The neglect of the arts in education is consistent with the focus on "the manageable, the predictable, and the measurable". Shortly before she died, she wrote:

> If we are going to affirm, extend, and expand the role of the arts in education, we must give up the kind of standardization that wipes clean the diversity, richness, and humanness that infuses the arts as well as human beings' individual— and sometimes collective— responses to the arts. Further, we must learn more about how to attend. We must be able to demonstrate to our students how the arts enable our full engagement in and of the world, allowing us to attend or be open to others and their possibilities (Greene, 2013)

A 2015 UK report (Warwick Commission, 2015) deplored the trend there that squeezes the arts out of formal education. As well as showing how schools were employing less teachers of arts related subjects, they cited evidence where 76 per cent of parents reported that their children regularly took part in arts clubs and cultural experiences outside of school, at significant cost. As well as the negative implications for the cultural and creative industries, the authors fear the development of 'a two-tier creative and cultural ecosystem' in which the well-off benefit and the poor don't participate. Their conclusion is clear: the arts have to be central to a broad and balanced curriculum in schools.

8

Nurturing Young Volunteers

'At the heart of our programme is the idea of devoting time so that young and old can enjoy each other's company,' says Dermot Kirwan of Friends of the Elderly. 'We have developed a programme for schools aimed at Transition Year and CSPE students,' he continues. 'Students who take part must make a friendship commitment to an elderly person. They can engage in activities such as designing and making friendship cards, producing a "Life and Times" biography or writing an essay entitled "When my elderly friend was young".'

'As part of their TY programmes students from the schools come to our Bolton Street headquarters and contribute to a range of activities,' says Dermot. He mentions St Vincent's in Glasnevin, St Declan's in Cabra and Catholic University School in Leeson Street among more than twenty schools currently involved with Friends of the Elderly.

However, Dermot's dream is to have more schools as sites where older people can visit and be entertained. He says: 'In a school you can put on cards, bingo, pool, darts and so on for older people but we are learning what they love most is a get together and a sing song. Schools are ideal locations because they are at the centre of most communities, they are accessible for those with limited mobility and there are plenty of enthusiastic young people who want to entertain.' Dermot points out that older people really love to be invited in to their local school.

Friends of the Elderly is keen to develop its engagement with the TY programme further. 'At one stage we looked at FETAC

Level 5 *Care of the Older Person* but realised that may be too specialised for TY. Now what they are offered is an amalgam of this and more social awareness building in what we see as responses to young people's needs. It's a work in progress that we believe is vitally important for the wellbeing of older people, TY students, schools and society generally,' says Dermot.

The technology connection

In Wicklow, Fintan Mulligan took a simple but inspired and inspiring idea into practice. 'The core idea in 121 digital[1] is that young people who are comfortable with modern technology such as phones, computers and cameras share their digital expertise with older people,' he says. In 2010, Fintan began working with five schools: Dominican College and Coláiste Chill Mhantáin in Wicklow Town, Coláiste Ráithín in Bray, Coláiste Craobh Abhann in Kilcoole and Gaelcholáiste na Mara in Arklow. 121 digital is now a TY module in more than 30 schools. Feedback from the programme has been very positive. 'The older adults report that their confidence in using the technology has been boosted and that they really enjoy the engagement with younger people,' says Fintan. 'Volunteer tutors report that initially they expected to feel awkward with the learners but discovered a lot of interesting "characters", he adds with a smile. 'A good number of the students liked playing the teacher role and some saw very quickly how well older people learn by doing. Others remark on what it taught them about patience,' he says, adding, 'Many TY volunteers commented that "this was the best thing I did in TY."'

Fintan says that the message back from the TY co-ordinators was that they were surprised at how successful the module was. 'I think it helped them realise that intergenerational contact can be very developmental for teenagers,' says Fintan. 'They also saw this module bringing some of the TY programme's aspirations to life,' he adds.

Feedback from parents was also very positive. 'Some of them emphasised how good it is that young people have this kind of op-

---

[1] For future information go to www.121digital.ie

portunity to engage in volunteering, to see something about community spirit in action and to "give something back". We'd like to think this will be a life-long benefit,' says Fintan.

A similar idea informs the An Post-supported initiative 'Log on, learn.' This project is driven partially by an awareness that the widening of the digital divide is excluding some older people from many aspects of modern life, partly because of their limited computer skills. In this model, the older person first registers with a school that offers the module in TY. Then she or he is paired with a TY student and, together and as part of a wider group, they engage in eight weekly training sessions. An Post runs this initiative in association with Microsoft.

Local action

The school chaplain in Newpark Comprehensive School, Blackrock, Dublin is Rev. Suzanne Harris. She also teaches religious education to TY students and co-ordinates the Community Action module through which students volunteer to work with local organisations. 'In Newpark religious education is an eight-week modular programme,' she says. 'Each year I vary the programme. In recent year we have covered Journeys of Faith, People of Faith, World Religions, the Alpha Course, Religion through Film, Moral Issues, Discussion based Religion. In Community Action, the central idea is that each TY student is expected to find a placement for two hours each week. They volunteer in a broad range of community situations, for example, youth organisations, charity shops, nursing homes and primary schools. Sometimes they volunteer to support elderly neighbours,' she adds. 'I think that engaging with the community through volunteering really helps achieve the TY goal of getting young people to reflect, try out new things and mature,' says Suzanne. 'For many the placement is an eye-opener, as they see people's needs up close. Also, giving practical help to other people can be a very positive experience.' She also explains that the Community Action module is well structured with the form teachers overseeing the weekly placements. The students have to make sure that their attendance, activities and attitudes are recorded on a standardised form. The credits students get as part of their final

TY assessment are informed by these reports. Suzanne says that, over time, the Community Action module has become a central feature of the school's TY programme. 'Like work experience, I think it's seen as a defining part of TY,' she says.

'As a chaplain and as a teacher, TY has also helped my development,' she continues. 'I work very consciously at nurturing a safe space to talk, an atmosphere that is relaxed and confidential. I have come to realise how much can be learned through games and discussion. I use ice-breaker games and short film clips to prompt discussion and, if you have the resources, teas, coffee and biscuits at the start are great.'

Research

Research commissioned by Volunteer Ireland has found that for 20 per cent of people the main barrier to getting involved in volunteering is not knowing where or how to find opportunities. More encouragingly, the same research found that one in four adults in Ireland is involved in some kind of regular volunteering activity. The most common motivation to volunteer was to support a specific cause (55 per cent), while helping out in the local community was the priority for 53 per cent of volunteers.

This data points to a major role for TY programmes to introduce young people to the idea of volunteering, starting life-long habits. Such a focus can also be very effective in linking schools more closely with local communities. Thus, in planning or reviewing a school's TY programme, a crucial question should be: This year, how will TY students interact with the local community?

9

MAKING FILMS TO PROMOTE
MENTAL HEALTH AND WELL-BEING

More than 400 teenagers and a small group of invited adults packed into the Red Cow Hotel in Dublin on the night of 23 April 2015 for the third annual CAST Film Festival. Young people from across the country dressed up for an occasion that looked like a fusion of a debs ball and the Oscars. We were there to witness and applaud short films, each with a positive perspectives on mental health. An Olympic medal-winning boxer, a Rose of Tralee winner and leaders of mental health and community organisations gave public recognition to creative endeavours by youthful filmmakers.

The idea behind the festival is both simple and brilliant: a group of young people get together and make a short film – no longer than five minutes – on a topic related to mental health. CAST stands for 'Caring about Society Together.' Thanks to modern cameras and computers making attractive and engaging films is relatively easy and need not be cripplingly expensive. As many TY programmes have discovered, filmmaking can also be a powerful learning experience.

Noel Kelly is keen to remind interested parties that the CAST project originated with and is sustained by TY students. The students emphasise that the project is a mental health one, as distinct from, say, a film project or a technology one.

CAST had modest beginnings. 'One day, in 2011, a group of students came to me and said they wanted to make a film,' recalls Noel, who teaches at Collinstown Park Community College, Neilsown, Dublin, near the Liffey Valley Shopping Centre. 'On foot of a tragic death in the area, a number of community groups had begun to focus on youth suicide. I think these students were sick and tired of what they saw as very negative talk. They had lost a friend. They said to me, "We want to make a film and we want it to be about positive mental health. Then we want to show it to the rest of the school". It seemed like a good idea. I suggested that they should make sure they were well informed. We talked about limited resources. We agreed it would be a cheap production, talking to camera. A few days later they presented me with a script. I was blown away. It was so real, touching on real-life issues including disability, drug abuse, relationships, anorexia, gender, bereavement. There was great empathy evident throughout the script,' recalls Noel.

The students filmed and edited their work. The end result was a short film, less than five minutes. Individual TY students spoke to camera on a range of issues. Each section ended with the student looking directly into the camera saying, 'But I'm okay. Talking helps.'

The next stage was to show it to the guidance counsellors in the school and then the principal. 'My first reaction was that it was a powerful piece. It didn't glorify problems and it put the emphasis on talking,' says guidance counsellor Alison Daly.

'The first time I saw it I remember thinking how powerful it was, almost overwhelming,' recalls Principal Pauline Duffy. 'I was very conscious that the students who made the film were watching and waiting for my reaction and I actually found it difficult to speak it was so powerful. There's great power in hearing these young people say, 'But I'm okay. Talking helps.' She adds, 'I couldn't but think of people across rural and urban Ireland who were now dead who might have heard this strong message from these 15 to 16 year olds.'

Noel reckons that the students approached him initially because he was a facilitator of Young Social Innovators (YSI) in the school. They saw YSI as offering the relevant time and space for implementing their idea.

'The students didn't want to show the film in isolation,' he continues. 'They came up with the idea of building a mental health week within the school. I remember a great meeting with Pauline where she listened to their suggestions and gave good advice – feasible, not feasible, manageable, not so manageable, who you might get in for this or that topic and so on. We ran a very well-remembered mental health week involving everybody in the school community. It was different. For example, we had a bring your teddy to school day, a wear your hair a crazy way day. There were birthday announcements over the public address system every day,' says Noel. He expands further, 'When I asked the TY students why they wanted things like crazy hair or wearing your clothes inside out, they said, "We can see the strange things and it's okay to see the strange things. We can't see the mental health problems. But it's okay if people have such problems." So the message is it's okay to be different, to be individual.'

While 'it's okay to be different' may be an important message to give young people, does having a week like the one described not undermine established patterns of order and compliance – often highlighted by the wearing of a uniform – that schools work so hard to develop? 'Well, as Noel, indicated, when I first heard their proposals I asked a lot of questions,' responds Pauline. 'You have to make judgements. In my experience when you have someone behind a project who is passionate, unless there are huge risks involved, the project is going to carry. There was great passion in this project, some from the students, some from their facilitator, Noel. So, in terms of a successful project I knew the key ingredients were there.'

While making the film and looking for reliable information, the students had gone to Beacon of Light, a local counselling service, and Pieta House, the suicide and self-harm crisis centre. Now they wanted to show the film in the school assembly hall to invited guests from these and other relevant organisations. 'Representatives from Beacon of Light, Pieta House, Ronanstown Youth Service, Mental Health Ireland and Rowlagh Women's Development Network turned up,' says Noel. As well as sharing their creation with the guests, the students were also focused on fundraising. There was tea and coffee and guests could avail of head massages offered by students from Collinstown's adult education department. 'We raised about €600 that day and, later on, in our own version of the TV programme the Cube, we raised another €600,' says Noel. This, he points out, also sent a powerful mental health message to the students as they observed adults, including parents and teachers, grappling with challenges. 'The audience could shout advice but could not actually go in to the Cube to help. They saw it like what's going on inside someone's mind and they got the point.'

On the day of the screening, while the guests and all the TY students sat in the assembly hall, normal classes throughout the school were interrupted; students in their classrooms also viewed the film through interactive whiteboards. 'We knew it was very powerful and that simultaneous viewing would increase this,' explains Noel. 'We had the counselling department on stand-by in case there was any fall-out from it.'

He continues: 'A tremendously positive wave went through the school. Two things happened. The TY students who made the film were catapulted into a little bit of fame. But also students started talking to them about the issues. Some didn't realise it was fiction, it was so credible. The effects rippled through the school for ages.'

'Immediately after the showing, when the guests had left, the students came to me and said, "We need to turn this into a film festival. We need to get other schools to do this as well." Initially I thought they were cracked,' he admits, laughing. 'I told them how much work would be involved. Would they be able to sustain this? I asked.'

By October 2012, Noel and his team of students had got the word out to other schools and youth groups. The second festival took place in the Clarion Hotel, Liffey Valley with over 500 people in attendance. By then the Collinstown students were working in close co-operation with Young Social Innovators developing the project further, calling it First Aid for the Mind. The invitation was to groups – from secondary students to senior citizens – to make a five minute film exploring the social issue of mental health through a positive lens. The theme 'Break the Mould' suggested looking at mental health in a unique way. Animated films, documentaries, fictional stories and films documenting the development of art projects came in. The entries engaged, intrigued and challenged.

The films explored difficult topics and proposed realistic and viable solutions in original ways. 'Seeing the ways they've explored the issues has been mind-blowing,' remarks Noel. 'It's just so uplifting. It's a completely unique event.' Past-entries can be viewed on the CAST website, http://castfilmfestival.com.

A year later, the festival showcased 15 films from 40 entries. The Minister for Health and Children formally opened the event, which had many of the glitzy hallmarks of show business celebrations. Mental health groups and commercial enterprises were attracted by the idea of young people making films on mental health topics. YSI and Dublin Dun Laogahire ETB were involved from the outset. The Clondalkin Partnership, Mental Health Ireland, Suicide or Survive, eDocs, Clondalkin Community Action on Suicide, Spunout.ie, FiT, Cura Pregnancy Support Agency, Crosscare Teen Counseling all lent practical support. The parents of Donal Walsh, the Kerry teenager who spoke publicly about his cancer and established the #LiveLife Foundation,[1] presented a trophy and attended the event. Vodafone Ireland and the Green Isle Hotel later became partners. 'It really seems to have captured people's imaginations,' Noel says. Rachel Collier of Young Social Innovators states that, 'This youth driven film festival shows us what can happen when we tap into young people's vision and energy.'

The original group of TY students left school, went to college but wished to maintain involved with this mental health project. 'Every second Thursday we get together to plan the next stages. It's easy stuff to facilitate as new things keep happening,' remarks Noel. Spin offs so far have included poster and ticket design as well as many good conversations with mental health organisations.

From a TY point of view, there is great versatility about the CAST project. Making a short film on a mental health topic is not tied to any one subject. 'Teachers in English, Art, Media studies, SPHE, CSPE and Religious Education, for example, find it a good focus,' says Noel. Furthermore, the mental health week that Collinstown Park Community College organised demonstrates cross-curricular or interdisciplinary work as advocated in the TY

---

[1] Further information is available at http://donalwalshlivelife.org/

Guidelines. They state: 'An interdisciplinary approach would help to create that unified perspective which is lacking in the tradition-al compartmentalised teaching of individual subjects.' A mental health week also illustrates the value of, occasionally during TY, suspending the 'normal' weekly timetable to insert a 'once-off' event.

Filmmaking is also a dynamic manifestation of how new technologies can transform learning. The teaching team in Col-linstown Park Community College have seen clear evidence of how the project nurtures imagination and creativity, teamwork, fresh engagement with mental health issues, links with commu-nity organisations, organisational skills and the sense of achieve-ment that comes from being involved in a successful enterprise. The CAST project can also be seen as a very positive response to what Hargreaves et al. (1995, p. 80) identified as the failure of secondary schools and their curricula to engage students in their intrinsic commitment to learning. In this regard, these researchers highlighted three problems: those of relevance, imagination and challenge.

Teachers like Noel Kelly, Pauline Duffy, Alison Daly and their colleagues in Collinstown Park Community College are also living examples of how listening to students' voices brings about trans-formation in a school along the lines described by Rudduck and Flutter (2004, p. 139). A key concept, they contend, is to create the school as a 'learning community.' This, according to Rudduck and Flutter, is about:

> ... re-casting teachers and pupils in a more participatory and collaborative relationship, reviewing perceptions of pupils' capacities to contribute actively to a range of school activities, and allowing them to move outside their assigned cells as learners of the statutory curriculum into learning associated with a wider range of roles and purposes.

Since its foundation, Collinstown Park Community College has worked at nurturing a culture of curriculum innovation. The principal's responses to questions about projects like this reveal some of that culture. 'We have learned a lot from experience,' says

Pauline. 'A starting point is to see suggested projects as ways of improving the school experience. There's always a group of teachers on the staff who are – perhaps because of their training, perhaps because of their nature – creative and well-disposed towards new initiatives. Then there is another group who are quietly supportive. The first group gives a new project energy and drive, the second group tends to recognise the value of this energy and drive; they lend support to initiatives.' This analysis almost inevitably invites questions about the third group. Might they be described as resistors? In some schools could they be the strongest group? 'In our experience, some who might not be convinced at the outset of a project, tend to come around because they see the benefits to the students or they want to be supportive of a colleague,' replies Pauline. She recognises that the culture of the school has given them the confidence to open windows as well as the confidence to close them again.

'I also know that in any organisation it is unlikely that you will get 100 per cent "buy-in" from everyone. But you have to be open to the possibility that they might "buy-in" next time around. In the case of the mental health week, I thought it was really important that students see what you might call "the other side" of teachers that's already visible to students through extra-curricular activities. But during that mental health week, they saw everyone – teachers, year-heads, home school community liaison person, deputy principal, principal – having fun and making the point that school is not all about following the regulations. What's also important is that they see you can have fun and then get back to work. I don't think I had any doubts about opening this up and being able to close it again,' she adds. Here Pauline touches on a point which, since its inception, has tainted TY: if you break too much with tradition and routine will some of the order and discipline of school life be lost? Experience in Collinstown Park Community College suggests that when the leadership in a school weights creative and even unusual suggestions on the basis of their educational merits, innovative and experimental practices become 'normal,' teachers and students feel empowered to propose initiatives and everyone adapts to a culture of some unpredictability.

Filmmaker David Puttnam, Ireland's digital champion, has argued[2] that society needs to give teachers more permission to harness modern technology so as to refine and improve teaching and learning practices. Examples like the CAST festival point to an exciting future.

Finally, the origins of the CAST project carry an important message to well-meaning adults worried about suicide: 'Focus on positive mental health not on suicide itself.' It's worth listening to the students.

---

[2] See, for example, http://ec.europa.eu/avservices/video/player. cfm?ref=I079556

10

ASSESSING LEARNING THROUGH PORTFOLIOS

A blue sky and blustery Atlantic winds welcome the visitor to Bundoran, County Donegal. In Magh Éne College, TY students Ben and Dylan have just completed their end-of-year portfolio assessment interviews. Both carry boxes with samples of their work as well as bulging reflective journals. 'In the interview we are asked about the whole Transition Year process, also about our favourite pieces of work, our blogs, how we have changed, how we benefitted from it,' says Dylan. 'Was I nervous beforehand? Yes, of course,' he continues. 'They're quite serious, interviews. Even though we had the questions beforehand, it was still a bit nerve racking. I'm happy enough at how I did. I took the approach more of a casual chat. I think I have improved all round during TY and I think I communicated that.' He talks insightfully about his work experience placements, first in an outdoor pursuits centre and later in a cafe. An ability to compare and contrast is evident.

His classmate Ben has a slightly different take on the process. 'During the year we got quite a lot of practice at interviews so I think I prefer it rather than a written examination,' he begins. He expands about interviews for the Build a Bank project and for work experience. He also represented the school in public speaking. 'However,' Ben continues, 'I was very unsure when I had the first assessment last Christmas. My communication skills were poorer.' He explains that English is not his first language, something not immediately obvious to the interviewer, charmed by Ben's fluent, lilting Donegal accent. The main language spoken at home is Polish; his family came to Ireland while Ben was halfway through primary school. As well as studying French at school, Ben is teaching himself Russian outside school 'in order to extend my language skills.' 'I like the way TY helps you focus on what you want to do – subjects, courses, careers and so on. It gets you more engaged,' he adds.

Both Ben and Dylan agree that interviewing as a form of assessment is something 'we were not used to.' Ben says that he thinks it fits in neatly with Multiple Intelligence theory. Magh Éne College's TY programme is explicitly constructed with Howard Gardner's[1] ideas in mind. Both students appreciate the instructions given in advance of the interview, for example, being asked to present evidence about five TY experiences which were of benefit. This prompts both students to discuss making new friends, linking with a school in Northern Ireland, stilt-walking, facing unfamiliar tasks, water safety, work experience, studying astronomy at third-level, completing a 10 mile run, mini-company, Gaisce, practical inventions, robotics class and supervising children. Dylan and Ben also expand on TY activities that help inform subject choices for the Leaving Cert. Their journals reveal weekly reflective accounts of their learning. During work experience placements students write daily reflections.

Despite all the positivity, surely there must be a downside? Ben mentions that he thinks interviewing to assess learning in some subjects might be more difficult than, say, in work experience. Dylan is realistic that the following September will see them back on a more traditional learning track, where written examinations dominate.

Developing boxes and folders

Magh Éne College Principal Jacqui O'Reilly-Dillon explains that portfolio assessment has been a central component of the school's TY programme since 1996. 'You could say we did it by the book, the *Guidelines*,' she recalls. 'We took these seriously. From the outset we required students to keep a log of what they we doing, a

---

[1] For an succinct eight-minute introduction to Gardner's MI theory and schooling see http://www.edutopia.org/multiple-intelligences-howard-gardner-video

reflective journal and we built that into everything they were doing. Initially we asked them to keep a three-dimensional portfolio, so, for example, in Construction or Engineering they made a box, a container for their work. They could then keep 3D things from the different modules. They also included an A4 portfolio. They kept samples of their work. This was before e-blogs and so on. Each student has to present all this to an interview panel. It has worked very well.'

The *Guidelines* Jacqui refers to are clear regarding assessment, yet anecdotal evidence suggests that even schools with very creative programmes do not always extend the innovation to assessment procedures.

'Assessment' according to the *Guidelines* (DE, 1993), 'is an integral part of the teaching and learning process. It should be diagnostic, so as to provide accurate information with regard to pupil strengths and weaknesses, and formative, so as to facilitate improved pupil performance through effective programme planning and implementation.'

If the implementation of innovative diagnostic and formative approaches to assessment has been weak in many schools, perhaps some of the fault lies with the next sentence in the *Guidelines*: 'Pupils should be assessed on all aspects of the programme as part of the normal assessment process of the school.' That 'normal assessment process' was, it seems, too often reduced to 'written examinations.' The *Guidelines* continue:

> Appropriate modes of assessment should be chosen to complement the variety of approaches used in implementing the programme and may include any or all of the following:
>
> • Summative evaluation: an overall statement of pupil performance by teachers
>
> • Written, practical, oral and aural assessment
>
> • Report of work experience
>
> • Project, portfolios and exhibitions of work
>
> • Pupil diary/log book to record personal progress
>
> • Rating scales, record of skills and competencies attained.'

Again, the evidence from many schools, is that TY assessment too often was regarded as 'an add-on' rather than as integral 'to the teaching and learning process.' The *Guidelines* explicitly demand student involvement:

> Pupil participation in the assessment procedure should be facilitated. This form of assessment involves dialogue with tutors and self-rating on various indicators should lead to greater self-awareness and an increased ability to manage and take responsibility for personal learning and performance.

The *Guidelines* conclude the section on assessment by stating that:

> The outcome of the assessment process should be a Pupil Profile. This would include a statement of achievement in all the areas of study and learning activities engaged in during the year and would incorporate an evaluation of a wide range of qualities. This appraisal should be compiled in the main by teachers/tutors but would include a significant contribution from pupils and, where feasible, some observations from parents. At the end of the programme each pupil should have:
>
> - A completed diary/log book or journal for his/her personal evaluation;
> - A pupil profile and record of achievement from the school.'

In many ways, a key factor in sustaining innovative approaches to teaching and learning in TY is the integration of appropriate assessment modes. Thus, the Magh Éne College experience of portfolio assessment is especially instructive.

Ripple effects

Echoing many of the comments made by Ben and Dylan, Jacqui explains more about portfolio assessment. 'We are not looking so much at the content, the information in their portfolios, as at their ability to present, to communicate, we are looking at their self-esteem and their confidence, their ability to reflect, to analyse, to self-critique, to apply what they have learned to different scenarios,' she says. She also remarks on how much students personalise and take pride in their portfolios. Even though Magh Éne students now have e-portfolios, the option to maintain a tangible box of work remains. 'Personally, I am still very attached to the 3D one,' Jacqui, who was the first TY co-ordinator in the school, comments. 'For example, I think there is a difference between an actual artefact a student has made and a photograph of it. But the students like the electronic ones. Every time they complete a module they write up a blog, upload photos, certificates or whatever is relevant. By the end of the year some will have more than 30 blogs, reflective accounts of their learning.' Jacqui also suggests that portfolios impact on students' confidence to ask teachers questions about subject choice. Now that the Donegal ETB gives students individual e-mail addresses the Magh Éne team plans to build on the possibilities this offers to enhance learning.

As principal, Jacqui is keen to locate portfolio assessment within the overall context of TY's mission. She emphasises links between assessment and teaching and learning. She is also very forthright about the need for schools to explain to parents what they are trying to achieve in TY, how and why approaches are different. 'When we meet the parents in third year we tell them very clearly that TY is about developing the skills of autonomous learners. We put a lot of emphasis on developing the ability to stand up in front of their peers, to speak confidently in public, to change information/data into knowledge and to know the difference.'

Each student is interviewed about their portfolio for a minimum of 15 minutes – 'sometimes it can run to 30' – at Christmas and Summer. 'By the second interview the growth is visible. Most can self-assess – this is where I was at Christmas and this is where I am now,' she adds.

A TY showcase in May, well attended by parents, connects well with the interviews. 'Two students MC the event. Students negotiate with their teachers so that everyone is involved on the night. They perform a short drama. This is followed by each student talking about some aspect of what they learned in TY. Then they are presented with certificates of completion.' Jacqui sees the showcase as adding to TY's profile in the school and in the community. She mentions a recent conversation with a father who described his son as the start of TY as 'a quite, anxious and nervous lad.' Through TY, 'the change has been remarkable. Now he's out there, in the thick of things, organising, making presentations and, overall, he is much more confident and happier.' Jacqui says that powerful evidence like this from parents reverberates throughout the community.

Assessment for learning

As principal, Jacqui O'Reilly Dillon sees portfolio assessment as a particular manifestation of a whole-school emphasis on continuous assessment for learning. She contends that continuous assessment allows teachers great flexibility. 'Depending on the subject, students might be given a task such as making an oral presentation, doing a project, making an artefact, writing and handing in a paper. Teachers have to give the students the assessment criteria in advance. The students self-assess their work. Then the teacher assesses it. A conversation ensures.' Magh Éne College has consciously been promoting assessment for learning throughout the school since about 2009. 'It sits well with a wider school focus on academic monitoring and raising academic standards,' says Jacqui. 'Assessment for learning, especially in TY , has been very beneficial. I know the national research showed that TY typically added 26 more points to LC achievement. I'd say, from our experience, it's more; it could be 70 or 80. Early on we realised that we needed to align assessment with the kind of teaching the TY programme favours. The teacher is not centre stage, doing chalk and talk. It's much more of a facilitation role. So, traditional end of term exams don't suit.'

'Of course, some students take a while to realise that the teacher is not going to do everything for them so they sit back. We believe that if they don't engage, they have to take the consequences. This is where the reports are important. They get marks for initiative and responsibility as well as feedback from the varied forms of assessments. So, inevitably, we spend time explaining to them why their marks are what they are,' she explains, adding that in TY the school sends home reports at Christmas, Easter and Summer as well as two work experience reports. 'Our thinking is very much focused on trying to teach responsibility,' she continues. 'We know that when they got to college nobody will be on their case, telling them to get up in the morning, to attend lectures, telling them to hand in an assignment on time and so on. Sometimes in TY you meet a student in a panic, saying, "I have 10 projects to hand in next week". This is usually the result of poor time management on their part. But we notice that in the next tranche of assignments, most manage them a lot better. There is great learning in this, a life skill is developed,' she says.

'In English, for example, there is a lot of emphasis on oral communication,' she continues. 'Recording and playing back and oral presentation allows for a lot of learning. Increasingly, there is peer assessment and that can be quite scary at first. Not only did we have lots of giggles at the start but I also got some notes from parents saying my son or daughter hasn't the confidence to try this and so on. In talking to them, I emphasise that it will be a safe environment. We've learned that this is important for innovation: trust and a safe environment. Usually when you explain the benefits, they see the point. You realise how deeply held is the view among parents that written tests is the only form of valid assessment. This, of course, is relevant to the Junior Cycle reform.'

How did the teachers react to the shift towards assessment for learning? Again, Jacqui is forthright. 'We sat down and talked about it,' she replies. 'Openly, frankly. We discussed "what works" and where do we want to go. Our staff meetings used to be about discipline and so on. We shifted to asking what's good here? What would benefit teachers in their classrooms? This led us into assessment of learning. We did it in bite-sized pieces, just like you eat any elephant,' she quips. 'Maths began with "traffic lights".[2] When we looked at co-operative learning we changed the format of our classrooms. Next we got involved with Barrie Bennett's "Instruc-

---

[2] Using green to indicate 'fully understood, ready to move on,' amber to indicate 'unsure' and red to indicate 'I'm stuck,' 'traffic lights' can be used by students and teachers to provide quick visual feedback about levels of understanding and learning within classes or when marking students' work.

tional Intelligence"[3] project. This was an excellent form of staff development – mind-mapping, lesson design, for example, checking for prior understanding, framing questions, higher order thinking skills,' she says. 'Teachers were doing much of it already. This put a formal language on what we were doing. We were also talking to each other about it. Workshops on teaching became integrated into our staff meetings. Our student journals now include Bloom's taxonomy and traffic lights so that students and parents have a clearer understanding of what we are doing. It has led us back to an appreciation of why we became teachers in the first place, our core mission.' She pauses. 'And do you know a funny thing,' she comments. 'Since we made the shift, discipline is not an issue any more. The school is very calm. There is a lovely open atmosphere.'

Conscious of the need for all staff to be aware of preferred approaches to teaching, learning and assessment, Jacqui explains that, 'We give all new teachers a crash course before the school opens in August – school ethos and values, restorative justice, instructional intelligence, TY, assessment for learning, and so on. Each is also assigned a mentor and we also do follow-up sessions. Subject departments are very powerful ways of inducting new staff members into school practices,' she adds.

To conclude the interview, Jacqui links together portfolio assessment, assessment for learning, active teaching and learning and the evidence base. Not only have LC scores and transfer rates to higher education jumped in the school, but she thinks students are more discerning in the courses they select. She acknowledges that high achieving students might get top points in almost any school, but maintains that 'they wouldn't necessarily get the social skills, the coping skills and the confidence that TY brings. Books, books, books needs to be balanced with the breadth of experience TY brings.' The second piece of compelling evidence she cites has to do with friendships. 'TY is crucial in cementing friendships that endure.' She recalls former students, 10 years on from TY, still talking to each other about trips to Dublin, Belfast, Cork for events like Concern Debates, Young Social Innovators, Junk Kou-

---

[3] See, for example, http://pketko.com/Unit%20Design/popups/ instructtactics.htm

ture. 'Some even keep their TY portfolio boxes and the stuff in it,' she laughs. 'I believe it's important that school gives students such memorable, positive experiences,' she concludes.

A teacher's viewpoint

Magh Éne College Teacher Noel O'Donnell talks frankly about his own conversion to assessment in TY. Noel has taught modules on woodwork, construction studies, technical graphics, road safety and coding. 'I think something like coding fills a big gap. There are kids out there who really love this stuff. You see the respect other students have for them. Kids are the best judges of each other. I have come to respect peer assessment. Take road safety. We use an instructional intelligence approach, a lot of collaborative work, mind-mapping, concept mapping, table mat exercises, say, on a road safety campaign. Then the whole class discusses each proposal. Everybody is an assessor. I was wary at the start. But then you see, because it's a group effort, that nobody is afraid of criticism. There's safety in that. Feedback gives them greater confidence to then do individual work. I think back to a time when I used individual questioning: "Well Jimmy, what do you think?" That can be very isolating, very inhibiting. Or looking for volunteers in a class; invariably it was always the same ones with the hands up. Think-pair-share is, I now realise, much more effective.'

'I think assessment for learning fits very well with TY, the emphasis on growth in maturity, in confidence.' As Noel looks back on the workshops he did with Barrie Bennett he says, 'It all makes sense.' Is that the key for teachers? 'Perhaps,' responds Noel thoughtfully, 'at the start he gave us small things that we could do, that improved our practice. You could take them away and use them in your classroom. It opened my eyes. Traditionally, I suppose my teaching was like a military operation. For a long time mine was the only voice you heard in the classroom. I probably still have some elements of military precision but the students are now much more involved in the learning. For me the bottom line is that I saw kids who wouldn't have participated putting more effort in, no longer afraid to try. Perhaps it's because I teach practical subjects but I could see assessment for learning working well for me'

As regards portfolio assessment, Noel says that at the beginning of TY students find the idea intimidating but as the year unfolds, 'you can see their growth in confidence and self-esteem so that you arrive at a day like today and they accept the interview as a logical part of the TY process and take it in their stride.' Noel pauses, 'Of course, it's a bit daunting but, overall, you can see so many students who benefit immensely.'

Influential ideas

'Inside the Black Box: Raising Standards through Classroom Assessment' (Black and William, 1998) has been a particularly popular and influential article on formative assessment. Distilling over 500 research articles, the authors conclude, unequivocally, that formative assessment can raise standards in achievement. Furthermore, everyone benefits. In particular, frequent assessment feedback helps low achievers enhance their learning. Traditional tests encourage, they suggest, rote and superficial learning. An emphasis on marking and grading is often at the expense of useful advice for learning. When pupils are compared to one another, they often see this in terms of competition rather than personal improvement; low-achieving students come to believe they lack 'ability.' Those who come to see themselves as unable to learn usually cease to take school seriously. Many become disruptive, others resort to truancy. Such young people are likely to be alienated from society and to become the sources and the victims of serious social problems.

Writing again a decade after the article first appeared, Black and William (2010) noted that 'The impact of "Inside the Black Box" has been a pleasant surprise.' They propose that being grounded in evidence led to its positive reception. They also suggested how teaching should change to make assessment more effective. They state 'interactive dialogue between teacher and learners and between learners themselves is at the heart of formative practice,' and that such practice should enrich the formative practice of teachers. The task is to engineer opportunities so that learners can become more expert in guiding and furthering their own learning. Black and William point out that formative assessment is:

... not just a collection of extra ideas to add to a teacher's arsenal ... teachers need to change how they relate to students, to become better listeners themselves and to learn to promote, respect, encourage and build on student contributions. Such change requires courage and calls for mutual support between teacher colleagues in sustained, in-school professional development.

The Magh Éne College experience also suggests that for something like portfolio assessment in TY to really take root, it cannot be an isolated initiative. It complements and is complemented by other fresh approaches to teaching and learning.

Finally, to emphasise the Irish dimension of a worldwide challenge, Anton Trant, the former head of Dublin's Curriculum Development Unit (CDU), remarked in 2007:

From second-level onwards, our curriculum is driven by examinations. We teach to the test and by doing so put the cart before the horse. We disregard warnings to the contrary – that assessment should never be separated from the curriculum but always be an integral part of teaching and learning. We forget the vital distinction between assessment as the service of learning and assessment for managerial purposes such as selection, certification and monitoring standards. We ignore the undesirable results that follow managerial assessment – the distortion of the curriculum, devaluing the work of teachers and students and lowering the very standards assessment purports to raise (p. 189).

11

LISTENING TO YOUNG PEOPLE'S VOICES

There is a close coincidence between Ireland's ratification of the United Nations Convention on the Rights of the Child (UNCRC), in 1992, and the mainstreaming of Transition Year two years later. In the subsequent two decades, responsible adults have begun to listen with more attention to young people's voices. Quite a dramatic example of this took place at the 2 April 2014 meeting of the Oireachtas Committee on Justice, Defence and Equality. Four TY students had been invited to speak about their project, *Life Leeches – Trafficking Changes Lives.*

'We all have strong feelings about this issue so we were delighted to be invited to address an Oireachtas Committee,' states Claire, one of the four. Everyone who listened to the students from Scoil Phobail Bhéara, Castletownbere, County Cork was impressed by their knowledge of the subject, the creativity of their proposals and their passion to bring about change. 'Their compassion and support for exploited people is great,' remarked Committee member Finian McGrath TD. 'Their sense of social justice is an example to us all and their determination to end human trafficking has got to be followed up on in the Dáil. I commend the pupils of Scoil Phobail Bhéara in Castletownbere for their magnificent efforts,' said the independent deputy.

Behind a significant performance like this by a group of TY students lies a range of initiatives and supports, as well as many individual stories.

Role of School Chaplain

Under the guidance of school chaplain and YSI guide Marie Murphy, the TY group researched human trafficking, including sexual exploitation and trafficking for labour. The students set up a Facebook page and victims got in touch, many thanking them for highlighting the issue. Subsequently, students interviewed victims. It was an eye-opening experience. This led them to contact other groups campaigning on aspects of trafficking. They publicised the issue within their school when they realised that their fellow students knew little about the topic. 'They know now,' adds Helen, one of those who addressed the TDs and Senators. The students also put together a photo exhibition and compiled a book for younger children.

In her opening address to the committee, TY student Ellen gave a succinct introduction. She said: 'Trafficking in human beings is a form of modern-day slavery. It can be rooted in poverty, poor education, lack of opportunities, gender discrimination, social and political violence and demand for services. Victims are often lured away from their homes with promises of better jobs. Instead, they are forced into dangerous, illegal or abusive work. For the purposes of our project, we set out to learn about human trafficking and to educate our peers and the community about it. We set out to raise awareness of the topic locally, nationally and internationally. We hope to use our research and make recommendations on the issue to the media, the Government and the travel and hospitality sectors and education bodies. We want to be agents for change in order that we might in some way make a difference. We discovered that both adults' and our peers' level of knowledge or awareness of the scale of this issue is poor.' She continued by demonstrating the thoroughness of the Castletownbere students' research by supplying extensive statistics, including the fact that '27 million people worldwide are trafficked each year and 2.4 million people throughout the world are lured into forced labour as a result of human trafficking.' The four students, Ellen, Helen, Elaine and Claire, proceeded to explain the breadth of their research. They concluded with innovative and challenging suggestions to address human trafficking.[1]

Guide on the side

As a YSI guide with a timetabled module in TY, Maire Murphy says that the work has been professionally developmental for her. 'The students cherish the opportunity to work on topics they are passionate about. I try to nurture their talents. I seldom have a disciplinary role. The YSI structure is very supportive. The annual showcase in May where students can present their work to their peers is excellent. We have also learned a lot collectively about harnessing social media, Facebook and Twitter in particular, as part of campaigning,' she says.

As a school chaplain, Maire sees her work in TY as building relationships with students. 'I work on the pillars of trust, personal development and maturity,' she explains. 'I gently aim to encourage, push, mentor and grow each student individually, preparing them for senior cycle and the world beyond. The relationship developed in TY is hugely beneficial for the rest of senior cycle.' Her advice to anyone starting to develop a TY module is to be innovative and creative. 'Dream big,' she says, 'and make it relevant to the needs, interests and experiences of the students.' This resonates strongly with a key insight from *Schooling for Change: Reinventing Education for Early Adolescents* (Hargreaves, Earl and Ryan, 1996, p. 80). They identify three common problems in the construction of curricula for adolescents: relevance, imagination and challenge. The human trafficking project undertaken by Maire and her Beara students illustrates relevance, imagination and challenge in action.

School context

As evident in other chapters, inspirational teachers flourish in supportive school environments. Kathleen Dwyer has been TY co-ordinator in Scoil Phobail Bhéara since 2008 and is a passionate enthusiast. 'I have seen a great improvement in the students'

---

[1] A transcript of the students' presentation is available at https://www. kildarestreet.com/committees/?id=2014-04-02a.415

self-esteem, the growth of a 'can-do' attitude and overall greater maturity as a result of TY,' she says. 'I see TY as a place where there are opportunities for each child to shine – in the drama, in the "build a bank", in a YSI project or whatever. It ties in very much with Howard Gardner's theory of multiple intelligences.'

Kathleen also notes the impact TY has on her own teaching of science and biology. 'I try to focus on skills for life. I cover common health conditions and link these to the various systems in the human body. I am also fortunate in that I can link with the Foróige office in the town to do the Real U programme on relationships and sexuality,' she says. 'I have come to realise more and more that it's not what you teach, it's how you teach it that makes the difference. A good relationship with the students makes a big difference in how they approach their own learning,' she adds.

Another teacher, Niamh O'Driscoll, a TY class tutor and teacher of an enterprise module, also emphasises how developmental TY can be for teachers. 'You can apply a great variety of strategies for student learning,' she says. She uses 'Think, pair, share,' groupwork, brainstorming and student presentations a lot. 'I try to develop and encourage a spirit of enterprise among all students. We start by generating ideas and follow through right up to making the product, advertising it and completing a business plan. So many skills are developed: communications, research, evaluation. Confidence and self-esteem increase as does their ability to work together. I have learned that there is so much more involved in teaching that exam preparation,' she adds.

As evident elsewhere in this book, teaching Gaeilge in TY can be challenging. In Scoil Phobail Bhéara, Caitriona Murphy relishes her work. 'I focus on active classes, always through the target language,' she explains. 'Students get to immerse themselves in the language in an active and fun environment. In our assessment we reward effort and participation. Tráth na gCeist and music lessons are very popular. I regularly use pair work and groupwork. I find that weaker students respond well to images and artwork. We also undertook a research project, comparing their schooling with that of their counterparts in the Gaeltacht. I think they enjoyed this, particularly the music, the songs and the ceilí. I attended Tionól

Teagais[2] and got a lot of ideas for active learning at that,' remarks Caitriona. A valuable insight she has gained from teaching Gaeilge in TY is that because of involvement in a range of activities, students may miss classes and so lesson plans need to be realistic, flexible and devised in consultation with students. Getting the correct balance between fun and challenge requires continual adjustment. She also states that it is vital for the assessment to be fair, especially regarding group projects. 'Clear rubrics are important,' she emphasises.

Co-ordination

Working in the relative remoteness of West Cork, Kathleen is in no doubt that 'being opportunistic' is a must for a TY co-ordinator. 'It helps if you know the community and who you might be able to invite in to support a module.' She cites the example of meeting the Principal of the Cork School of Music on a plane journey that resulted in a magnificent performance in the school. She recalls working with an architect on a prize-winning project a few years ago that was triggered by seeing an advert in the post office window. 'I have also learned that you have to take a chance and that not everything will work,' she adds. Asked to locate TY in its wider educational context, Kathleen does not hesitate. 'It's a lifeline,' she exclaims. 'Education,' she believes, 'has been so narrowed. Teaching for understanding has been paralysed.'

The supportive environment in Castletownbere is also nurtured by the fact that a former TY co-ordinator, Mary O'Sullivan, is principal of the school that serves over 300 pupils drawn from the length and breadth of the Beara peninsula. Both Mary and Kathleen emphasise staff co-operation and flexibility as key ingredients of a successful TY. They also show a sensitivity to costs associated with the TY programme. 'We do seem to hire a lot of buses and most trips are long trips,' comments Mary. 'But we have to balance these costs against the wonderful benefits of bringing students to Dublin for the YSI events. We also put on a week at

---

[2] A national series of workshops for second-level teachers of Gaeilge organised by the PDST.

an activity centre that is magnificent for team building. We also encourage Gaisce activities and each year is different as we seize opportunities that arise.'

Evaluation

As co-ordinator Kathleen is also keen to emphasis TY as a team effort. 'It's great to work in an atmosphere where you can bounce ideas and ask advice from colleagues,' she says. Kathleen is very open to learning from mistakes and sees evaluation as vital to keeping TY vibrant. 'At the outset we emphasise that "you get out of TY what you put into in yourself". I try not to measure achievements in terms of competitions won – though that helps – but in terms of indictors such as seeing a student who previously would have had a heart attack if asked to speak in public making a short speech confidently. Personal development is hard to measure but you can see a growth in confidence, their horizons broadened. As a co-ordinator you can see this when you get to know the students.'

Regarding evaluation, the DE *Guidelines* state the following:

> **Evaluation** The programme should be regularly reviewed and evaluated internally by the co-ordinating team in close co-operation with school management, staff, pupils, parents, work providers and community interests. As part of this process, schools should attempt to develop appropriate quantitative and qualitative indicators as the means of raising and assuring the overall quality of the programme provided in the school. Regular monitoring and external evaluation of Transition Year programmes will be the responsibility of the Department's inspectorate and psychological service (DE, 1993).

As regards internal evaluation, the team in Scoil Phobail Bhéara continually seeks students' views. Listening to these young voices assists the school in deepening everyone's understanding of TY. One student, Seán, for example, articulated an understanding of TY by emphasising learning by doing, developing emotional intelligence, working in groups, interacting and improving social skills. Seán then proceeded to devise an imaginative list entitled,

'The five habits of highly successful Transition Year students,' based around a book called *The Seven Habits of Highly Effective Teens* by Sean Covey.

The first is 'putting first things first,' that is, learning to prioritise. Will I watch Coronation Street or finish the history project? One of the big lessons this student took from the mini-company experience was how to prioritise.

The second habit involves having a clear end in sight. This was nurtured through a range of project work where visualising what you want to achieve and devising a purposeful plan were discovered to be helpful. For teachers looking for structured approaches to project work, a resource developed by the Transition Year Curriculum Support Service, *Supporting Active Teaching and Learning Project Work*, may help.

The third habit this student identified was communication, spelling out the three dimensions of speaking, listening and understanding. Making oral presentations in a range of classes supported this, as did working with Toastmasters.

The fourth habit is intriguingly called 'destroying boxes.' This insight is based on recognising that a drawback of a small area is a tendency to categorise, to divide people neatly into different boxes – he's the smart one, she's the artistic one, they are the athletic ones. Opportunities like outdoor pursuits – kayaking, orienteering, raft building, canoeing – and other TY projects gave everyone a chance to destroy boxes.

Finally, 'sharpening the mental saw' refers to developing 'a well-rounded mind' not just one that is examination-focused. Here Gaisce, community service, horse riding, sporting activities, countdown in Maths, writers' workshops and scrapbooking in French are cited as contributing to the sharpening of intelligent well-rounded citizens.

Parent voices

As regards engaging the parents of TY students in evaluation, Scoil Phobail Bhéara uses a simply structured, single page questionnaire. There are five questions with three lines for a response after each one. The questions are:

1. What did your son/daughter gain from Transition Year?

2. What were the main advantages for your son/daughter taking part in Transition Year?

3. What were the disadvantages of participation?

4. Any suggestions for next year?

5. Any useful advice to students starting the programme next September.

What kind of comments do parents make? 'Generally, they are very affirming,' says Mary O'Sullivan. 'It's important for schools to know what they are doing well and have it supported with hard evidence. We also pick up pointers for improvement.' Parents can be very nuanced in their replies, she adds. For example, one parent noted that her son didn't particularly like the core subjects but added, 'I understand why they need them.' Another saw great advantage in her son being allowed to excel at what he was good at while being given the opportunity to work on his weaker side. One parent remarked, 'It was a super year for her from beginning to end ... she proved she is a great manager, super worker, never gives up no matter what the project on hand.' There were also suggestions about spreading the activities, about encouraging students to get stuck in to projects from the start, more work experience and reducing the costs.

Outdated?

Finally, in *How to Improve Your School, Giving Pupils a Voice* Rudduck and Flutter (2004) contend that while young people's opportunities for choice, individuality and self-expression have expanded, thus altering their experiences of the world, schools have been slow to respond. They argue that many schools' organisation, structures and practices are outdated. They strongly advocate closer attention to student voice as a way forward. Scoil Phobail Bhéara students' presentation to the Oireacthas committee suggests that this school is responding innovatively to such challenges.

12

THE EVOLUTION OF TY
OVER 40 YEARS

It was during the week of the annual teachers' conferences, in 1974, that the notion of a Transition Year first emerged. The Education Minister of the time, Richard Burke, sprang his brainchild on an unsuspecting audience, and public, at the TUI Congress in Dun Laoghaire. Using the hurling vernacular of his native Tipperary, 'it was a solo run,' he said in a 2001 interview. There was little or no planning within the Department for the initiative. He expanded: 'nobody in the administrative or educational sector of the Department of Education had – good, bad or indifferent – anything to do with this idea. It was just sprung upon them and they were just told to go and introduce it.'

A year in office at the time, Burke described his initiative as 'potentially the most important idea to emerge from my Ministry'. The kernel of his innovation was as follows: 'Because of the growing pressures on students for high grades and competitive success, educational systems are becoming, increasingly, academic tread-mills. Increasingly, too, because of these pressures the school is losing contact with life outside and the student has little or no opportunity "to stand and stare", to discover the kind of person he (*sic*) is, the kind of society he will be living in and, in due course, contributing to, its shortcomings and its good points. The suggestion was made that perhaps somewhere in the middle of the course we might stop the tread-mill and release the students from the educational pressures for one year so that they could devote time to personal development and community service' (Burke, 1974).

His noble aspirations – and counter-cultural proposals – were met, initially, with scepticism and indifference. Only three brave schools embarked on the TY voyage the following September: St Joseph's College, Garbally, County Galway; the Municipal Technical Institute in Limerick; and the Holy Child Community School, Sallynoggin, County Dublin. A year later, five more schools offered the programme: Newpark Comprehensive School, Blackrock, County Dublin; St Louis High School, Rathmines, Dublin; St Mary's Convent of Mercy Secondary School, Nenagh, County Tipperary; Convent of Mercy Secondary School, Roscommon; and Presentation College, Athenry, County Galway.

Looking back on his initiative, Richard Burke had no illusions that one of his 'pet projects' could easily have been scrapped. As he saw it, TY was 'a subversive idea which was not part of the current educational or administrative culture which would take time to take hold and the principal thing was to guard it in a regulatory fashion'.

This he did by ensuring that a description of TY was included in the *Rules and Programmes for Secondary Schools* (DE, 1976) The former Minister cited this inclusion as critical to TY's survival. 'That meant,' he recalled with some satisfaction, 'that a Minister would have to make a political decision to remove it and then face parliamentary questions to explain the decision.' In his opinion such a move was highly unlikely. Burke identified the role played by Seán MacCarthaigh, a Senior Inspector, as most important in supporting the early development of TY. This inspector's encouragement of teachers to embrace TY is cited by many early participants in the programme as particularly inspirational.

TY was introduced at a time of limited financial resources, exacerbated by the effects of the 1973 oil crisis. Richard Burke was aware that few additional resources could be diverted to TY but, he said in 2001, he had faith in teachers: 'I knew from my own personal experience (as a teacher) that if you put people into the deep end here (in TY) they would really have to sink or swim.

But I knew they would swim because I had a high regard for the teaching profession in the sense that I knew that if circumstances could be such they would be delighted to be liberated to do that for which their basically idealistic calling had prepared them. So it (TY) was in a sense an emancipation of the teaching profession to educate as distinct from grind.'

But, uptake of TY over the next decade was slow. By 1985 less than one per cent of Intermediate Certificate or Group Certificate examination candidates participated in TY the following September.

An unexpected boost for the programme arose in the late 1980s with the decision to introduce a three-year Junior Certificate for all students. Schools that had traditionally offered a four-year pathway to the Inter Cert discovered that including TY would enable them to keep a six-year cycle. TY numbers jumped. Furthermore, the Curriculum and Examinations Board, a precursor of the NCCA (National Council for Curriculum and Assessment), issued imaginative guidelines for schools. By 1993, the figures had climbed to 8,499 students in 163 schools, about 13 per cent of the cohort.

By far the biggest shot-in the-arm for Burke's creative proposal took place in 1994. Senior Cycle education was re-structured. All schools could now offer four programmes: TY, Leaving Certificate Applied (LCA), Leaving Certificate Vocational Programme (LCVP) as well as the established LC. European funding was secured for teacher development. The Department issued fresh guidelines for TY, sharper and more focused. For the first time, schools were obliged to engage in a programme of staff development as a condition of TY participation.

Formal support structures were put in place to enable such development and the model that was developed – a team of seconded teachers supporting regional networks of schools – later became the preferred form of support by the DES for other curricular innovations in the 1990s.

Those who worked on the initial support service for TY recall contradictory responses in staffrooms: teachers enthusiastic to devise educational experiences for their students that were relevant, creative and challenging sitting cheek by jowl with more sceptical colleagues. The latter, often very dismissive of the project, had no shortage of dire predictions of TY's imminent collapse. Consequently, there were many times in those early days of 1994 when support team members wondered whether TY would become widely accepted.

A dramatic surge in TY numbers suggested progress. In 1994 21,085 students in 450 schools began a TY programme. Growth continued. Schools and individual teachers became more courageous and innovative in the programmes they offered. For example, many schools developed close links with community organisations. The original concept of devoting curricular time to personal and social development through activities outside the classroom, especially community service and work experience, became a reality.

Inspection and evaluation

During the initial year of mainstreaming, teams of inspectors looked at TY in 146 schools. They found that nine out of ten schools were following the guidelines in a 'satisfactory' manner. They added that:

> The consensus among principals, teachers and pupils is that the Transition Year Programme is a very worthwhile initiative, allowing the school to engage in genuine in-school curriculum development, offering teachers an opportunity to break free of overly compartmentalized subject teaching, and giving students the space and time to grow in maturity and to develop in self-confidence (DE, 1996, p. 20).

This report, while echoing many of the points in the *Guidelines* and praising schools for enthusiasm and innovation, also suggested:

- More attention to interdisciplinary, cross-curricular approaches

- LC subject choices to be delayed until the end of TY (some schools had been operating what looked very like a 'three-year LC')

- Further develop links with the local community

- More compensatory teaching

- More informal networking between schools for 'improving and revitalising' programmes

- Better assessment procedures

- Improved evaluation within schools.

The Irish Times decided that the findings deserved front page treatment, though, rather than focus on the 89 per cent satisfaction, opted for a heading that read 'Department tells 10% of secondary schools to improve their transition year programmes' (*Irish Times*, 1996).

In fairness to *The Irish Times*, it subsequently adopted a very positive attitude to TY, developing a dedicated page to the programme entitled 'Transition Times' which provided a valuable platform for popularising aspects of the programme. This page evolved into a media studies page, 'Mediascope', and later reverted to 'Transition Times.'

By 2004, as noted in the Introduction to this book, an official account of the Irish Education system stated that, 'Transition Year, which has been one of the major innovations in Irish education, is an option which is now firmly embedded in the system.'

The following table illustrates the growing participation rates in TY, at school and student levels:

Year	Number of schools offering TY	Number of students following TY	Number of students following TY as a % of numbers sitting previous year's JC exam (or Intermediate/Group Cert prior to 1991)
1974-75	3	66	0.4%
1979-80	8	174	0.78%
1984-85	Not found	425	n/a
1989-90	Not found	5,564	n/a
1994-95	450	21,083	31.3%
1999-2000	502	22,797	37.1%
2004-05	522	24,798	44.4%
2009-10	555	28,657	53%
2014-15	614	39,348	65%

Source: Department of Education and Skills

Beyond the department

The evolution of TY has been greatly supported by a range of imaginative projects and initiatives, sometimes by agencies with no direct educational brief. The Irish Film Institute, Trócaire and Amnesty, to mention just three, produced some superb resources of great benefit to TY teachers and students. Perhaps the most spectacular example of creative initiatives beyond the Department of Education and outside the formal school system is the Young Social Innovators (YSI) project. This is a powerful indicator of what is possible within the TY framework for increasing social awareness.

Today, two-thirds of the relevant age cohort follow TY. Educators in other countries show increased curiosity about this uniquely Irish innovation. Minister's Burke's solo run has opened up some wonderful educational opportunities.

13

INSIGHTS ON TY FROM RESEARCH

Way back in the early days of Transition Year, when only a very small number of schools opted for the programme, the Department of Education commissioned the Educational Research Centre in Drumcondra, Dublin to evaluate TY. The researchers, Egan and O'Reilly (1979, p. 49), identified some of the tensions associated with the programme. Reflecting the school completion rates of the time, they noted that the TY project was for 'both early school leavers, for whom the Transition Year will constitute a final year of formal education, and students who will return to do the Leaving Certificate'. They suggested that the name Transition Year was 'a little confusing since it refers in effect to two different transitions, the transition from school to work, and the transition from junior cycle to senior cycle'.

In addition to the major tension between the transition from school to work, and the one from junior cycle to senior cycle, these evaluators reported other tensions: between the emphasis on practical living and the focus on philosophy and logic; between the linear subjects (English, Irish and Mathematics) and the 'new' subjects. Attitudes in schools varied: 'linear subjects were deemed an irritation in many schools and received the minimum possible emphasis'; along with philosophy they were 'generally seen to be of little importance compared with the other subjects'.

Egan and O'Reilly compiled a list of 12 TY-related themes, which they regarded as identifying the differences of emphases in TY curricula:

1. **Linear subjects:** ensuring that students stay in touch with Maths, Science and Languages as academic subjects.

2. **Philosophy and Logic:** introducing students to the content and methods of these disciplines.

3. **Student–teacher relations:** expanding the traditional roles so that students and teachers can meet person-to-person.

4. **Social skills:** giving students more confidence in their public speech and behaviour.

5. **Arts and humanities:** offsetting the intellectual bias of the academic curriculum by adding music, art, poetry, the study of culture as units.

6. **Community service:** giving students the experience of working with the poor, the sick, the old.

7. **Transition to work:** preparing students for the role of the working adult, giving them job experience, getting them jobs if possible, teaching them job skills

8. **New subjects:** introducing new subject-areas, e.g. Media, Astronomy, which otherwise would never be presented.

9. **Self-analysis:** some formal attempt to encourage reflection and self-assessment such as retreats, group discussions on leadership and personality, meetings with the counsellor.

10. **Education for practical living:** imparting skills and information likely to be useful in practical day-to-day living, for example, consumer education, household repairs.

11. **Education for leisure:** teaching specific skills and interests for the use of adult leisure-time, for example, listening to music, photography.

12. **Non-academic students:** enabling the non-academic students to feel that school is for them too.

While identifying basic problems within the conceptualisation of TY, Egan and O'Reilly observed that:

... they have not by any means brought the project to a halt. Nor are they likely to. The reason for this is that many of the most enthusiastic and enlightened participants are the same people who have little time for problems of definition. From their point of view the Transition Year, as they are implementing it, is working satisfactorily; and if it does not conform with some blueprint in the Department – well, too bad for the blueprint. (*ibid.* p. 57)

Egan and O'Reilly also noted that students claimed 'to have become more aware of themselves and others, more confident in social settings, more informed about the world outside school, and surer about the careers they might follow' (*ibid.* p. 57). They added that many of the students' claims were confirmed by the teachers, that in some schools TY had 'a definite impact on the climate of the school' and that TY had improved the 'attitude of the school towards early school-leavers.' Finally, they noted that TY had introduced the school to the experience of educational innovation, to the idea of *éducation permanente*, had increased parental involvement, and had removed some of the barriers between school and the world outside (*ibid.* p. 58). Commenting on the evaluation, Doyle remarked:

> Unfortunately, the most important advice given in this report was not followed, namely that the Evaluation Report would be part of a systematic programme of research that would include the opinions of the Inspectorate of the Department of Education and the evaluators. Such a professional evaluation was a prerequisite of effective continuity and development of the TY. The envisaged programme did not take place (Doyle, 1990, p. 19).

Despite Transition Year being hailed by the DES as 'one of the major innovations in Irish education,' commissioned research has been limited. Some MA, MEd and PhD theses have shed valuable light on aspects of TY.

Longitudinal study

A longitudinal study of those students who sat the Junior Certificate examination in 1994 attracted much public attention to TY (Millar and Kelly, 1999). Comparing those who sat the Leaving Certificate Examination in 1996 with those who took the examination a year later, this research indicated that the latter group – the vast majority of whom had followed TY – tended to achieve more CAO points than the former. The raw difference was 46 CAO points and, when adjusted for gender, school type and previous performance in the JC, 26 points. The report also noted the positive impact TY appeared to have on the progress of boys in both disadvantaged and non-disadvantaged schools. This study also suggested that students following a TY were most likely to be educationally adventurous with regard to the subjects they selected for LC, for example, more likely to take up a subject *ab initio*. The commentary by the National Council for Curriculum and Assessment (NCCA) accompanying the report noted:

> While it cannot be concluded that participation in TY is the cause of this gain in CAO points, the data do point to a strong relationship between enhanced academic performance and TY (Millar and Kelly, 1999, p. xxvi).

Perhaps ironically, numerous schools found this data more effective at convincing students and their parents about the value of TY than extolling the virtues of a holistic educational experience.

ESRI assessment of TY

In 2004, researchers from the Economic and Social Research Institute (ESRI) published an important study of TY, *Transition Year: An Assessment*. Smyth, Byrne and Hannan (2004) noted how the experience of Transition Year varies from school to school. Schools differ in the kinds of subjects students can study, the nature of their work experience placement, the kind of assessment used (for example, project work or formal exams) and the extent to which all (or most) teachers in the school are involved in the programme. These researchers reported that school principals and teachers saw TY as broadly successful, especially in developing personal and social skills among students. However, they noted that principals in designated disadvantaged schools, smaller schools and those in the vocational sector were somewhat less likely to see the programme as effective.

When it came to students' views, the researchers found that young people felt that TY exposed them to different experiences, provided a 'break' after studying for the Junior Certificate and made them more mature. They also found that other students considered the year to be a 'doss' and 'boring'. Students who were not very positive about school life in general tended to have more negative views about TY, especially if they attended schools where the programme was compulsory.

Like the earlier study by Kelly and Millar, the ESRI study found that TY has an impact on students' academic outcomes, even taking account of initial differences between participants and non-participants. 'On average, students who take part in Transition Year achieve higher Leaving Certificate exam grades and are more likely to go on to higher education than non-participants,' they concluded.

However, they also pointed out that not all students did better academically as a result of taking TY. This was the case for two groups of students: male students who worked part-time and continued to work up to their Leaving Certificate year; and students in more disadvantaged schools where the programme was compulsory.

Smyth, Byrne and Hannan concluded that a successful Transition Year programme has a number of features: a whole-school commitment to the programme; time for co-ordination activities and for co-operation among teachers; varied programme content, covering a range of different subject areas; a structured exposure to the world of work; the use of more innovative teaching methods and forms of assessment and accreditation; and on-going evaluation and redesign of the programme within the school.

They identified the main constraints to the successful operation of TY as lack of time and insufficient financial resources for funding activities and outings.

Report to the DES on attitudes to TY

I was commissioned by the DES to research attitudes to TY and published a report in 2007 (Jeffers, 2007). The brief was to focus on a small number of schools where TY was 'well regarded', eliciting attitudes from students, parents and teachers. Many of the themes, tensions and issues mentioned above re-surfaced from the six schools studied. A consistent thread through the data from all informants was that students are more mature as a result of the TY experience. There was also consensus that TY promotes young people's confidence, improves bonds between classmates and facilitates better relationships between students and teachers. Opportunities to explore adult and working life, particularly through work experience placements, were seen as distinct benefits of TY. Many teachers indicated that TY has a positive impact on school climate.

TY students were generally enthusiastic about the programme, frequently contrasting it with their experiences in Junior Cycle which many of them described as pressurised and examination-driven. They highlighted activities that involved learning beyond conventional classrooms. They valued classes where their opinions were sought and listened to.

Focus group sessions with third-year students suggested that decisions to do TY are often arbitrary. In the two schools in the study then designated as 'disadvantaged', the evidence suggested that teachers can play a significant role in assisting students in this decision-making process.

As might be expected, fifth- and sixth-year students echoed many of the points made by their fourth-year peers. Some also spoke about TY in terms of personal freedom and becoming more responsible for their own learning. In some cases, these students indicated tensions between the emphasis on a broad education for maturity in TY with the demands of the LC and the associated points system.

Parents valued in particular learning situations outside the classroom – trips, musicals, fund-raising projects etc – as opportunities that enabled their children to relate to each other and to their teachers in more varied ways than in conventional class-rooms. Parents frequently stated that their knowledge of TY was limited. Their desire for more knowledge contrasted with teachers' perceptions, as a majority of teachers believed that parents were well informed about TY. Parents' anxieties centred on a fear of a drift from 'an academic focus' and a worry that a student might leave school before completing the LC.

Teachers' responses were more nuanced than students' or parents'. Teachers were very supportive of the aspirations of TY and recognised that many young people benefitted from the pro-gramme, especially in their personal and social development. They also regarded TY as having positive effects on school climate but expressed reservations about TY in practice. While a majority appreciated the freedom and flexibility TY offers, opinions were sharply divided when it came to questions about a prescribed syllabus for subjects or a three-year LC. About half the teachers surveyed believed there was a lack of resources for TY, with one-third disagreeing, suggesting that the perceived shortage might be subject-specific.

The evidence also suggested that while schools adapt the TY *Guidelines* to their own circumstances, they can also underplay, and even omit, some essential features of TY.

The research concluded with the following observations:

> Coherent TY programmes appear to require, in particular:
>
> Involving the whole school community in planning and writing a programme that focuses on learning experiences that are relevant, imaginative and challenging.
>
> Clear communication with parents about the goals and format of TY
>
> Co-ordination that is imaginative and efficient
>
> Overt and consistent support for TY from principal and deputy-principal.

Teachers indicate a need for greater support for designing, de-veloping and implementing TY programmes. Support for 'linear' or 'continuity' subjects seems particularly urgent. Low uptake in schools designated 'disadvantaged' may be partly related to perceptions of high costs associated with TY, and the non-increase of the TY grant for students from the DES since 1994.[1]

Finally, perhaps one of the long-term legacies of the mainstreaming of TY is that it has generated, and sustains, debate among students, parents, teachers, school leaders, policy makers and the wider society about the purposes of schooling (Jeffers, 2007, p. 28).

Subsequent research (Jeffers, 2008) highlighted fragmentation and incoherence, suggesting that being 'ring-fenced' into a 'parallel universe', keeps TY isolated from what precedes it – the JC – or what follows it. That study stated:

> For some young people and their parents, a consequence of fragmentation, discontinuity and incoherence is a somewhat bemused view of TY as a slightly unreal, parallel universe, disconnected from the perceived 'core business' of schooling: achieving in certificate examinations. In this context, it becomes relatively easy for the more instrumentalist and pragmatic to dismiss TY as irrelevant (ibid, p. 366).

Research on personal and social development

In a comprehensive overview of TY-related research, with particular attention to personal and social development, Clerkin (2012) concludes that the future development of the programme will be determined by the manner in which a number of challenges are resolved. At the school level, he points to tensions between the values of TY and the LC. He notes, 'Although questions of academic performance are, on a formal level somewhat tangential to the main rationale for the programme – that is, supporting stu-

---

[1] Following the inaugural Transition Year National Conference' on 20 April 2007 in the Osprey Hotel, Naas, Co. Kildare, Minister for Education and Science Mary Hanafin spoke of her desire to see more schools offering TY to their students and announced that the TY grant would be increased to €100 per student from September, the first increase since 1994.

dents' personal development – it is clear that research findings of superior LC performance among participants do go some way to allaying concerns that participation in the year out from examination-based education might have a negative impact on students' achievement.' One consequence of these tensions, he observes, can be a 'rather conservative approach to designing the content of the programme'.

Clerkin suggests that such views reflect one of the consequences of measurement-driven instruction in high-stakes testing environments, quoting Madaus (1988, p. 43) who observed, 'when test results are the sole or even partial arbiter of future educational or life choices, society tends to treat test results as the major goal of schooling rather than as a useful but fallible indicator of achievement.'

Clerkin also identifies the threats arising from Ireland's financial difficulties. He states:

> Public and political debate on the value of continuing to invest in the programme is fuelled to some degree by the perceived difficulty of quantifying psychosocial outcomes such as those targeted by the programme in comparison with academic and economic outcomes, with a relative dearth of psychosocial indicators evident in previous research. Informed debate on ways in which the implementation and content of the programme could be improved – and just as importantly, recognition of ways in which the programme fulfils its goals – is dependent on the availability of appropriate information (Clerkin, 2012, p. 12).

He poses a valuable question, quoting Zimmer-Gembeck and Mortimer's (2006) review of adolescent work and vocational development. 'They lay out a key question for policy-makers worldwide: how can adolescents begin to be incorporated into the adult world without distracting them from school and personal development?' (Clerkin, 2012, p. 12).

14

A Conversation on Co-ordination

This conversation took place in Maynooth University at the end of the 2014-15 school year. Glenda Groome is co-ordinator of Transition Year in Cross and Passion College, Kilcullen, County Kildare. Aisling Savage co-ordinates TY in Ratoath College, County Meath. Both schools are co-educational. The former has a student enrolment of about 700, the latter of approximately 1,000. This is an edited version of the conversation.

Gerry Jeffers: Let's start with your involvement in TY co-ordination.

Glenda Groome: I began co-ordinating in 2004. At that stage I had been working in the school for four years as a teacher of English and Religion. I was involved in a lot of initiatives and was timetabled for a significant number of TY classes. I absolutely fell in love with TY. I was involved from an early stage with Young Social Innovators. The school had introduced TY in 1994 and there had been two co-ordinators ahead of me. When the co-ordinator's role became vacant, I applied and was selected, though it was not an official post (of responsibility). Then, in 2007, we had a Whole School Evaluation (WSE) and the inspectors said that, while they were impressed with what we were doing in TY, they thought it was ridiculous that co-ordination didn't involve a post. So, after that, it was decided that to make the role of co-ordinator (of TY, LCA and LCVP) a post. More interviews. I got the post.

A Conversation on Co-ordination

Gerry Jeffers: Aisling, you have a different story?

Aisling Savage: Very different. I started teaching in 2000 in another school. From the start I set my eyes on that job of TY co-ordinator. I would always say to the co-ordinator: I love your job, I love your job! I'm also a teacher of RE and English and I was heavily involved in TY: Model United Nations, the musical, any kind of peer education, Gaisce, whatever I could get my hands on to do with the students. I was a tutor to a TY class and I just loved TY, you know, working with the tutor group, being involved in work experience, phoning employers, I loved the community care module. Students always described that as a 'gamechanger'. I thought it was a fantastic idea to have students out in the community like that. I was there for eight years. I really wanted to be TY co-ordinator but knew it wasn't going to happen for me there and I was living a long distance from the school. Ratoath was nearer. It was a new school. It was very progressive. When I got the job there, after two interviews, the co-ordinator's post was gone. Anyway, I got heavily involved in TY. I brought Model UN to that school and it just didn't work. Similarly, YSI didn't take off. I was on a real learning curve then, seeing things working in one school and not in another. Then the TY co-ordinator went on maternity leave. I'd no post but I said I'd throw my hat into the ring. I did the presentation, did the interview and got the job last December. So, I'm very green compared to you, Glenda. I'd love to pick your brains. I just hit the ground running and loved the experience.

Gerry Jeffers: Does everyone do TY?

Aisling: In the previous school it was compulsory. Here it's optional. I think everyone doing it is better. If I could make one change it would be to make TY compulsory. We will have 100 TY students in September.

Glenda Groome: We will have 120 students in September. It's compulsory in our school and has been since it was introduced. Occasionally, we have individual cases that might be fast-tracked, mainly because otherwise they might not complete school at all. I also recall one student, highly academic, who did everything in her power to avoid TY. We put in a lot of time and concluded that it was in her best interests to do TY. The student's parents appealed the decision to the Board of Management. However when the Board did not uphold the appeal, and applications to other schools for a fifth year place did not materialise, the parents worked with the school to ensure that their daughter was supported in addressing the challenges faced over the first few weeks. TY turned out to be an amazing experience for her. In fairness, even though she was, initially, passionately opposed to TY, she did put her heart and soul into it and it was very important to her. She got a lot out of it. I can think of a few other cases like that. Of course, there are also some who, for whatever reason, don't get as much out of it.

Aisling: That girl who was very anti-TY, was she enthusiastic from September or did you have to bring her around?

Glenda Groome: I think it probably took about a month. I think her preconceived ideas got smashed very fast. I consciously make the first induction day a mix of information, team-building and goal-setting. Then day two is always a day out of school, bonding on an adventure day. I also think an important challenge is to strike a balance between moving away from a very exam-focused Junior Cycle programme while maintaining an educationally sound yet fundamentally experiential approach to learning during TY. So, our TY is very structured. We have developed a specific journal. Even if it is just for me, they have homework every single day. There is a massive range of assessment. As co-ordinator, I'm constantly talking about goal-setting, about making wise choices. I get them to do a career investigation. They have to present that so it links public speaking skills with doing research. I also emphasise TY as a platform vital to research leading to subject choice (for LC).

Gerry Jeffers: I imagine those features make TY in Kilcullen strong. Are there other things?

Glenda Groome: I use my co-ordination time very carefully. I have one class period each week when I have the whole year together.

I'm also timetabled for an individual period each week with each class group. That allows for clear communication, a focus on deadlines, in mimicking, as much as possible, the real world, in terms of talking about the work to be done but mixing it with a variety of ways of working. It's never just research and essays.

Gerry Jeffers: So, structure, orientation, goal-setting, good use of co-ordination time. What about the programme itself?

Glenda Groome: A strong and well balanced mix of academic and experiential learning. We have 42 subjects. There are core subjects. We have subject sampling. We have subjects that are TY specific. We use a wide range of methodologies: individual and group research, primary and secondary source research, group work, think/pair/share, jigsaw group work method, teambuilding activities like 'Building the Tallest Tower', individual and group logging of activities, discussion, debate, lower and higher order questioning (Bloom's Taxonomy), project work, use of appropriate film/audio clips, matching games, practical applications of a skill such as how to wear a Sari, graphic organisers. It's a long list! Then, on top of the 42 subjects we have external experiences. For example, every year they go to the museums in Dublin, of course accompanied by teachers and worksheets. This year, in the natural history museum, we had a competition for who could do the best selfie with the animal exhibits.

Gerry Jeffers: How do you see it, Aisling?

Aisling Savage: Like Glenda, I think I would prioritise the orientation, the goal-setting. We also do bonding as an overnighter in that first two weeks. We used go to Carlingford but last year went to Lilliput Adventure Centre in County Weatmeath. Amazing. I would recommend it highly. Water sports, adventure, team building, camping, cooking all on site. Fantastic.

Gerry Jeffers: Expensive?

Aisling: I think it was €60 per head and that was everything included.

Gerry Jeffers: Don't you also do an extended trip to Dublin?

Aisling Savage: Well, we actually do Belfast and Dublin. The trip to Belfast is great – the Titanic museum, a walking tour of the city, they hear both perspectives. They love that day. There is a lead-up to that in the classroom and a follow-up afterwards. This year they did an urban challenge in Dublin. It was linked to a subject called 'Twenty-first Century Skills'. They did different projects around the school and in the local community. They designed and created a wall in the school of handprints of every student. They did a mock refugee camp. Sounds a bit unusual! They camped out overnight. They were without certain resources which they had researched in advance. Then, about two weeks ago, they went to Dublin city centre and had a series of challenges, like, find the Shelbourne Hotel and take a selfie with the doorman. They had to find specific sites; find their way to certain meeting points. They had to take a Luas trip on their own, buy their tickets, get from A to B within a time limit. They had to measure the diametre of the Spire! It was brilliant, a great list of challenges. Thank God it didn't rain!

Gerry Jeffers: So, is the idea of teachers coming up with imaginative trips part of the culture of the school?

Aisling Savage: Yes, they have been to the Planatarium. They went to a chocolate factory, the art gallery, the natural history museum. Accounts of these trips feed into the memory box which is part of our assessment. At the start of the year, we explain that throughout the year they have to build a memory box. It has to include assignments, photographs, maybe a clock they made, pictures of buns they cooked, different elements from the year. I ask them to put in a word to describe TY. Then at the end of the year they have to present this to me or to one of their tutors or their year head. They reflect on their year in that way.

Gerry Jeffers: Some schools refer to this as portfolio assessment but I like 'memory box'.

Glenda Groome: Do you do this once a year?

Aisling Savage: Yes, once. Throughout the year I remind them regularly about putting items in the box. The interview is at the end of the year.

Gerry Jeffers: Trips beyond the classroom, which I know make demands, sound exotic, exciting. In both programmes you seem to travel a lot. What about the 'stay-at-home-teachers'? Are they as enthusiastic about TY? How do teachers in the core subjects feel about continuity?

Aisling Savage: There would be about six or seven trips spread throughout the year. Like Glenda said, we try to aim for a balance between classroom-based work, written assignments and so on, and the trips.

Gerry Jeffers: So, who monitors that balance? Is it you as co-ordinator?

Aisling Savage: Well, this year, I came in to a programme that was already planned and up and running. But I have been planning for next year. We have made some changes.

Gerry Jeffers: So what do you emphasise with those changes?

Aisling Savage: Well, we already have a fantastic programme but it has been this programme from its birth. I want to see what else we can do. So, we have introduced the idea of a modular timetable. So, imagine four classes, four timetables: blue, red, yellow, green. A student in one tutor group starts, say, in the blue timetable. Then after eight weeks, he moves to red, then after another eight weeks, to yellow and eventually to green. So, eight week rotation for the student. The teacher teaches a module four times in the year. We presented it to the staff, offering them the opportunity to teach something they had never done before and would like to teach

117

with TY students. We also introduced the idea of a theme for the year, to integrate the year in very real but also subtle ways. Our theme is 'superheroes'.

Gerry Jeffers: How does that work out for the continuity subjects, English, Irish, Maths, languages?

Aisling Savage: So, the four of us teaching English work together as a team, making lots of links with each other.

Glenda Groome: We do a mix of that. I'm very conscious of students choosing subjects for fifth year and regretting what they pick. Sampling is important. We used to do four terms but we moved to three. This gives you a true eight weeks. It used to look like eight weeks on the calendar but in reality it wasn't. Now the teachers really do have eight weeks of class time per term. Two weeks are spent on work experience – and I'm fighting hard to keep that rather than one day per week. We have integrated the musical into the programme so that it is a true educational experience for all not just a chance for the musically gifted to shine. Throughout the year we have a quadruple class for musical rehearsal and preparation. During the two weeks leading in to the show it is total nine am to four pm – sometimes later – focus on the musical: performance, songs, rehearsals, but also stage management, dealing with advertisers and all the other necessary jobs.

I also streamlined trips, partly because of the big numbers and not wanting to bring 120 students into one place at the same time. So, one group goes to the Kairos Studios in Maynooth to study the media, another has an Introduction to Golf day, another group does Driver Education and the fourth group does a Historical Walking Tour of Kildare town. This happens on four different days so each student experiences everything. For other trips, to Dublin or when we go surfing, for example, it's the full group together.

Gerry Jeffers: I love the enthusiasm you both have for TY but what are the challenges?

Aisling Savage: Time is always a challenge, as any schoolteacher will say. I found towards the end of the year, teachers were saying I'd love to do this or I'd love to have done that. But you can't fit everything in. On reflection they often say: this would have been brilliant; can we have them for an afternoon? No, I say, you can't, we need to do this or that.

Gerry Jeffers: What about less motivated students? Do you have problems with attendance or engagement, for example?

Aisling Savage: No. We don't have problems with attendance with this year's group. They were especially engaged, no matter what you threw at them. There might have been in the past.

Glenda Groome: I would imagine that because your programme is optional there are high levels of motivation. When everyone does it, you really have to work on motivation. I constantly refer to school as a training ground, as a safe environment where it's OK to make mistakes, multiple mistakes. We're there, I tell them, to pick up the pieces. In the working world sometimes if you make mistakes three or four times, you're gone. I like things to be clear. So, 20 per cent of the overall grade for the year is based on attendance, 40 per cent is for classwork and application. You could have someone who is quite brilliant academically and doesn't engage at all with classmates and yet is able to produce an amazing project at the end. So, we try to reward consistent work. Finally, 40 per cent goes for their portfolio and their journal. The journal is examined at the time of the portfolio interviews as well. So, some similarities with Aisling's memory box. In our school they are constantly building their grades. Students have to get 85 per cent to get a distinction in TY. A merit is between 64 per cent and 84 per cent. Yes, we have had people who haven't achieved 40 per cent. In most cases there have been concerns that have been worked on and the pastoral care system seriously kicks in. We interview them and their parents and we put in place support systems to help them settle into fifth year.

Aisling Savage: I find that, because it's not compulsory, it's very hard to deal with disappointed students, the ones who didn't get

119

in – 230 students for 100 places. It's not easy. You have to tell them this is not the end of the world. All that is a big challenge for me.

Gerry Jeffers: If TY is optional for students, should it also be optional for teachers?

Aisling Savage: No! Well, I don't actually know. As teachers we are given a timetable review form every year. You can indicate on that what you would and wouldn't like to teach again, or what you're happy or unhappy with on your timetable. This year, because of the new modular timetable, teachers found out in April what they will be teaching in September. I felt very strongly that teachers need to know so they can plan their module, give good notice if they want to bring in a speaker, or whatever.

Gerry Jeffers: Aisling, I'm wondering if being a 'stand-in' co-ordinator brought particular difficulties, especially when it came to working with older, more established colleagues?

Aisling Savage: (Laughs) No! I was just so excited about TY and getting the dream job. What I did learn was about my own style as a manager. I was very conscious of going in to a very busy staff, a very dedicated staff, a very hard-working staff, and I wanted to present this idea I had for TY in a way that was appealing to them, but I also wanted them to get on board. I think I did find the balance between all that. Then we had a launch night for the students and the parents; they are excited too.

Glenda Groome: Where I am all teachers are expected to participate in TY. I'm glad to say we have a dynamic staff anyway and that's a huge bonus. Teamwork on the staff is very important and, thankfully, we have that already. I can't imagine what it must be like to be in a school where people are not about 'team.' I imagine it could be very difficult. Certainly there are people who enjoy TY more than others. We have one or two who would not consider TY their favourite part of teaching, but there are 38 teachers teaching TY. Most enjoy it. I think that's partly because it's quite embedded in the school, part of who we are. As a school we are very much about pastoral care and self-development anyway. That ethos allows TY to flourish. We have a module on Mindfulness which is proving very valuable for the well-being of our students. There is a module on Hinduism. It aims to develop their knowledge, research skills, empathy for and understanding of another culture and belief system. We have a teacher who is absolutely passionate about the equine industry. This is very relevant as we are situated in the heart of the thoroughbred county. He has created an equine studies module with a strong business perspective. Aisling was talking about teachers deciding on trips. Well, he arranges trips associated with this module.

Gerry Jeffers: Perhaps conveniently that brings us back to money. There can be a lot of expenses associated with some TY activities.

Glenda Groome: Rather than trying to collect the money each time we have a trip, we have a flat rate. That allows us to provide a varied and holistic programme. I think it would be very stressful collecting money all the time for each event. It also means as our programme is compulsory everyone attends workshops, trips and speaker presentations.

Aisling Savage: We also look for a flat rate. Our students pay a deposit when they are offered a place and the balance later on. I think ours is a little more than yours. I took a look at your website before I came here.

Glenda Groome: We charge €400 expenses.

Aisling Savage: €450.

Gerry Jeffers: So, for that a student is getting Belfast, Dublin, a lot of speakers as well as other trips?

Aisling Savage: Yes, all that and more but, you know, we spend an awful lot of money on buses. I'd love them to use public transport more but it's not that reliable or even available.

Glenda Groome: Yes, I think location has a big influence when it comes to costs for TY. In a way, I think that turns us back to the local community. Much and all as I value the trips, two of the most rewarding community things we have done were educating local people in the use of computers through Log-on Learn. We then moved to 121digital.[1] They are innovative and they are locally-based. Bar the price of tea and biscuits for our guests at break time, there are no costs to the school for these.

Gerry Jeffers: That's a really good example of an innovative idea that's low cost. Are there others?

Aisling Savage: We have a triple period community block. The students go in to local primary schools and, say, assist with reading. They also had a drama class and a presentation skills class.

Gerry Jeffers: Are those school visits separate from work experience?

Aisling Savage: Yes.

Glenda Groome: Another good activity is Poverty week. I recall students at both ends of the spectrum of academic achievement who told me that, for them, Poverty week was the most important thing that happened to them in TY. It was about meeting reality.

Aisling Savage: We run a Mental Health Week. Very powerful. Next year we are going to link it with fundraising – Pieta House. Some did the *Darkness into Light* walk this year. We also have a group who are going to come in to do project management with the students.

Gerry Jeffers: What about other leaders in the school, principal, deputy principal? How do you connect with them?

---

[1] These are programmes where teenagers show older people how to get good use from computers, mobile telephones and other hardware and software. See also Chapter 8, 'Nurturing Young Volunteers', p. 66.

Aisling Savage: Well, I knew what I wanted to do but every second Friday was my meeting time with the Principal and initially I didn't know what the response might be to my next big idea. To have a management team behind you, supporting you, is great. I'm the kind of person who believes everything in life is possible. So, I need someone to pull me up on the logistics, to say, 'Ah, come on now, Ais, this is the reality of a school.' But it's great when the principal says, 'OK we'll give that a go.' Having that faith and confidence in your principal is good and then it's so important that they have faith in you.

Glenda Groome: Yes, even on basic things like timetabling. The Principal will say to me, 'Who's your dream team?' or, 'If you could choose anything for the timetable, what would it be?' She's brilliant. She takes that away and thinks about it. The Principal before that was the same. I was able to put in my wish list. Obviously, I do that in consultation with other people. I also want to say that evaluation is a vital component for a successful TY. Time is allotted to TY at the staff meeting. Staff are put into groups and I have a number of A2 sheets each with a question on all aspects of the programme – trips, assessment, parent-teacher meetings, everything from big picture stuff to specific details. The A2 sheets move from group to group around the room. Everyone gets to give their opinion and input as to how the year went. The students also evaluate the programme. They reflect on each item and activity. Based on a critical mass of feedback, we decide whether to continue or to drop something. It's so important to listen. A danger for co-ordinators is to say: well I know this works. You have to be open to the possibility that something else might be better. I've just e-mailed my core team colleagues with 12 points to ponder on ideas for next year, reflections on this year's programme, asking them for feedback and contributions. I'll bring all that into the mix.

Gerry Jeffers: You are both very committed and enthusiastic co-ordinators. But as Aisling said, time is a big issue. You also have heavy teaching loads. Personally, I think the *Guidelines* are quite wise in recommending core teams.

Glenda Groome: I agree. I didn't have a core team from '04 to about March of this year. It was very, very tough. At times it seemed that every spare minute I had when I wasn't teaching a class was spent on TY. I job-shared for one year. Absolutely no point as I spent all my time in school. What also happened was that I was working at home very late on my teaching subjects when my children were gone to bed. Normal preparation time during the day was gone on TY. Especially when you are trying to be innovative, time gets eaten up.

Aisling Savage: Do you co-ordinate LCA as well?

Glenda Groome: No. Even though I have the co-ordinator's post, the hours were divided up between myself and two others. So one is doing LCVP and one is doing LCA.

Gerry Jeffers: Tell us more about the TY core team.

Glenda Groome: The inspector from the Department of Education recommended that we have a core team. We have a fantastic team now of seven people. I approached them, asked them if they would consider being on the team. Everyone said they would. We are very fortunate to have a wide range of subjects areas represented, as well as a broad range of teaching experience within the group. They are a very dedicated group of people.

Gerry Jeffers: Do you meet regularly?

Glenda Groome: We meet every three to four weeks with the provision that it may need to be more often during busy times. We meet during lunchtime. It totally depends on good will.

Aisling Savage: I've a different experience. There would always have been a core team of teachers: the tutors, the year head and the co-ordinator. We meet regularly but we also have, on Tuesday afternoons, a timetabled core team meeting. Also, the whole TY teaching team meets on three occasions during the year, for about 30-40 minutes.

Gerry Jeffers: Throughout the year, I presume there is a lot of e-mail communication.

Aisling Savage: Yes, a lot of e-mail. It's brilliant. It's quick. 'They will be out of class today for three classes' – and everyone knows immediately. It's great. But, I know it is actually very time consuming, but I love the personal touch. But if you want someone on board and you want them excited and enthusiastic, you have to speak to them in person.

Glenda Groome: I agree. I use e-mail and I also have a noticeboard in the staffroom for TY. On that I have our TY mission statement, our theme for the year, the timetable for the year, as well as various pictures. I also do an item, 'What's on in TY', that's refreshed every week. As Aisling says there's also a lot of one-on-ones. I sometimes find it seems to be the same people all the time who come forward. The musical is a huge undertaking. Not everybody on staff is going to buy-in to three nights. And in some cases they simply can't. We have some people travelling very long distances to work.

Gerry Jeffers: Is there a bigger question here? Why do you think some people, including both of you, are so enthusiastic about TY, especially given what you are saying about all the time-consuming work?

Aisling Savage: I think the style of programme TY is, it is going to appeal to some people more than others, whether students or teachers. I think it also has to do with the management style of the co-ordinator. I got a very nice e-mail at the end of the year from a parent, thanking us, but it began, 'I did not want my child to do TY. I wasn't enthusiastic about it. But he's had a great year. He has come out of his shell and learned X, Y and Z.' So, I think with teachers there's also a little bit of 'just try it and see'.

Glenda Groome: Yes, but I do think it is very much about your value system. If you believe that the person and their self-actuali-sation is the most important thing then you will love TY. If you are someone who is very focused on exam results and grades and your worth is defined by how your students do in an English paper or a Maths paper or whatever, you will be less enthusiastic. I know I am putting this in a very black and white way, but I genuinely believe that is a key point.

Aisling Savage: I sometimes describe TY as a slip-road. Students are on this exam highway. They come in in first year and its exams, Christmas tests, Junior Cert, Leaving Cert, it's just boom!, as fast as you can put the pedal on to reach that footbridge to get to college. In TY it's like they take a slip-road off the crazy highway. I know they will have to merge back on eventually.

Glenda Groome: I suppose I see TY very much in terms of teaching responsibility, for your own learning, for your own life, self-management skills. It really frustrates me that we do this amazing work in TY and – I'm not sure if it's a slip-road – but after it, when they have taken ownership, we put them back into a fifth year and a sixth year programme where it's, 'Oh, let's spoon-feed again.'

Aisling Savage: Because TY is optional, I can see very clearly in my fifth year English class, in September, when it's boom!, here's an essay from a LC paper, the ones who have done TY are the first in with the assignment. They are more focused; enthusiastic might be stretching it, but definitely more focused.

Glenda Groome: The maturity is there after TY.

Aisling Savage: They are ready for it. Even now some of them are saying I'm sad TY is over – some even jokingly ask, 'can I repeat TY?' – but I'm ready for fifth year.

Glenda Groome: I don't disagree, the maturity is there. But what frustrates me is that the system we're in doesn't allow the use of a lot of these great methodologies for learning that we use in TY. In fifth and sixth year students are put back to a system where they don't have as much ownership over their own learning, where they have to meet certain criteria, regurgitate information. It's as if they are not getting the rewards, the benefits of what they achieved in TY. I see students who really shone during TY and it is as if they are put back into a box, as if they were shown a glimpse of an amazing world of opportunity and then the door is shut. They have the resilience to get back on the road but it is still frustrating. As teachers we have to say, well, we don't have time to use those methodologies because we have to cover the course for the LC. There is a disconnect. This is much bigger than you and I. The disconnect is there in the planning, in the Department of Education planning and assessment of LC curriculum.

Gerry Jeffers: We're coming towards the end. Imagine a school is starting TY for the first time, and the co-ordinator comes to you and says, 'point me in the right direction'. What do you say?

Aisling Savage: Well, it can be overwhelming. What do you say no to? I'd say put in all the basics: work experience, community care, Gaisce[2] because Gaisce in a way sums up what TY is about – the four elements of Gaisce – Model UN, as well as your core subjects, your sampling layer, your TY-specific layer, your goal-setting, the induction we talked about.

Glenda Groome: I think that's a really important point: trying to figure out what to say no to. I think when you are planning, particularly from scratch, you need to have a very clear vision of what is the point of TY. Why do we want to do this in the first place? What is our end goal? What are the short, medium and long-term goals? That's about values. Then you have to create structures, based on the resources available to you, everything from geography to financial back-up. You have to look at best practice. I read a lot, everything from parenting books to the recommendations made by the inspectorate in other schools, interacting with colleagues at conferences, reading research like *Attitudes to Transition Year*. It's a kind of melting pot, everything contributes. I think you also have to take into consideration the ethos of the school. What are we about? Then you so have to look at the particular cohort of students. What is best for them, for their personal, social and aca-

---

[2] See also Chapter 29.

demic development? And, I'd say, be very open to change. That's a massive thing.

Gerry Jeffers: Thanks. That's a helpful summary. Do you think the 1993 *Guidelines* state what TY is about clearly enough?

Glenda Groome: I think they do. But I think part of the problem is teachers like to have very clear processes that will lead to clear outcomes. Many teachers like rules. They like the idea that if I do X, I will get Y as a result. Sometimes teachers seem to want really rigid rules. Because the TY *Guidelines* are quite skeletal, giving a lot of freedom, some teachers are quite fearful of that. They worry: what are the parents going to say? What will the students actually learn? Some find it hard to cope with the intangible benefits of TY. They prefer what's tangible, concrete, measurable. And we know an awful lot of good stuff that happens in TY is not measureable until a lot later in life. I think that is a huge difficulty.

Aisling Savage: Yes, it's one of those things, where on reflection, parents or past students come back in and say, it really benefitted them. And I agree with everything Glenda says about setting up the programme but it can also depend on your skill set as a co-ordinator, the talent you have on staff. I met a parent last week talking about a friend of hers teaching in a different school who felt there was nothing in it for the students. She was very disappointed. There are a lot of factors at play.

Glenda Groome: But that sometimes adds to the freshness. We had a module on candle-making. It was very well received. Then the teacher went on maternity leave: no candle-making. Another guy started off with a photography module, making pinhole cameras and then we invested in digital cameras. That kind of evolution keeps TY fresh. We're celebrating 21 years of TY. I think it's so important to keep it fresh. I'm always looking out for new ideas. That's one of the reasons why I'm involved in the TY Teachers Professional Network.

Aisling Savage: Yes, one of the advantages of being in a growing school is that new staff are coming in every year. New skills, new interests. What would you like to do? We have chess coming on, philosophy also. Even changing the name of subjects or modules. Calling English 'The Word'.

Gerry Jeffers: Maybe that's a good word to end on. Glenda and Aisling, thank you both very much.

15

THE CHALLENGE OF KEEPING TRANSITION YEAR 'FRESH'

Michael O'Leary is uniquely positioned to comment on the main-streaming of the Transition Year programme. 'Back in 1994, I was a teacher of Maths and Science in the CBS in Kilkenny. I was invited to join the team that was being put together for the mainstreaming of TY. In all there were 68 of us, from all over the country. In the first year we ran workshops and visited schools while still teaching. In 1995 I was selected for the support team of fourteen seconded teachers that worked together for the next three years.' Like many others on that team, Michael has vivid recollections of those times. 'We were all on a sharp learning curve,' he says. 'Teachers talking to teachers about a curriculum innovation was new in Ireland. Some-times teachers were very unsure about the whole idea of TY. There was fear – about the lack of structure, about the lack of curriculum, as they saw it, and, of course, without a big exam some feared they would not be able to motivate students. There were times when this fear spilled out as hostility to us. But, as a group, we shared a lot of our experiences, became better and more confident.'

When the full-time support service was downsized to six in 1998, Michael continued as a member of that team. Subsequent-ly, as the service shrunk further and new structures such as the SLSS (Second Level Support Service) and the PDST (Professional Development Service for Teachers) emerged, Michael was, even-tually, as he puts it, 'last man standing,' having been national co-ordinator of the service from 2003 onwards. Michael retired as a full-time teacher in 2013 but continues to work with teachers in individual schools and as an occasional staff member in the University of Limerick.

Standing back from twenty years of very fulfilling work, Michael focuses on one word: creativity. 'It's clear that a good TY programme brings out creativity in young people. But I have also seen teachers' creativity flourish. At the beginning, the idea of a flexible curriculum and the absence of the "stick" of public examinations frightened the life out of some,' he explains. 'Many doubted their own abilities. They were called on to dig into their own teaching imaginations, extend their repertoire of skills, relate to young people in different ways. Many rose to the TY challenge,' he adds. Michael knows that working with schools also nurtured his own creativity. 'Looking back, at first, I wasn't that aware of my own potential. I think that working closely with great co-ordinators, teachers and colleagues brings out your best.'

Asked for examples of good practice, Michael O'Leary pours forth dozens of incidents, events and innovations. He begins with a recent TY graduation night where the school had the courage to allow the students to decide on the format and they had opted for each student 'hosting' a table with friends and family. 'A wonderful occasion,' he remarks.

As a former science teacher, Michael cites various examples of initiatives to advance scientific literacy, to connect science with everyday life: students analysing aspects of local swimming pools, hotels, businesses, restaurants, as well as mapping local flora and fauna. A growing awareness of climate change has prompted numerous environmental studies, he says. 'Some TY programmes lead to real change in school environments as students investigate energy consumption, waste, carbon footprints, pollution, sustainability and so on. Linked to that can be great examples of TY students really educating younger students through presentations, question and answer sessions, film-making and so on. Those encounters in turn cultivate leadership.'

Michael O'Leary remarks that some of the best TY Mathematics programmes he saw in the early days had much in common with Project Maths, which emerged following a review of post-primary Maths in 2005. 'Creative teachers were looking at Morse code, bar codes, linking art and co-ordinate geometry, the history of maths, analysing games and puzzles, re-enforcing basic concepts in Algebra. Very powerfully, there was a new emphasis on approximation. I think that is such an important idea, especially with the rise of calculators.' Michael's reference to 're-enforcing basic concepts' captures two of the most under-appreciated and difficult dimensions of TY. The first is remediation and compensation, the second is TY's relationship with Leaving Certificate syllabi.

Two relevant extracts from the *Guidelines* state:

> **Remediation and Compensatory Studies** A central aspect of Transition Year should be the development of basic competences in key areas according to the needs of individual pupils, including remediation where appropriate. The aim should be to identify and eliminate weaknesses, and to develop the confidence and attitudes of pupils so that they will be better placed to give optimum consideration to their future study options for Leaving Certificate or other programmes. This will extend to enhancement of their study skills for more effective learning and to the development of their capacities for self-directed and open learning.

> **Curriculum content.** The programme content for Transition Year, while not absolutely excluding Leaving Certificate material, should be chosen largely with a view to augmenting the Leaving Certificate experience, laying a solid foundation for Leaving Certificate studies, giving an orientation to the world of work and, in particular, catering for the pupils' personal and social awareness/development. Where Leaving Certificate material is chosen for study it should be done so on the clear understanding that it is to be explored in an original and stimulating way that is significantly different from the way in which it would have been treated in the two years to Leaving Certificate (DE, 1993).

Unfortunately, some have interpreted 'not absolutely excluding' as a licence to overload some TY subjects with LC material. 'The effect is more like a three-year LC, with little of the original and stimulating,' says Michael. 'Properly understood, TY can strengthen the foundation for LC, but, like so many other features of TY, you need people to be creative, he adds.

Michael O'Leary also wonders whether the 1993 *Guidelines* might benefit from a revision. 'Some of the ambiguous views about TY and LC material come from the section immediately before the 'not absolutely excluding' section. The section reads:

> The Transition Year should offer pupils space to learn, mature and develop in the absence of examination pressure. The school should ensure therefore that, in all areas studied, there is a clear distinction between the Transition Year programme and the corresponding Leaving Certificate syllabus. A Transition Year programme is NOT part of the Leaving Certificate programme, and should NOT be seen as an opportunity for spending three years rather than two studying Leaving Certificate material. This is not to say that Transition Year programmes should lack intellectual content; it is essential that they offer a challenge to pupils in all areas of their development. Pupils entering the Leaving Certificate programme on completion of a Transition Year should be better equipped and more disposed to study than their counterparts who did not have the benefit of this year. Those who enter the world of work after the Transition Year should do so as well developed and reflective young adults.

'It's far from a black and white issue,' adds Michael, as he outlines the value of creative writing and of language skills. 'For instance, creative writing skills and oral competency can enrich the LC experience. Many TY programmes do these well,' he says. In passing he mentions a popular strategy used by many teachers of English. 'Two boxes at the top of the class, each full of a range of unusual objects. Each student is invited to pick an item – unseen – from each box. Then, spurred on by their feelings and thoughts on the objects, they make connections between the two objects. Magic!' he says. The drama of such creativity resonates with Michael's long-term involvement, as actor and director, with the Watergate theatre group.

When asked about imaginative resources produced to support TY, his first mention is of lesson plans related to the TG4 soap opera *Ros na Rún*. 'This was a few years ago but they are excellent models for teachers of Gaeilge,' he says. Michael is also enthusiastic about the imaginative ways that some teachers of Gaeilge have moved towards emphasising oral and aural skills in TY. 'I have also seen some good initiatives under a Celtic Studies umbrella,' he adds, expanding on how language, folklore, poetry, history, music and set dancing can be combined.

Michael has supported dozens of schools to shape their own TY programmes. 'The once-off events and the TY-specific modules often get a high profile – work experience, outdoor pursuits, mini-company, the musical, trips, visiting speakers and so on,' he continues, 'but the sampling and continuity subjects are also vital. Being creative with them can be more challenging. When done well, giving students meaningful tastes of, say, Physics, Chemistry and Biology can help students in the important area of LC subject choice. Similarly with business-related subjects, Accounting, Business, Economics,' he says. Michael also recognises that TY can 'showcase' lesser known LC subjects through 'tasting' or 'sampling'. For example, the LC uptake rates of Spanish, Music, Design, Communications Graphics, Religious Education, Technology and Classical Studies are lower than the figures for Geography, French, Art, Home Economics and History.

'As you know,' he says, 'the *Guidelines* propose interdisciplinary or cross curricular work and the experience is that teachers like the comfort of their own subject areas. So, it's not easy. Staging a musical or drama can be a good example. It's also very evident in minicompanies. I also like the idea of a school devoting a whole week to a topic or theme, such as a Europe Week or a Justice Week,' he says.

Co-ordination

'In my opinion, the best co-ordinators are totally enthused by the TY rationale. They really understand and appreciate it,' contends Michael O'Leary. 'They have a real strong belief in the power of TY to benefit students. They are the people who are always looking for something to keep TY fresh, to keep it evolving. They have to be both creative as well as organised. I don't think it's a good idea to give teachers such responsibility simply based on seniority,' he continues.

Michael acknowledges that keeping TY fresh can be a continual battle. 'Like everything, there can be the temptation to settle for mediocrity, to repeat this year what seemed to work last year,' he says. 'People may say things like "if it's not broken, why fix it", but dull repetition leads to boredom, not just for the students but for the teachers. The idea of a co-ordinating team is a good one. In the long run, putting responsibility on the shoulders of one person (the co-ordinator) is not sustainable,' he says. 'Ideally, there should be a whole-school approach. Yes, I've seen principals who don't seem to value TY, who are happy to leave too much to the co-ordinator. But I've also seen enthusiastic principals, people who really "get it", who refuse the reduce everything to LC points or numbers moving to third-level.'

Michael O'Leary is wary of making judgements on TY programmes based on their timetables. 'A timetable tells you very little of what's happening in classrooms. A central feature of TY is that students are actively engaged in their learning, that what they are doing contributes to their maturity and their personal, social, vocational, educational and academic development. That's hard to measure,' he says.

Having given twenty years of his life to supporting schools develop their TY programmes, Michael has mixed feelings about a 2004 statement about TY. The Department of Education published a brief description of the Irish Education system. It said that 'Transition Year, which has been one of the major innovations in Irish education, is an option which is now firmly embedded in the system.' 'Now at one level, this was great, because it was a public confirmation that we had been successful at mainstreaming TY, something that was in no way guaranteed in 1994,' explains Michael. 'On the other hand, maybe it generated complacency. Sometimes you meet an attitude that, in effect, says, "it's there now and it's grand!" I think the best TY programmes consistently renew themselves, responding imaginatively to needs and opportunities,' he says forcefully, adding that assessment for learning is so important for TY. Michael is also a strong believer in the value of teachers working together to update the written version of the TY programme. Here Michael echoes a vital point made by the Department of Education in the first circular letter of the new millennium:

> Successful Transition Year programmes have well developed written programmes, in which the overall aims and objectives of the programme, as well as the specific aims and objectives of each curricular area, module or subject are clearly stated. The elaboration of such a plan requires team-work between the principal, the TY co-ordinator and the teachers concerned. This team-work, manifested in the writing of the programme and in its implementation, is one of the distinguishing features of a good TY programme (DES, 2000a).

One of Michael's biggest concerns has to do with the high turnover of co-ordinators. 'New co-ordinatiors and teachers new to TY need a lot of support. TY can easily slip down a school's agenda. Keeping it fresh is a continual challenge,' he says.

Throughout the interview, Michael mentions dozens of TY-related initiatives and projects. 'In the early days, various agencies and individuals developed some great resources for use in TY,' he says. 'Mental Health Matters is a brilliant pack. The RIAI developed Shaping Space on the built environment. A great pack emerged from the Citizens Information Centres. There have been some great projects: Young Social Innovators, Log-on learn where TY students work with older people around technology, a beautiful initiative. There's Gaisce. Fantastic! There's Junk Kouture, Get up and Go mini-companies, Junior Achievement, the work of the Irish Film Institute, Press Pass. The EPA did a pack 'The State we're in'. There is some excellent material available from Sustainable Energy Authority Ireland (SEAI). Sports organisations like the GAA, IRFU, FAI and SARI (Sport Against Racism Ireland) continue to enliven TY. There is so much,' he says. Overall,' concludes Michael, 'for any school wanting to refresh its TY programme, they can build from some great resources that promote active learning. They don't need to buy in expensive activities from outside to keep TY fresh. They just need time for imaginative and creative planning.'

16

FIVE FORMER PRINCIPALS'
PERSPECTIVES

*This chapter is a conversation between five former school princi-
pals. The event took place in Maynooth University on 9 October
2014. Some questions had been circulated in advance so each came
prepared with some memories, challenges, views on teachers' attitudes, resources, support, inspection and possible regrets about
Transition Year. To ensure maximum freedom of expression regarding potentially difficult issues, the agreement was that all five would
remain anonymous. Hence, names have been changed. The actual
conversation lasted over 90 minutes. This is an edited version.*

Gerry: Maybe we can start with some memories of TY?

Liam: The joys of teaching are sometimes found through extra-
curricular activities. When Transition Year came along, suddenly
these sort of activities could be brought into the curriculum. I
think that was a fantastic liberation of teacher creativity. The idea
that you didn't have to be staying on after school – when some kids
couldn't stay back for the activities – was tremendously liberating.
People who had that sort of commitment to education saw that
very quickly and were very enthusiastic about it.

Gerry: Was that engagement with extra-curricular activities because teachers found the existing curriculum restrictive?

Liam: I think it was more a vocational thing, an intellectual evaluation of what curriculum actually was. Individual teachers were

trying to find time whether it was football, hurling, a history project, a mini-company, time outside the regular Intermediate or Leaving Certificate , where they could do things that were developmental for students. Some teachers have a tremendous facility for engagement in an educational relationship with students beyond the classroom. I think it was more an impulse to bring the students on, to engage them in the adventure of learning. The narrow syllabus didn't necessarily lend itself to that. A lot of teachers used to do this sort of thing in fifth year. They saw fifth year as an opportunity but then they found themselves under pressure when they came to sixth year. Maybe in English, or Maths or whatever they were doing they were forming film societies, or mini-companies, or mental health associations which spilled out into lunchtime or after school and sometimes eating into classtime.

Gerry: So, liberating the creativity of teachers who found conventional syllabi restrictive was a big plus of Transition Year. That's a good starting point.

Noel: I'll start with two aspects. I was the first co-ordinator of Transition Year in the school where I worked. I had been asked by the Board of Management to research it, to prepare for it and to meet all the various resistances that arose in a traditional all-boys secondary school. One of the attitudes was that 'we're very academic here; we have no time for that.' So I remember a huge amount of preparation before the start date. Many traditional teachers saw it as Leaving Cert 'lite'; 'we'll go there but we'll see it as a three-year Leaving Cert.' So preparation and scepticism from staff were one thing. However, there was also a view that the boys were too immature to attempt the Leaving Certificate programme. There was a wide awareness of that. I think that awareness allowed us to turn the corner, to introduce it with both parents and teachers. Kids were going into fifth year, after the Junior Cert, and switching off. I remember arguing strongly that this year would facilitate maturity. As a staff we engaged with the idea of multiple intelligences, that a narrow curriculum would not allow children to reach their potential. Later, TY became the focal point for drama and public speaking throughout the school. I also found that one of the greatest sceptics about TY taught a module on local history and through it did a complete turnaround. I was fortunate that my daughter was doing TY in a nearby girls' school. It had been going strongly there so I took their model and adapted it for the school where I worked. Subsequently I became deputy principal and then principal. As principal I saw that the appointment of the right person as co-ordinator was key to sustaining the initiative. I didn't want TY to become diluted so I put a lot of effort into working with the new co-ordinator.

Maureen: I would agree with the importance of the appointment of the TY co-ordinator. It is absolutely critical. In the school where I worked, which was co-educational, TY was a compulsory programme, though when we introduced Leaving Certificate Applied we did allow a small group to go straight through to a two-year LCA. We ran a tutor and year-head system so that, generally, the team of first-year tutors and year head would stay with that group of students right through to sixth year. When it came to TY there was also a TY co-ordinator who would work closely alongside the year-head. The TY co-ordinator remained with TY. There are so many possibilities, events, modules, projects that land on the principal's desk. As principal in a big school you wouldn't have time to introduce all these to the staff. So I could route these to the co-ordinator who was able to assess them, direct them towards a particular class or set of students. I think that worked really well and helped keep TY fresh and current every year. One of my strong memories is of our constant review of the programme: what worked, what didn't work; we have to change that module, or the timetable or the calendar; we'll never do that again at that time of the year; too many things happening in this term and not enough in that, and so on. I also think it's important to adapt it to the different group of students coming through. Another memory was despite that the school had it for years and years before I became principal, there was a constant need to 'sell' the programme to the students, to their parents and to the teachers. The negativities associated with Transition Year always seemed to rise to the top.

139

Noel: The 'doss year' syndrome.

Maureen: It was easy for students to say 'we're doing nothing' so you had to explain the philosophy behind Transition Year, not just say we are doing mini-company, we're doing musical, we're doing whatever but what are the personal skills being developed, how does it position students for the Leaving Certificate and so on. The challenges of promoting TY to parents at the end of third year never changed. We also addressed parents at the start of TY, throughout it and then at the end. You just couldn't sell it to some people and a few students opted out and we actually lost a few students to other schools. I regret that we lost them.

Patricia: I was a TY co-ordinator, succeeding a very high profile co-ordinator who ran a well established programme in an all-girls school. Like Noel, my experience from my days as co-ordinator until my recent retirement is that a great benefit of Transition Year for young people, and I include my own children here, is the way it helps the whole growing up process. Whether they are academic or not, they often gain a maturity that firstly enables them cope better with fifth year. It also allows them space to develop other skills. They are not as pressurised into the narrowness of reading, writing and arithmetic. They are freed from this pressure of 'I have to get these As in my exams.' The maturity the comes from all this is great. Much also depends on the programme. In my case I was heavily involved in the musical where I saw new skills being developed, especially teamwork, learning how to work with people they had never worked with before. I also saw a great social mix (mentions contrasting geographical locations) and girls often said to me how much they valued sharing trips, accommodation and activities with a wide cross section of their peer group. I think the personal development aspect of Transition Year is very strong. As a parent I had experience of good programmes and ones that were not as well developed, but in all cases the friendship bonds formed in TY remained very strong. I can think of one close friendship group, now in their mid-thirties, which formed in TY. I can think of another child who had been subject to bullying when young and

Transition Year made him; to this day he says Transition Year was the beginning of a new life.

Gerry: What was it like moving from co-ordinator in one school to principal in a different one?

Patricia: Unfortunately, when I moved I was not impressed with the TY co-ordinator. I think the view was that this was a step towards retirement, an easy option. Consequently, as principal I devoted a lot of time to developing aspects of the TY programme, pushing certain things forward. I attended the TY core meetings. We were fortunate that, unlike in Maureen's school, we didn't have to sell our programme. Parents were very open to it. They were aware of the maturity benefits and also the extra points. Yes, it was compulsory. Maybe once or twice people left. When Maureen and Noel talk about the co-ordinator making a huge difference, I fully agree. It is essential. I think if I had not pushed it, it would have fallen off the table.

Maureen: What Patricia says underlines that as well as a good co-ordinator, you also need a principal who believes in the programme. Before being principal I had experience, not as co-ordinator, but as a year-head and I believed in Transition Year. So, as principal, when you believe in it, as you obviously did, Patricia, you make it happen, you facilitate possibilities because you do have to make allowances for TY, for example priorities when timetabling. Sometimes it might be more convenient to chop it and streamline it. I also think the co-ordinator can't drive TY on his or her own. Neither the co-ordinator nor the principal on his or her own can drive TY, it has to be in conjunction with other people.

Noel: Yes, a team person, a process person.

Patricia: We had the year-head position in my last school but when I was co-ordinator I wore both hats. I agree with Maureen, having two positions is ideal.

Oliver: I was never a co-ordinator. I was a deputy principal before my appointment as principal. Before that, one year we came back from summer holidays and Transition Year was on the timetable. We were all looking around at each other wondering, 'where the hell did that come from?' That was a long time ago, in the bronze age. One guy, very liberal, very laissez-faire, had persuaded the principal to include TY. We also had a series of changes of principals, two nuns and a lay person. The laissez faire approach led to what you were saying there, Noel, the 'doss year' syndrome. There were some great aspects to it. I remember a European Studies module that linked us with schools in Holland, Belgium, Denmark and France. Mini-companies and Young Social Innovators were also good. My own daughter did it and it made her so self-confident it was unbelievable. But TY was up and down, good reputation for some parts of it, bad reputation for other parts. It was totally voluntary, we didn't make it compulsory. Some years it went really well, next year it was down there and nobody wanted to do it. Sometimes it survived, just about. My son came to me after a week and said, 'Da, please, take me out of this, I can't stand it. If I have to fill in another map of Ireland green I'll go.... I listened and he went back into fifth year and it was plain sailing after that. It went up a step with a change of co-ordinator. I agree that the co-ordinator is key. A process person, a team person and, most of all, an inspirational type of person. There's a terrific person there at the moment. She just lives for Transition Year. My only fear is that she will wear herself out.

Gerry: If you go back to the 1993 *Guidelines for Schools* regarding Transition Year from the Department of Education, they are very clear about appointing a co-ordinator but there should also be a coordination team. I think that may be with a view to the burnout problem.

Patricia: Yes.

Gerry: But the evidence is that it is very difficult to get a team going. Most schools seem to depend on the individual co-ordinator rather than a team.

Various voices: Yes. Yes. Yes.

Maureen: A few years ago on the timetable we put in a class period for a team meeting, that was the year-head, the four tutors and the co-ordinator. It was very good for communication. It's not good if you are a tutor and you just hear that your group is going off to Croke Park or a speaker is coming in or whatever. It was an extra period on the timetable but I think it was valuable because it was a regular meeting involving the main people leading TY in the school. Then there would have been sub-teams as well, the musical and so on.

Oliver: We had a difficulty in that nominally Transition Year was under the year-head for fifth year, but in reality it didn't work so things fell to the co-ordinator.

Maureen: I think the year-head is very important for the day-to-day discipline and attendance, the usual issues. The co-ordinator can be the organiser, the person who speaks to the parents, who suggests to the students that there is this project or that module. They can be the bearer of good news.

Noel: I agree, Maureen, but it's also very important that the year-head and the co-ordinator act as a team. I have heard of one school where they was conflict between the two and the programme suffered.

Maureen: And that can change from year to year as different personalities come into play.

Noel: They become a mini-team.

Patricia: We had a variation in that we had the same team of tutors for TY classes for a number of years. What was good was that they opted in. There would be some who wouldn't want to have anything to do with TY. We had a big module on social work and that involved a lot of work outside the school, visiting homes and that was extra work. The four tutors who volunteered for this work knew what they were letting themselves in for. On the other side they also got going on the skiing trip as well!

Gerry: I'd like to go back to Liam's opening point about unleasing teachers' inner creativity. I remember interviewing Dick Burke (the Minister who, in 1974, first introduced TY) back in 2001 and he was very strong on this point of TY enabling teachers as professionals to engage in true education. Link that to Maureen's point about the challenge every year of having to convince people, including teachers, of TY's value.

Maureen: Every year at the end of TY the co-ordinator did extensive evaluations. Teachers, students and parents were surveyed. The feedback from parents on forms was generally excellent. But there would always be some negativity, maybe only one person. As regards teachers I think there was a difference between what you might call the core subjects, academic subjects if you like, English, Irish, Maths and the modules that were specific to TY. The teachers doing the modules were much more engaged. Sometimes teachers of Irish or Maths indicated they were more comfortable with a traditional textbook approach. Also, when it came to assessment, they often favoured a written exam format as opposed to a portfolio or project work. There was also division between those doing the core subjects and the teachers who always seemed to be taking the students out of school to do various things: mini-company trade fairs, exhibitions, fundraising, that sort of thing. I think the 'stay-at-home teachers' sometimes felt they were left with the students who didn't volunteer. Overall, it was much more difficult to get the core subject teachers to try to be creative in their classroom methodologies.

Gerry: There seem to be two tensions here. We know from research that learning beyond the four walls of the classroom is very popular with TY students. That tends to be exacerbated with the classroom work in what Maureen refers to as the core subjects. This can extend to Science, French, History, Geography.

Oliver: I found that some of the parents wanted it that way, an assurance that there would be continuity in Maths and Irish and so on, maybe English to a lesser extent, with a view to the Leaving Cert.

Noel: Oliver is right. I had to convince parents and teachers and a cohort of students who were very academically focused that there was a strong academic element in TY. Nobody wanted them going into fifth year feeling 'now we get back to real learning'.

Gerry: How did you do that?

Noel: We did that through assemblies, but also by reviewing the programme with teachers so that while not doing a three-year Leaving Certificate programme, the subject had real academic challenge. We had huge communication with parents, at the end of third year, the start of TY and the end of TY, always reassuring them that subject continuity was a feature.

Patricia: We also had a regular newsletter that kept parents in the picture.

Noel: Some parents seemed obsessed that there might be 'free' classes. So it was good to show them how rigidly timetabled the TY programme was.

Gerry: As well as the timetable, in TY there is also a calendar of once-off items. It can seem that, say, because there is a trip to the zoo, it can seem like fun and games, somehow not 'real' learning.

Maureen: Yes, but you don't have to be out of the classroom to have experiential learning. It can't be just about going places and doing things beyond the classroom. That was the challenge for teachers: to adapt their classroom strategies, their modes of assessment. I think that ties in with the new Junior Cert. And the project work that has become more a feature of the Leaving Cert, for example projects in History and Geography. I think being introduced to project work in TY may have helped students and teachers for Leaving Cert.

Liam: I identify with everything that is being said. Initially in our school I think we tried to be the ideal, that everything had to be different, to have an element of 'transition', to be a step sideways, including Maths, English and Irish. The teachers were willing to try it. But what we discovered was that students were wondering where the handrail has gone. After a while teachers were wondering where the handrail has gone. And parents were definitely wondering where the handrail had gone. So, it became evident that we needed to build that handrail that was going to provide the continuity between the Junior Cert and the Leaving Cert. The timetable itself became a very creative act. It was the programme, the timetable and the calendar. While the normal curriculum was inclined to take care of itself once the timetable was in place, in Transition Year the timetable was multi-dimensional. It also had impacts beyond Transition Year. Right from the start there were boundary issues. And boundaries were exceeded. Toes were stood on, both within the Transition Year team and beyond it. It was like trying to discover the lost chord, except this one wasn't lost at all; it had never been found. You had all these elements that you were trying to bring into harmony.

Gerry: So, if there is a slight discord, can the principal play a critical role?

Liam: Absolutely. It's essential. Whether the principal wants to be or not, people take their cues from the principal. If the principal is lukewarm about anything, then everybody else is going to be lukewarm about it as well. If the principal isn't convinced then nobody else is going to be. We were talking about communicating. Communications within our school were transformed by Transition Year. I would recast the word 'transition' and call it 'transformation year'. It does transform people. It's enormously influential on people's lives. Transition Year is about self-discovery; every learning experience is a vehicle for self-discovery. It's not what you discover about the Alps, or about the quality of snow under ski, it's what you discover about yourself as you are doing these things. In Transition Year kids discover potentialities about themselves that they hadn't realised. Oliver, you talked about confidence. It's central. The thing about communication and conviction, and this is not just about Transition Year, is that you sometimes can think because you have done something well once this should permeate the whole community, as by osmosis, forever. As if it's an inoculation against doubt and negativity. But it isn't. You have to do it again and again. You have to do it with first years as well and the parents of first years. Particularly when parents have choices, you have to say: these are the reasons why we think this is a good place for your child. The most important PR is not what you claim, it's what the kids tell their parents around the tea-table.

Gerry: Patricia, you mention a transformative experience, the boy who had been bullied and now, in his thirties, he has friends from his TY days. Do the rest of you have evidence of similar transformations?

Oliver: I'm thinking of a young lad whom I saw working in a shop yesterday. He is gay and he came out in Transition Year. Where else could he do that? He was well supported, especially by other Transition Year students. He was also supported through fifth and sixth year. A couple of others also came out then.

Noel: That's the kind of community spirit that's generated in Transition Year. We mixed them around so that by the time they went into fifth year they all knew each other. That was a change from the time before TY's introduction when one fifth year group didn't know another and it had a bit of a snob element.

Patricia: Tuppence halfpenny looking down on tuppence.

Gerry: This is related to streaming.

Patricia Yes, we had been streaming. The mix in Transition Year was great especially when they were doing projects together, like the show, like Co-Operation North as it was then, like the skiing trips I mentioned. I liked the idea that the person who couldn't sing for nuts was backstage hammering nails while at the same time with an A1 in honours Maths under her belt. To go back a little bit, to the idea of selling the programme to parents. Sometimes they would say that, for example, there are only three classes per week in English. My reply would be to point to the modules like drama, creative writing, media studies, helping writing the yearbook and say it's all English. Sometimes we have to help parents to join the dots about the programme.

Gerry: I'd like to hear a little more about teacher resistance and how to deal with it.

Liam: It depends on the situation. Like, Oliver, how did the teachers react when they found TY just landed on the timetable?

Oliver: Shock and awe! I think some thought European Studies was Transition Year. There was some 'Mary will you teach Transition Year Science?.' 'What will I teach?' 'Ah sure, we'll work out something?'

Noel: That ad-hocery is dangerous.

Liam: Yes, terribly dangerous.

Patricia: Yes, very.

Noel: Preparation, preparation had to be the message especially with the more traditional teachers.

Oliver: Something similar happened with LCA when that came in. You were told in September that it was happening.

Patricia: Consultation mustn't have been part of the ethos.

Oliver: Well, as I said we had rapid changes in principals over about five years.

Noel: In relation to Gerry's question about teacher attitudes, I found that you needed at a staff meeting to put aside time for an open forum session where we could engage with the question 'what exactly is our philosophy of education?' I found the same with parents, a lot of whom were points-driven. You had, at the night meeting, to pose questions like 'what do you want your child to be?' So, you could reply, 'well this is what we are trying to achieve'. With the staff it was the same thing.

Liam: Yes, I think that's crucial. Fullan talks about 'Ready, fire, aim'. I think that's an interesting formula but it can be absolutely disasterous. Like, who's ready? Is the principal ready so he puts it on the timetable? Then it takes about seven years afterwards to get the aim right. In the meantime there's a lot of fallout. The problem with something like Transition Year, or LCA indeed, is that if you haven't prepared meticulously for it, the kids end up as the victims of experiments.

Patricia: Exactly.

Noel: Disaster.

Liam: Initially, one of the experiences we had in an attempt to buy the vision wholeheartedly and contextualise it in our own school, we were very liberal. We let anyone in who wanted to do it. It was optional. We never made it compulsory. A number of kids were let in and they didn't get to the end of fifth year afterwards. They were not suited to it. It wasn't right for them. If there is a regret I have about Transition Year, that's the kind of thing I'd regret. It's still optional and four classes of twenty-four are doing it. I think being optional has been a good thing. I know other schools have different experiences. But if it wasn't good, they wouldn't opt for it. It's like voting for Transition Year. If it's a good programme and it's evolving, if it's reviewed annually and there is good communication with parents and students it will work. I think that communication with parents is so important. When they come in with new ideas it's useful to be able to say we did that eight or nine years ago and this is what happened. None of the parents had experience themselves of Transition Year so they needed to be educated about it. Tapping into their creativity too was an important part of the process. Parents need to be able to express their views, to say to the school, 'why don't you do this, why not try that?' Even if we tried something two years ago and know the outcome, parents still need to be heard.

Patricia: With regard to teachers, Gerry, as a principal I would never have timetabled anybody for Transition Year who didn't want to be in it. Some might have struggled with being as creative as others, but they were opting in. Others wouldn't touch it.

Gerry: Were there many?

Patricia: Well, a few. There was one teacher of Irish who would have sat at her desk and delivered her lesson.

Noel: Programmed for transmission only!

Patricia: Exactly. There is no point in putting somebody like that into TY. All it does is it kills it. There were some Maths teachers also, a couple of English teachers as well who would not have wanted it.

Maureen: You know your teachers and you can predict certain things. Resistance comes mostly from fear, fear of the unknown. Transition Year is seen as a strange animal and so on. But over a period of time, especially if you have four classes doing it every year, it involves a lot of teachers. Even if they get positive feedback from their colleagues that they haven't 'died' that helps. One of the transition elements was to give students a chance to sample Leaving Certificate subjects. This was very relevant, for example, if you hadn't experienced Home Economics, Engineering or Art in Junior Cert. That brought in a lot more subject teachers who were comfortable in saying, well, I have this group of students in front of me for 10 weeks and I am going to engage them with my subject. I think that brought a lot of people around. I agree that as there is no student choice about English, Maths and Irish, they are seen differently. Generally, you know your staff and if people are positive about TY I think you can bring people along. But you may have to decide 'no, with that teacher it's not going to work'. I don't think we have ever excluded anyone.

Patricia: I certainly have. The teachers who were involved in TY were very positive about it. Some of the others would have had the perception that there was a lot more work involved in preparing for Transition Year.

Gerry: That has been very useful, especially in relation to the challenges of getting Transition Year embedded in a school. Then when TY is up and running, does it lose some of its 'edge'?

Various voices: No. No. Definitely not.

Noel: Provided you had a process going, that it was reviewed every year, that you could say to teachers, 'Look, that's not working; we need to do something.'

Patricia: Especially with the modules you can take them off and put new ones on. During the year you are having conversations with teachers and they are saying, 'I have this idea', and you can encourage them to try it out. If they have been thinking about it and they give you a programme and tell you how they will assess it, there is a good chance it's going to work.

Maureen: This may go back to teacher resistance. Sometimes teachers may have great ideas but when you ask them to write down the programme they struggle, especially with learning outcomes and so on. On a different point, towards the end of my time as principal I began to wonder whether Transition Year should be the full year. I began leaning towards the idea that during the final term you need to include transition elements that prepare students for the immediate next step, fifth year.

Oliver: I found that there were some Alice in Wonderlands when they went back into fifth year. They found it very formal, very rigid, and they were shocked.

Gerry: So, is the problem Transition Year, or fifth year, or that these youngsters have discovered the power of hands-on learning?

Oliver: I don't think it's a major problem. It's a bit of a difficulty.

Patricia: I think they find it (fifth year) hard but they are actually ready. They have had this wonderful experience and now they can move on.

Oliver: I just thought of one word there and it was 'homework'. That is where we had a few problems: nine classes a day and maybe nine bits of homework for the next day or over the same week. Whereas in TY you might have been doing a project or a report that was more long term with time for planning and so on. Now it was about tomorrow and, 'Where's your Maths, your English, your Irish?'

Maureen: Just to be clear, I don't mean cut it (TY) totally dead at Easter. We have two key planks that students love in terms of bonding. One is the outdoor pursuits trip to Delphi at the start of the year which is a great beginning. They come back to school knowing everyone in the year group. Then in the Spring term we had a musical or fashion show, a major big production that involved all of them. Great bonding. I think if you ask many students about Transition Year these are what they would mention first. So there is a lot of coming and going, a lot of time outside the classroom and I think there comes a time, maybe the last four or five weeks of term, when that should stop. Even in terms of running the school we need that.

Patricia: Towards the end our students would have been focused on a final night where they demonstrated what they have been involved in, like a massive exhibition of their work, with videos and examples, where parents attended.

Noel: Lots of schools have that final TY night.

Liam: Maureen is identifying the discontinuity between Transition Year and fifth year. There is also a discontinuity between third year and Transition Year but it is a liberation. The other one (TY to fifth year) is like going back into prison. We identified this and so it became part of the guidance function to map what's coming. There are certain skills, certain attitudes and certain adjustments they are going to have to make when they are finished Transition Year. Over a period of a couple of years this was addressed seriously so there wasn't this cold bath in September. It worked. I don't know whether it is working still. Transition Year throws up a lot of challenges. I think it raises questions about what it means to be human in an experiencing world, how can we deal with that, how can we make it better, make it more positive, how can we remove the bumps and the splinters and so forth. Isn't it a constant process of looking at the programme and adapting it all the time? Some of the things you come up against at the beginning could cause you to say this isn't going to work at all. I can tell you if it had landed in our school on the timetable in September it would not have had a chance.

Oliver: It was touch and go in ours for a good number of years. Evoling would be a good word but...

Liam: Another thing that strikes me here relates to our experience of Leaving Cert Applied. The school had been involved in the Senior Cert back in 1986 so, in all sorts of ways, LCA was our training for Transition Year. The action focus on tasks, and some excellent modules, particularly in social education, were good. Some of the teachers who went into Transition Year brought modules like that into it. The communications modules was also adapted from Leaving Cert Applied. What was also very helpful in preparing the ground was the team focus with the co-ordinator model and regular meetings. The meetings took place during lunchtime and this continued with Transition Year. The school bought them their lunch and if they didn't get the business finished they met again after school, at four o'clock. At staff meetings TY also got a substantial slot. I know the industrial relations landscape has changed since but that worked well.

Gerry: That idea of LCA nurturing TY is a rich one and prompts a question on the relationship between TY and the emerging Junior Cycle. I know some of you have been retired longer than others but how do you see it?

Noel: I think it's a good preparation.

Patricia: A lot of people would say that what we have been doing in Transition Year is a fantastic preparation for the new Junior Cycle. I think the English teachers starting this year are comfortable with it because they have done so much similar work in TY. I also think teaching TY modules feed well into short courses.

Gerry: So, do you think we're going to have one, two, three, four years that have a similarity and then the cold bath or the prison Liam spoke about?

Maureen: Students love Transition Year because it is different – projects, different ways of working, freedom and so on. But if they have had a certain taste of that on the way up over the previous three years, the change won't be as dramatic. That will be a challenge for Transition Year, to adapt. I think something similar happened with LCA when JCSP (Junior Certificate School Programme) came along. Initially LCA was very different. The collaborative work for students and teachers was fantastic. Many JCSP students went on to LCA and the difference wasn't as noticeable.

Noel: Yes, I see that unless we are going to continue the approach into fifth and sixth year, to use another analogy to complement Liam's cold bath, you're going to be climbing a ladder into the upper echelons of five and six.

Gerry: So, the case for Leaving Cert reform is strong?

Various voices:. Oh yes. Absolutely. Yes.

Gerry: Conscious of the time – we have now been talking for an hour – are there any major points from your preparation for today that have not been mentioned?

Noel: You asked us beforehand about resources for Transition Year. In the initial stages I found convincing the Board of Management that TY needed extra resourcing hard. They needed convincing themselves about its merits.

Gerry: Can I ask did you have a fee for TY or was there a specific amount to pay for buses and so on?

Noel: Initially we worked on an ad-hoc basis but then we came up with a set fee that covered all trips including the one to Delphi (for outdoor pursuits), paid in instalments.

Oliver: Was there much of a shortfall?

Noel: A small amount. Generally they had to have paid the final segment before the Delphi trip in April.

Patricia: We charged a fee of €350 that didn't include an outdoor pursuits trip to Carlingford nor, obviously, the skiing trip. It covered a bonding day at the start in Causey Farm that was great and a lot of trips. Much of the 30 or 40 thousand euros spent on TY came from the students. Unless you put the resources in you won't have a good programme. I'm thinking about being able to pay a first aid person to come in, having qualified swimming instructors, a public speaking person, stationery and so on. I felt very strongly that the money taken in should be spent directly on Transition Year activities with no slush fund diverted to the heating or the lighting. That way I think the students got good value for their money. I had some arguments with the Board about that because they often said we have no money and things are tight and getting tighter.

Maureen: We didn't charge a fee but it was always a challenge to keep the cost to an individual child down. We didn't want children excluded from any activities because they couldn't afford to pay.

We collected the cost of the Delphi trip before the summer. For a number of years we were strong on that trip being compulsory but over the last couple of years we had to row back on that because some students just could not afford it. We subsidised what we could but we had to make hard decisions. Other activities where we had to bring someone in, for example First Aid, there was a charge to individual children. Again we did some subsidising but overall it made a difference what you could or could not offer.

Gerry: You made the point earlier, Maureen, that you don't have to go outside the classroom to do experiential learning.

Maureen: Yes, but if you bring in a drama group there is a cost. The co-ordinator was very good at finding people who took a nominal sum but we can't deny that there are costs. Moving away from that, we had groups of international students and sometimes it was difficult to explain Transition Year to them and their parents. Some were very focused on getting the points for third-level and asked why we were focusing on all this personal and social development. There were appeals to the Board that visas might run out and we did make exceptions. There were also issues that some Muslim parents did not want their children to go on the outdoor pursuits trip. The point I am making is that new issues emerge for schools with migrant children. Transition Year has particular challenges. We also had lots of international students who did Transition Year and did extremely well, so it's a complex picture. The other point I want to make is that we are here all very positive about Transition Year and our school delivered very good TY experiences for our students. But I think there are schools out there that may not have the same commitment. You could still find unsatisfactory Transition Years. When you are promoting Transition Year as a whole global thing, people, especially parents, may have varied understandings of what it means.

Noel: You are dead right, Maureen. I remember asking one parents who was resisting TY so strongly for her reasons and she said, 'my daughter did it in another school and it was a disaster'. So, one poor Transition Year has a knock-on effect throughout the whole society and also on journalists.

Liam: I think your are right about reputation, there are poor Transition Years but there are also poor Junior Certs and poor post-Leaving Certs and poor everything out there.

Maureen: But you can have a very high points school, supposedly a fantastic place, and they are paying lip-service to Transition Year.

Liam: They shouldn't be allowed to have it. A poor Transition Year does damage to the students and to the collective reputation. Looking back, there was a view that school was some sort of waiting room, that life began after the Leaving Cert. Transition Year, and also LCA, has brought out the idea that education is life, that there is joy in it. There's also blood, sweat and tears and that's what life is. You don't wait for life to begin until after the Leaving Cert. It happens in school. If there isn't that sort of engagement, especially emotional engagement – Noel mentioned multiple intelligences – at all levels, then it is a waiting room. I think Transition Year has opened our eyes that school is life.

Maureen: Back to the point Gerry made in relation to Leaving Cert reform. Not only are the students older and more mature, they are also leading very adult lives. Yet we still have them wearing uniforms and demanding they ask 'An bhfuil cead agam...' and so on. I'm not sure that schools have adapted sufficiently to this more adult reality, to more 19-year-olds with the car, the vote and whatever. I think that's a challenge for the Leaving Cert course as well.

Gerry: That's a big challenge for school leaders to shape an environment that is friendly for 12-year-olds and also appropriate for 19-year-olds.

Liam: Regarding making a school friendly for first years, Transition Years have played an enormous role in our school as mentors. Once you learn those attitudes of empathy, they stay with you and are good for future leadership. In that way Transition Year is a transformational process not only for the kids but for the school.

Patricia: Yes, mentoring the first years gives wonderful opportunities. We also had a peer mediation team trained that enabled Transition Year students to mediate in little rows the first years have. I found that this training equipped them very well to engage with adult issues in fifth and sixth year. Transition Year is so rich with possibilities and opportunities that don't cost the students anything extra. That peer mediation training was led by a teacher. .

Maureen: A further point. Because there is now no regular in-service for Transition Year, it puts a huge responsibility on the school to bring the staff together and train them in. You can have new teachers every year not familiar with the ethos of Transition Year and you have to devote resources to their induction.

Noel: There also has to be some continuity in terms of a philosophy of education from first year to sixth year. You can't have TY as too different from other years and teacher induction has to be underpinned by that. Collectively I think it is about all staff engaging in a conversation – no holds barred – about fundamentals, what are we about as a school?

Liam: I think it is very healthy to have those conversations, especially in discrete groups.

Patricia: One of your questions in advance, Gerry, was to do with support from the inspectorate. I have never seen an inspector for Transition Year.

Liam: Neither have I.

Patricia: The school has been inspected about almost everything but not Transition Year. I would have loved to have them look at Transition Year.

Gerry: Did you not have a WSE (Whole School Evaluation)?

Patricia: Yes, but they barely looked at TY.

Liam: In our case they looked but they weren't that interested.

Oliver: They did in our case.

Patricia: I was involved in two WSEs, one as a deputy principal and two years later as principal in a different school. OK, we gave them the Transition Year programme and so on but they were not particularly interested. One of the last inspections was an incidental inspection and I asked, 'Is there any chance I could have a Transition Year inspection?', because I would have loved it at that stage, and she said, 'I'll see what I can do'.

Liam: We had a WSE where they specifically inspected LCVP but we got the impression that they were not that interested in Transition Year.

Noel: I don't think that many inspectors are comfortable with Transition Year. I remember one conversation I had with an inspector who said, 'I don't know enough about it'.

Maureen: A few years ago we had a TY-specific inspection. Like all inspections there was a lot of preparation, form filling and gathering documentary evidence. We also told them a lot about the unique modules and so on. It was fine. The inspectors visited a lot of classes, asked a lot of questions. I think the co-ordinator found it quite gruelling. 'Is it all written down?' was a recurring question. Having twenty to thirty modules written to the same standard is the hard bit.

Patricia: I would have hounded people to have their modules written down, learning outcomes clear with some thinking outside the box. But what's on paper is different from the dynamic you see in classrooms, the enthusiasm of the teachers that filters down to students.

Maureen: Yes, in our case I think the inspector got a lot from interviewing the students and encountering their enthusiasm. The students telling the inspector what they had done, what they liked and didn't like was very positive.

Liam: How did the report back read?

Maureen: It was an excellent report. Ther students and staff were highly commended for the richness and effectiveness of the TY programme and for the success in attaining the programme objectives.

Oliver: I checked back with previous co-ordinators and they said the support service that operated in the 1990s was excellent.

Patricia: Yes, that was excellent.

Liam: We'd all say that. It was terrific. The support for co-ordinators through formal and informal networks was great. The meetings that were organised were invigorating and energising. The specific grant from the Department for Transition Year also made a difference.

Oliver: Isn't it amazing how Transition Year has survived, even excelled, with limited support from the Department? It's a credit to schools. Maybe they should just leave us to it.

Patricia: To go back to resources, a few years ago I literally didn't have enough people to run a timetable. So instead of having Transition Year go out in block on work experience we changed to one day per week. I have reservations about that but such were the constraints that I felt I had little choice.

Gerry: What reservations?

Patricia: I think it was educationally damaging. On a block they can be followed up easier. It's a more coherent experience. When it's one day a week the marginal kids are more likely to skip it altogether. I also have questions about the quality of the work experience they are having on those days. It was a cruel decision and against my own inclinations but I had a school to run and not enough resources. Now we still say they have to do three different placements in the year and many of them get so much out of it. But the monitoring is not as good. We also had a problem with some employers treating the placement more like a part-time job when it was one day a week.

Maureen: When you come under pressure for teaching resources, Transition Year often gets hit. We dropped a period from the TY week and it was the one negative thing the inspectors' report noted.

Liam: I think work experience one day a week is nuts.

Gerry: Any last comments?

Oliver: I think Transition Year has had a very positive effect on the development of subject departments within schools. Methodologies, especially innovative and active ones, were being talked about, were being shared. And a teacher is never just a teacher of Transition Year. Teachers began to use these active methods in other years.

Noel: A final personal comment is that I found being TY co-ordinator a very good preparation for the role of principal.

Patricia: I agree. I remember a principal telling me when I was co-ordinator that if I ever became a principal I'd find it a doddle compared to running Transition Year.

Maureen: It gives you an overview of everything, especially insight into how the timetable works.

Patricia: You had to deal with staff, get teachers on board for co-ordinating everything, dealing with people saying, 'I'm not doing that' or whatever.

Oliver: I came to it a different way. I was an SDPI (School Development Planning Initiative) co-ordinator and so was going to schools and seeing at first hand how different they can be, particularly their approach to Transition Year.

Patricia: We shouldn't forget about the opportunities TY offers to develop oral language skills.

Maureen: It's also a place where teachers have to practice differentiated learning because the groups tend to be so mixed.

Oliver: Another benefit was ICT (Information and Communications Technology). In our school ICT came in through Transition Year, specifically the European studies module I mentioned earlier.

Gerry: Notwithstanding Liam's warning about victims of experiments, TY is a relatively safe place for trying things out, for unleashing that creativity mentioned at the outset.

Maureen: But as principal you have to protect teachers because the enthusiastic can get burned out. The big danger would be to develop a good programme and then rest on your laurels, presuming that everybody knows what it is about. It is constantly evolving and it need fresh inputs every year, but you have to review it and sustain the teachers.

Gerry: Maybe that's a good note on which to finish. Thank you.

17

Irish Language, Culture and Learning

'Of course there are challenges in teaching Irish in TY,' replies Gearoidín O'Dwyer,' but in my experience, there are also great opportunities. For example, in TY not only can we focus on speaking the language, but there is the time and space to make mistakes without being constantly interrupted, as often happens in exam-focused classes. Then there is the richness of Irish culture. TY Irish is also a great place to reinforce the fundamental learning objectives of TY itself. So, it's full of possibilities,' she says.

Gearoidín teaches in Newpark Comprehensive School in Dublin, a school with a distinguished history of curriculum innovation. When the idea of TY was first mooted in 1974, Newpark principal John Harris was enthusiastic but hesitant. He has written:

> We told the Minister.... that we wished to take a year of planning before introducing such a different kind of curriculum. The Transition Year was started in Newpark in 1975 and was the first school to run this programme for the entire fourth year cohort and doing this has been the practice ever since (Harris, 2010, p. 48).

Gearoidín acknowledges the school's continual engagement with innovation. She mentions that, as well as Irish in TY, she also teaches a module on Lateral Thinking where she shares insights from neuroscience with her students.

'I think as teachers we sometimes underestimate how dominated our work is by the exam system. That's TY's great strength, the liberation from a terminal exam. So, we have that great flexibility to pursue the interests and passions of both teachers and students. In TY a teacher can be more sensitive to the process of learning than just covering content, for example, going in-depth on topics that command attention and using a wider range of experiential learning activities,' says Gearoidín.

'Hence,' she continues, 'in the Irish TY classroom, we can spend time on oral skill development. This can give the students great confidence in their ability to communicate, even if imperfectly. I have noticed that during TY some students realise for the first time that communication is not primarily about linguistic perfection but about communicating.'

Applying the principle of starting from where the students are, Gearoidín finds it more effective to explore the richness of Irish culture through classroom discussion *as Béarla.* 'English is their everyday language and, as they discuss the historical context of the Irish language and wider themes of cultural identity and pride, the possibilities of emotional engagement and understanding are greater,' she asserts.

Gearoidín increasingly sees an intercultural educational relevance in such discussions. 'The presence of a wider variety of nationalities, cultures and belief systems in Ireland today, gives a new urgency to understanding Irish heritage and identity. I sometimes see a new confidence and pride as students realise the global achievements of Irish people and the respect and affection in which we Irish people are held, generally,' she says. She adds that the exploration of language and Ireland's changing cultural landscape often leads to discussion on the value of bilingualism.

A particularly practical way of using Irish in TY is to extend students' vocabulary about their own learning in TY. 'Getting the students to talk in Irish about their voluntary work, mini-company, work experience, research and other components of the programme deepens both their language skills and their understanding of their learning. I think it is so important that they don't see education as just textbook driven or classroom contained. TY's focus on the bigger picture: maturing, opportunities to travel, to develop social skills, to explore work possibilities, to volunteer, to dream, is very important. We don't put enough emphasis on these in the other five years,' says Gearoidín. She quickly adds, 'That is not to say that there is no place for reading skills, aural comprehension, written work or the mastery of grammar; there is, but it is much more than that.'

The Newpark programme also encourages TY students to make individual choices to opt in to a wide range of activities. 'In TY the students can, if they wish, involve themselves in Irish-languages groups, competitions and other activities. It fits well with the emphasis on self-directed learning, on personal motivation,' says Gearoidín.

As indicated, Gearoidín is a strong advocate of classroom discussion. 'Most classes are based on active learning in pairs or groups,' she says. With a strong background in CSPE, she is comfortable with experiential learning activities. 'I also employ research, project work and debating. Dramatic improvisation and adaptation of work or stage can also be effective. I also invite students to be innovative, to design their own educational activities,' she says.

If Gearoidín, who has more than twenty years experience of teaching TY, was advising someone starting out to teach a module, what would she say? 'Firstly, take time to "start with the end in mind". Ask what you want the students to have experienced and achieved and then, work backwards,' she replies. 'Secondly, enjoy and make good use of the flexibility you have in TY regarding content and time. Thirdly, be courageous enough to engage honestly with your students. Listen to them. Let them know you wish to cater better for their abilities, interests and possibilities. Go further and look for honest feedback so that you can take strong ownership of the module. Fourthly, remember the big picture of TY's mission and encourage your students to "think big", to undertake activities that are new and even frightening – I'm thinking dance, singing, public speaking – and remind them that you don't have to be wealthy to find ways to experience new adventures, to discover new learning,' she says. 'It's a great opportunity for students to get to know themselves better, to discover their learning preferences, to dream about their future,' Gearoidín concludes with seasoned realism: 'If you think the school management is not fully with you, start small, keep them and your colleagues in the picture. Remember that while TY might be closer to "real" education, we work within the constraints of a "system" where perfection is seldom attained. But continue to strive for it, especially in your own classroom.'

Guidelines

The TY *Guidelines*, reflecting the thrust of the programme generally, is broad and invitational rather than prescriptive when it comes to Irish. It encourages teachers to shape their own courses, as Gearoidín has done in Newpark. The opening paragraph states:

> The Transition Year offers an opportunity to place increased emphasis on speaking the language and on creating environments which support this approach. In general, the use of projects will greatly help to provide the basis for spoken and written communication, including participation in debates, plays, Irish dancing, singing of traditional Irish songs, Irish language competitions, etc. (DE, 1993, p. 22).

The *Guidelines* continue:

> Particular attention could be focused on projects in Irish culture and history, and on current affairs in local, national, European and World contexts.

Many of the examples cited to realise this, though written in 1993, continue to be relevant. However, one can imagine the list being extended, particularly to embrace developments in information and communications technology. The examples with a *Gaeilge* focus are:

> ... history of the locality; places of historical interest in the locality or region; important local organisations or events; radio and television programmes in Irish; Irish and other media; classroom talks and discussion in Irish with personalities from different walks of life; visits to the Gaeltacht including exchanges with schools.

18

IN HISTORY'S FOOTSTEPS

In the CBS Secondary School, Kilkenny there are four TY classes. Each group studies history for two 40-minute periods each week throughout the year. Significantly, the classes are taught by the class tutors which include the TY co-ordinator Gerard Morrissey. 'Most subjects are taught as modules that rotate,' explains Gerard, 'but with history we move out of the classroom quite a lot so the full year approach makes sense.' At Christmast and in May, Dublin is the destination; locations visited include Kilmainham Gaol; War Memorial Gardens, Islandbridge; Arbour Hill; Glasnevin Cemetery; Croke Park Museum and Stadium Tour. There are also regular excursions to savour Kilkenny's rich heritage and the school gives an imaginative historical twist to an optional trip to Bavaria in February.

'Genocide is one of the topics we look at in depth in TY History,' says Gerard. 'Armed with some knowledge of Nazism, the students recognise the significance of No 12 Arcisstrasse, Munich. This year we – TY students and teachers – sat in silent awe in Room 105, Hitler's office, where the Munich Agreement was signed on September 30, 1938.' He sighs and says, 'this was the room from which Prime Minister Neville Chamberlain emerged and then returned home to declare to an anxiously awaiting British public the ironic phrase: Peace in our time.' Gerard adds: 'When students and teachers share experiences like that, the bond that's forged can be very strong.'

As TY co-ordinator, Gerard has become very aware of the need to keep modules relevant and stimulating. 'In History, we work hard to strike a balance between interest, enjoyment and engagement, avoiding boredom, so that we build a foundation on which all students can appreciate the topics as well as the evolving world politics,' he says.

The focus on the rise of Nazism was given a poignant sharpness by a visit to the school by Tomi Reichental. Born in 1935 in Slovakia, Tomi's book *I was a Boy in Belsen* tells the story of how he survived a concentration camp. 'Even the most lethargic learners were impressed by the story of such a witness to history,' remarks Gerard. The school also has an annual Tomi Reichental Award for a TY history project. 'The recipient is invariably the student who throughout the entire year has revealed and displayed a fascination and enthusiasm for the subject irrespective of standardised and measured academic testing,' adds Gerard.

The genocide dimension of TY history is enhanced by the study of films such *as Schindler's List, The Boy in the Striped Pyjamas, Hotel Rwanda* and *Letter to Daniel,* as well as the BBC Documentary *Valentina's Story.* Through their TY history programmes students not only gain insights into Nazism but also study what happened in Rwanda in 1994 and Bosnia in 1995 as well as the Al-Anfal campaign against the Kurds in Iraq.

Local history

When it comes to local history, readers might say that Gerard Morrissey and other teachers of history in Kilkenny are exceptionally fortunate with what's on their doorsteps. 'True, we are lucky here with Kilkenny Castle, St Canice's Cathedral, the Black Abbey in the city and then Jerpoint Abbey, the coalmines at Castlecomer, Woodstock House and Dunmore Caves within the county,' concedes Gerard. Furthermore, for interested students there is a remarkable richness of historical books relating to Kilkenny.

The interdisciplinary challenge

The TY *Guidelines* locate the teaching of history – as happens with many school systems across the globe – in the wider context of Environmental and Social Studies, linking Historical Studies, Geographical Studies, Social Studies and Civic, Social and Political Studies together. A co-ordinated, interdisciplinary, thematic approach is suggested. The overarching vision is that 'environmental and social education prepares pupils for active responsible citizenship in local, national and international life.' Under 'Historical Studies', local history, history of arts and crafts, archaeology, architecture, classical studies, social history, heritage studies, etc. are mentioned. The list under 'Geographical Studies' is the local landscape and environment, planning and development, tourism awareness, etc. For 'Social Studies', the *Guidelines* list practical applications of scientific principles and theories; influence of science on industry and the environment; human beings and the biosphere; ecology; pollution; population trends. Finally, under 'Civic, Social and Political Studies' citizenship, rights and responsibilities, systems of government, European Community, development education, etc. are listed.

In the 1990s, shortly after the mainstreaming of TY, the Department of Education, with support from the European Commission Representation in Ireland, published an interdisciplinary, thematic resource for schools: *In Search of Europe*. Two copies were sent to each school and there were regional workshops on implementing the pack. Teachers of history reported that a booklet included in the pack *An Overview of European Integration since 1945* was much appreciated. Indeed, in response to requests, the Commission reprinted thousands of copies. However, other feedback, while positive about the resource, suggested that interdisciplinary modules were not popular. Interdisciplinary modules, particularly when they require a number of teachers to work in harmony, seem, in many schools, to remain a largely unfulfilled aspiration from the *Guidelines*.

Flexibility

Gerard Morrissey believes that in TY teachers need to be both flexible and opportunistic. 'When something is stirring in world politics, the currency and urgency of an issue can engage students greatly,' he says. He cites the American Presidential campaign, the Arab Spring, tensions in Ukraine as topics that presented themselves in recent years. 'As a teacher of history opportunities to illustrate that what happens today becomes history tomorrow should be grasped. We also see, so often, that following war a peace must be negotiated as much as those individuals guilty of war crimes must be brought to account, something learned from the Nuremberg Trials Courtroom No. 600; he says.

Another strand of the TY history programme in CBS Kilkenny looks at Ireland at the start of the twentieth century, inviting comparisons across a 100-year timescale. 'We look at the Celtic Revival, the new Nationalism and present profiles of the signatories of the 1916 Proclamation but daily life at the turn of the century is a big theme; says Gerard. 'With the wonderful resources from the National Archives of census data from both 1901 and 1911, there is a natural link with family history; he adds. 'Students construct family trees, analyse heraldic coats of arms and gain clearer insights into their own identities; says Gerard. Each student undertakes a project on a significant event or personality connected to his family.

In a valuable development from what students have studied in CSPE at Junior Cycle, the history programme also explores key concepts associated with political ideologies including pluralism, socialism, communism, capitalism, left wing, right wing and nationalism linked to a brief account of Irish political parties.

Finally, and perhaps unsurprisingly in a county with such a distinguished hurling history, the TY students look at the development and heritage of Gaelic Games, the GAA's contribution to Irish sporting, cultural and social life. 'Online newspaper archives are a great resource for this; says Gerard.

Assessment

'With a view to encouraging TY students to become more self-directed learners, we require them to record all personal and group work on their own personally developed website which we call the E-portfolio; explains Gerard. This work is subsequently examined by interview with at least two teachers in early May, with the students revealing their work using a data projector. The interviewers pose questions relating to the design, content and presentation of

their E-portfolio. 'We always find that the five-day Bavarian educational trip features hugely for the 64 per cent to 74 per cent of
students who were fortunate to participate on this tour,' he says.

In addition to the portfolio interviews, individual teachers of
history also assess their respective classes aurally, examine the
essays and formal project work, and conduct class tests. 'I think
that oral presentations in class where a student has to condense
project work into six or seven slides and make a presentation
to peers and a teacher is very effective. They learn from the experience, from the feedback and advice from the floor. These
presentations are also useful practice runs for the end of year
E-portfolio interviews,' says Gerard. He also believes that developing communication skills and self-confidence resonates very
well with TY's wider goal of gaining social maturity in order to
interact with the wider world.

As evident in other chapters, project work presents opportunities but also has pitfalls. 'In TY history you can encourage
students to pursue avenues of personal research that pique their
interest,' remarks Gerard. 'Of course,' he warns, 'you have to be
alert to the possibility that he will simply "google" the topic, cut
and paste bits of what he finds and then present the teacher with
a clichéd response,' he says. 'We try to be more imaginative than
that!'

Other legacies

Gerard Morrissey sees the interest sparked and kindled by the TY
history module translating into between 30 and 35 students opting for LC history in fifth year. He adds that, over the years, many
students have admitted that, despite a love of history, they opt for
other subjects as they anticipate that the amount of work required
to research and write essays to higher level English standards
would be too much of a workload.

Finally, as a teacher of history and TY co-ordinator, Gerard
had consistently observed how, at the end of senior cycle, when it
comes to final graduation and students are reflecting on their time
in school, TY is central to positive memories. 'They talk about
friendships, about camaraderie and so much of this is tied up with

the various history trips at home and abroad,' he says. 'When we talk about levels of maturation and personal development in TY, you can see, as the year progresses, one manifestation being how well they form friendships with each other. Another is the way many show their respect for teachers not simply as figures of authority and knowledge but as persons.'

19

FUNDRAISING FOR CHARITY

Irish Times columnist and teacher at Muckross Park College, Dublin, Breda O'Brien, remarked in a 2014 newspaper article that:

> People regularly talk about how passive and apathetic young people are. They rarely talk about how, for example, so many charities in this country would fall apart without the fundraising done by transition year students alone.

Walking down Dublin's Grafton Street, particularly on a Friday afternoon, the unsuspecting visitor can be assailed by numerous young people, often in school uniform, rattling collections boxes. On enquiry you will usually discover that many are TY students. Sometimes, on further probing, the youngsters in question articulate limited knowledge of the work done by the charity whose name is on the box. Uncomfortable questions can arise. Are they volunteers or conscripts? How well prepared are they? What role, if any, does the charity play in the process? How exactly does fundraising fit into a school's TY programme? Is this a lazy way of filling Friday afternoon's timetable?

One school with extensive experience of TY-related fundraising is St Mary's Secondary School in Ballina, County Mayo. 'We build three distinct fundraising efforts into the TY programme,' explains principal Patsy Sweeney. 'In the first term we concentrate on a local need. Then, often coinciding with Lent, we focus on a global issue. In the final term, we do a big fundraiser for a national charity.' This formula has served the school and numerous charities well. 'From the beginning we were adamant that while fundraising would form a core element of the Transition Year social outreach programme, it would be planned, timetabled and strictly controlled,' adds Annette Leonard, a long-serving teacher at the school and an energetic driving force behind many imaginative campaigns. 'Innovative fundraising has become a distinct feature of our TY programme,' she remarks.

While the school has refined its approach to fundraising, it still maintains some flexibility so that students can respond to emergencies and disasters. For example, the school funded the purchase of a boat following the Indian Ocean tsunami in 2004, donated a night's proceeds from the TY Musical in 2010 to victims of the Haiti Earthquake, and more recently assisted Cystic Fibrosis West reach their target figure to complete a CF unit in Mayo General Hospital.

'In the first term, a local charity, the Ballina branch of St Vincent de Paul, is supported in varied ways, one of which is by fundraising,' continues Patsy. Within the framework of the social outreach programme and as part of the Gaisce award, some girls volunteer for Junior St Vincent de Paul. 'All TY students get involved in the term's major fundraising effort at Christmas when we collect food items as well as toys, make-up and jewellery,' she continues.

Every school builds its own rituals and traditions which in turn shape its ethos. Since the early 1990s, the Staff Christmas Panto has become established as a much anticipated annual event in St Mary's. All proceeds go to St Vincent de Paul. 'Lovingly and wittily crafted each year by our talented drama department, the Panto celebrates and scandalises staff and students in equal measure and has a cast of over 30 staff participating,' enthuses the principal. 'No secret or event is spared,' she adds, her eyes twinkling. The finale is a presentation of collected gifts as well as cash to local St Vincent de Paul volunteers. 'We know that these are sensitively distributed to families in need, many with children here in the school.'

Trócaire, Concern, Goal and the Mercy International Trust – where one of the school's retired staff members now works – have all benefitted from fundraising by St Mary's TY students in the second term. 'Many undertake a 24 hour fast,' adds Patsy. 'Then at Eastertime someone from the relevant charity comes in to the school, talks about their work and the students present them with a cheque.'

Third term fundraising by TY students for a national charity has catapulted the school to national, even international, notice. 'It began humbly enough in the early 1990s with a basketball marathon,' explains Annette Leonard. 'It was mainly the TY students themselves. There were guest appearances by our local Ballina National League Basketball Players such as Liam McHale and his brothers. In 1995 the TY girls, with help from some basketball players, staff and other students, played basketball continuously from 11.00 a.m. to 3.45 p.m. The games, refereed by PE teachers in the school, raised over €2,000 for the Children's Hospital, Crumlin. This was part of the hospital's fledgling 'Jump for Joy' campaign. I remember the students got a set of singlets from the national organisers for their efforts. Precious,' remarks Annette.

'Jump for Joy' has morphed into a national programme Kellogg's 'Fun Raise 4 Kids.' Proceeds go to the Medical and Research Foundation at Our Lady's Hospital in Crumlin, Dublin. To encourage school participation, the hospital initiated the 'Tom Collins Trophy' and St Mary's have won this annual award on a number of occasions. Other schools to distinguish themselves in recent years include St Michael's College, Listowel, County Kerry, Ardscoil Rath Iomgháin, County Kildare and the Ursuline Secondary School, Thurles, County Tipperary. Part of the challenge is to come up with an imaginative new fundraising idea every year. St Mary's Secondary School, Ballina hit the jackpot in 2009 when, in a very clever initiative for an all-girls school, they organised a race where all runners had to wear high heels. Not only did they raise €10,000 for the children's hospital but they became official entrants into the Guinness World Record Holders. The entry reads: *The most people running in high heeled shoes is 763 in an event organised by St Mary's Secondary School in Ballina, County Mayo, Ireland on 24 April 2009.*

Achieving Guinness World Record status can be addictive and in 2012 TY students were central to another record breaking effort. Almost 1,600 people performed the well-known 'Rock the Boat' dance routine – surpassing the 1,428-strong record previously set. You can check it out on YouTube. 'Of course, getting these awards is wonderful for morale,' comments Pasty Sweeney, 'but it also supports real needs and highlights for the students the power of innovative thinking, a central feature of Transition Year,' she adds. She should know. Prior to becoming principal, Patsy Sweeney was seconded from St Mary's, where she had been TY co-ordinator, to the TY Support Service. In 2001-02 she served as national co-ordinator of that service. During those years she introduced dozens of schools to innovative teaching and learning projects and saw at first hand the powerful impact fresh thinking can have on a school.

But, she continues, the fundraising stories are not finished. A further venture was to take the 'Beat the Apprentice' challenge. This not only resulted in the precious accolade of 'Guinness World Challenge' with the innovative and catchy title of 'Snap, Record, Crackle and Rock' but a visit to the school from *Apprentice* stars Bill Cullen and Jackie Lavin. Bill Cullen had been a vocal critic of Transition Year. In 2009, the *Irish Independent* ran a headline 'Cullen wants transition "doss year" scrapped.' The report, by John Walshe, began, 'Apprentice star Bill Cullen last night branded the transition year a "disaster" which should be scrapped.' He continued by adding that, 'They can fall into bad habits and bad company, and get into a habit of just being lazy.' However, on local radio in Ballina after his visit to St Mary's, he made a public retraction of his views, praising the school's TY programme and claiming it was one of the best schools he had ever stood in!

Having representatives of the benefitting charities present at fundraising efforts is central to the St Mary's, Ballina strategy in TY. Furthermore, TY students have also visited Crumlin hospital. 'They are treated like celebrities there,' remarks Annette, 'particularly in St John's Oncology Ward which is the focus of so much of their efforts.' Fiona Whelan, head of Marketing and Communications at the Children's Medical and Research Foundation at Crumlin, says that she regards the Ballina students as 'absolutely incredible.' Fiona adds that the charity works with many schools and values their support very much. 'Another great example,' she explains' is from Clongowes Wood College in County Kildare. 'They have been fundraising for us for about twenty years. They have an annual duck push which is a virtual rite of passage for TY students,' she says.

Contrasting perspectives

The word 'fundraising' does not appear anywhere in the DE *Guidelines* on TY. Yet, it has become a central ingredient of the programme in many schools. One can argue that, like in St Mary's, fundraising activities are especially well-suited to realising some of the 'interrelated and interdependent' aims of the programme:

1. Education for maturity with the emphasis on personal development including social awareness and increased social competence

2. The promotion of general, technical and academic skills with an emphasis on interdisciplinary and self-directed learning

3. Education through experience of adult and working life as a basis for personal development and maturity.

Charities themselves, many under pressure in recent years due to various scandals, are sensitive to the need to be more transparent about their activities, especially how they spend money. The website www.GoodCharity.ie proposes five of the most relevant questions everyone supporting a charity should ask. These are helpful signposts for schools, TY co-ordinators and TY students:

1. What problem is the charity trying to solve?

2. Does the charity's approach to solving that problem make sense?

3. What has the charity achieved to date?

4. Is the charity signed up to any professional standards?

5. Does the charity make information on its finances publicly available?

Locating fundraising activities in the context of a continuation of the Junior Cycle subject Civic, Social and Political Education (CSPE) may lead teachers and students to explore other dimensions of the work of charities. A United States sociologist, Janet

Poppendieck, poses questions about whether people favour charity over justice. Does participation in – and awareness of – charitable efforts act as a 'moral safety valve'?, she asks. Participating in a walk-a-thon for the homeless or donating a box of macaroni and cheese to a food drive may keep us from confronting the underlying injustice of a society where great wealth exists alongside grinding poverty, she contends.

Irish researchers Bryan and Bracken (2011) found that, in the arena of development education, schools frequently tend towards 'soft' forms of activism which they characterise as the three Fs – fundraising, fasting and fun. Their concern is that uncritical understandings of development 'endorse individualistic, charitable acts and simplistic "quick-fix" solutions as legitimate responses to complex and intractable development problems.' However, they continue, 'This is not to deny that involvement in charitable activities may lead to a longer-term commitment to development, nor to critique individual forms of social activism *per se*.' They acknowledge that small steps can lead to bigger transformations and that 'there is much to be said for the Gandhian philosophy of being the change one wants to see in the world.'

As the St Mary's Ballina experience suggests, a well-structured fundraising programme can link well with wider educational goals. Such activities can play a valuable role in heightening the social awareness TY aims for in nurturing responsible and participative citizenship. Skills of project management, research, budgeting, campaigning and public relations through experiential learning can be fostered. Young people can harness their energy, skills and enthusiasm to address local and global issues. Finally, fundraising can scaffold schools' efforts to realise their responsibilities of socialising young people into dispositions of giving, volunteering and increased social concern.

20

CREATING SPACE TO CULTIVATE SENSITIVE BUDDING TALENT

Prior to lecturing in English Pedagogies at the University of Limerick, where she works with student teachers, Carmel Hinchion taught in Carrigaline Community School, County Cork. 'Supporting students to find their voice through writing has been one of my big passions. I am continuously astounded at the insight and writing capability of young people,' says Carmel. Indeed, she can still vividly recount poems and stories written by her students more than twenty years ago. She quotes Seamus Heaney who said, 'finding a voice means that you get your own feeling into your own words and your words have the feel of you about them.' Carmel says that over the years she has seen:

> ... how all students can be nurtured and scaffolded in saying something important, intriguing, fun, powerful, moving, real, magical, different, emotional, personal and thoughtful as they play with ideas and words, as they tune in to themselves and others. I have seen too their rising confidence and sense of pride in their growing identity as 'writer.' What an exciting achievement, 'I am a writer.'

Carmel continues: 'As teachers I think we need to promote aliveness, interest and awareness in young students. Educationalist Maxine Greene reminds us to be liberated from "right angles" and to wear the "sombreros of possibility". Creative writing liberates us into ourselves and others. Greene (1995, p. 123) said: "At the very least, participatory involvement with the many forms of art can enable us to *see* more in our experience, to *hear* more on normally unheard frequencies, to *become conscious* of what daily routines have obscured, what habit and convention have suppressed".

Other possibilities

Under the heading 'English' the TY *Guidelines* offer a rich list of possibilities. Starting with, 'Broad reading for the sake of enjoyment', the *Guidelines* proceed to encourage, 'Attendance at drama productions; viewing of films; listening to radio; the staging of a play (even a prescribed one); the writing for and production of a school magazine; the development of the individual pupil's talent for writing in a particular genre, and entry into competitions for same where possible; radio and video production by the class; debates within the school and between schools; talks from pupils to the class on projects done by them, e.g. on a favourite writer; the study of words, the origins of words, and related words in different languages; coverage of a short history of English literature.'

The list of possibilities concludes by suggesting an interdisciplinary approach to a topic or period (e.g. a World War) from the points of view of English literature, History, Music, Art, Media coverage, and so on.

Twenty years on, the evidence suggests that not only has this broad framework worked in TY programmes, but that boundaries are being stretched. Indeed, some creative writing initiatives are healthy indicators of educational imagination in action.

Listowel Writers' Week

There are many examples of writing-related activities which reach beyond conventional classrooms. For example, in recent years TY students from Kerry schools have been invited to hear published writers read from their work and see them being interviewed as part of Listowel Writers' Week *Operation Education*. 'Students really enjoy hearing a writer's own voice, reading from his or her own work,' says Katherina Broderick, Principal of Presentation Secondary School, Castleisland and a teacher of English.

'The popularity and value which schools place on *Operation Education* is such that trips to Writers' Week now form part of the school calendar and examinations are sometimes planned around it,' explains Katherina.

'Meeting a living writer can be quite a powerful experience, whether it is Niall McMonagle interviewing Paul Durcan or John Boyne describing his writing techniques and sharing some of the ups and downs it takes to complete a best-seller are experiences the students will not forget and will value forever,' she adds. 'The setting is quite informal and the conversations flow. Students pose their own questions and that is both memorable and worthwhile,' she says. 'In my experience here and in the previous school where I worked, students return to school from their visit to Writers' Week full of enthusiasm, aware that they have been part of a very special literary experience,' says Katherina. She is also a strong believer in bringing writers into the classroom. 'When I taught in Causeway Comprehensive School in North Kerry, I witnessed the magic a writer like Tommy Frank O'Connor could work when talking about his writing with TY students. I remember him saying, 'Students I work with get to understand the creative process, thereby enabling them to approach the writers on the syllabus with greater confidence,' says Katherina.

'Fighting Words'

In 2009 Roddy Doyle and Seán Love set in motion a creative educational initiative called *Fighting Words*. They wanted to give children and teenagers an outlet for their creative writing. 'We thought it was daft, in a country that prides itself in being a land of writers, that there was so little opportunity for writing,' state the founders.

In the first six years of *Fighting Words* the centre, located in Behan Square, Russell Street, Dublin, not far from Croke Park, hosted over 50,000 teenagers and children. This has been possible because of 500 volunteer tutors and mentors. TY students and teachers from all over the country sing the praises of *Fighting Words*. The project gets no state funding and Seán Love emphasises that 'all of our workshops, programmes and summer camps etc. are provided free. All children from every background are welcome and they participate on an equal basis.'

The Irish Times published its fifth *Fighting Words* supplement in April 2015. Testimonies from 'grads' give a taste of its value. 'I first stepped through the doors of *Fighting Words* in September 2010 as a Transition Year student and have remained there since,' remarks Kevin Bird. 'In those years I've been given a place to do something I love and get great opportunities from it. I've got the chance to get short stories published in a book and in *The Irish Times*, have a play performed in the Peacock Theatre and simply meet people with a similar interest in writing. Since then I've gone on to study English at Trinity College and volunteer for primary school workshops at *Fighting Words*.'

Sarah Merriman, a DCU student currently studying in Beijing, first set foot in *Fighting Words* during TY work experience. She describes her experiences there as 'amazing'. Sarah has also seen her work performed on the Peacock stage and continues to volunteer.

Researchers Francesca Lorenzi and Irene White[1] evaluated the *Fighting Words* creative writing model in 2013. They concluded:

> .... the Fighting Words model has positively impacted on participants' personal, social and academic development and the analysis highlights specific areas where this impact is evident. The findings, among others, indicate that participants in Fighting Words demonstrate increased levels of engagement –with creative writing and with the school experience - and motivation, improved confidence and self-esteem, recognition of and pride in creative ability, a greater ability to work collaboratively, and improved literacy.

As evident on the *Fighting Words* website, as well as encouraging creative writing, Seán Love and Roddy Doyle always saw their project as having a civic and a social purpose. Seán encapsulates the vision of the project in a quote from President Michael D. Higgins who visited the centre in 2013:

---

[1] These researchers work at the of the Centre for Culturally Responsible Research and Evaluation in the School of Education Studies, Dublin City University. The full report is available at http://www.fightingwords.ie/publications/dcu-report-fighting-words-model

When we learn to read and to write, to understand letters on a page and to create our own sentences using those letters we are handed a great gift, a gift that allows us to engage fully in society, to educate and inform ourselves to open our minds to realise our possibilities and to discover new worlds and new ways of thinking.

The evaluation noted, 'Openness, creativity – as the opposite of rote learning – and empowerment are cited as defining purposes of the activities offered by *Fighting Words* by both of its founders. Self-esteem is also mentioned as a recurrent outcome resulting from engagement with *Fighting Words*.

Interviewed as part of the evaluation, NCCA CEO Anne Looney stated:

Fighting Words to me is about voice so it's about giving students the tools to articulate views, opinions, ideas, concepts, questions even if they're challenging ... giving them the tools, giving them the space and ... giving them the confidence as well to find that voice.

One of the principals interviewed for the study remarked: 'I know when we get to the end of TY and we ask them to assess the different activities they've been involved in, *Fighting Words* will always be one they have up there as one of their favourite activities.'

The writing starts in a collaborative way with a group of about 25 students. As Roddy Doyle remarks, 'It's the blank page that terrifies people more than anything else.' So starting with a scenario based role-play, participants are given the opportunity to develop dialogue, create characters and establish a setting, all of which gives participants the inspiration and confidence to start writing. Typing and projecting the initial words on to a screen is particularly effective. Seán Love says: 'When they would start orally with an idea ...we'd give them scenarios that they could ad-lib and kind of act out and we'd type up these brief dialogues. It works without fail, no matter who the students are, once they see it become real, written up on the screen, they start to edit it and they take ownership of it.'

Teachers who took part in the study reported a transfer of the positive atmosphere of *Fighting Words* into the school environment. One teacher said, 'it helped us to bond as a group of people who love stories.' A dedicated space for creative interactions is among the suggestions made to improve creative writing in schools. Others include the support of tutors and the involvement of established writers.

Seán Love says that one of the unexpected benefits of *Fighting Words* has been the engagement with learners with special needs. He says: 'Some of my favourite workshops are with children and adults with special needs. The feedback from themselves and from their parents and teachers, or whoever's with them, is that it can have extraordinary benefits for them ... particularly, I'm struck by parents of children with Asperger's about what it has opened for their children ... and for the visually impaired ... I think the workshops with those students are just the best fun ever.'

Principals interviewed for the research comment on the positive power of creative writing for young people with mental health issues, for shy and inarticulate children and for those with behavioural issues. One principal in particular puts nurturing creativity in a school context: 'While we offer a broad curriculum the syllabi are very constraining so the imagination of the child is very constrained ... generally they are reminded to regurgitate the facts, the facts, the facts and sometimes there isn't space for expression aside of the facts ... generally they don't get the opportunity ... kids have imaginations and we forget that they have imaginations and ye know positive day dreaming and visualisation again from a de-stressing perspective is very important ... it's a way of releasing. Imagination is very, very important and it's something that is not encouraged enough at second-level and it's something that should be cherished.'

Slam poetry

Poet Stephen Murray is an increasingly familiar figure in TY classrooms. Stephen is director of Inspireland, an ambitious group of artists whose mission is 'to push the limits of the Transition Year project to its maximum potential'. According to the website:

Inspireland is where creativity, magic and education come together in the classroom to deliver innovative, exciting arts and literacy programmes that will live in the memories of students forever.

Stephen is an advocate of Slam Poetry, a movement that began in the USA in the 1980s. Writers perform their own work in front of a live audience, judges vote and, in some cases, a slam poetry competition may involve eliminations over a number of rounds. Stephen organised a competition for young Irish writers and 5,000 took part. Four winners were selected to travel to the USA during the summer of 2015 for the HBO-televised slam poetry competition *Brave New Voices.*

One of the four and Irish co-captain Melissa Kavanagh traces her involvement in slam poetry back to TY. She says: 'My teacher Ms. Connolly introduced us all to the *Brave New Voices* through YouTube videos. It was she who brought Stephen Murray to our school, and in his workshop I wrote *Winter's Night.* From there I entered the piece into the All Ireland School Slam competition and came in second place, and haven't put the pen down since.'

Melissa says that poetry has become such a positive force in her life: 'I have great faith in the use of poetry to express one's innermost thoughts and feelings, especially when students don't have the opportunities to do so normally. It might sound clichéd to say but it can be a life changer. The way I see it is the further I progress with my own poetry, the greater potential I have to help others. Recently, Team Ireland performed at the Sunday Best Fest in support of the Green Ribbon Campaign. It felt so amazing to speak in a room full of strangers about my own struggles with mental health with such acceptance, but the highlight of the night was in knowing that by doing so, I was helping others. I've been quoted before as saying, "As a Spoken Word poet, I know that one voice can be enough. One voice can still be heard by hundreds. One voice can make a difference" and I stand by it.'

Melissa's teacher in TY, Lisa Connolly of Coláiste Bríde in Clondalkin, Dublin works hard with her students in opening up creative spaces. Asked how she sees her role, she articulates it like this: 'I am not a writer but I am story. I am not a writer but I teach creative writing. I am not a writer but I recognise talent. I am not a·failed writer and thus a teacher. I am not a failed teacher and thus a frustrated writer. I am an observer of flow and I honour it when it appears. Creativity is essentially unpredictable and it cannot be forced. It's not about making sense and imposing structure and logic. It's about openness, trusting, intuiting, sensing and connecting. We are all story. You don't "teach" a story, you share it. Teachers are overly concerned with physical space, texts, literary techniques and traditions. These are stifling and confusing in equal measure and can be constrictive.'

OK, Lisa, the reader might say, but how does all this translate into practice in the TY classroom? She continues: 'The space that creativity requires is an inner space, an opening, located in a type of sanctuary, where the students can draw from their own deeply familiar and feel safe in sharing without inhibition. You don't need to go looking for inspiration, you are inspiration. Critical comparisons with establishment can be counterproductive to any true sense of freedom and flow resulting in insecurity and impotence.'

And, the pragmatic questioner might continue, how does one know what 'works'? Lisa says: 'What is a good student? A teacher in the making. What is a good teacher? A successful student. The system is hypnotised by the illusion that if you pump content and assimilate technique, just as you might force feed geese for *foie gras*, the outcome will be better content and more sophisticated technique. Actually the outcome is usually terminal in terms of creativity, the pressure of such unreasonable expectation simply stifles flow and confidence. When the student doesn't measure up the system just gives up, paradoxically being written off en route to being a writer.'

And, finally what advice might Lisa offer to other teachers? She responds: 'Be counterintuitive with your practice and don't be in a hurry to throw the weight of established writers over sensitive budding talent. Create a space and cultivate the climate so that they can be spontaneous. Ultimately convention and creativity are at odds. I doubt they can co-exist; one has to collapse in order for the other to have any kind of real footing. For me risk taking and flow are natural to teenagers. They are not yet locked into firm identities, rather, they're feeling their way and testing all kinds of water. As a teacher, my role is to make them feel safe in their personal exploration, to maintain a climate such that they can play and not be judged or discouraged. This, of course, means I have to be very self aware and present and see them as equals, which is not a traditional teacher perspective, but then I have not yet been fully assimilated!'

'Don't be a sleepwalker in your life or in your classroom. Be alert, conscious and fresh. Watch as your students surprise and delight you, but more importantly as they surprise and delight themselves. That way no one is left in creative limbo waiting for Godot.'

21

THE POTENTIAL OF SCIENCE

Teaching science in Transition Year is sometimes seen as a case of unrealised potential. Researcher Sarah Hayes and her colleagues at the University of Limerick contrast a focus on science in society in the TY *Guidelines* with the narrowness of Junior and Leaving Certificate syllabi. They state: 'The opportunity provided to teachers by the Transition Year could be a crucial factor in the development of scientifically-literate citizens, the promotion of positive attitudes towards science and interest in and uptake of science, if it were properly utilised.' (Hayes, Childs and O'Dwyer, 2013, p. 739). They also see TY science as having the possibility of 'laying the foundations for a rich and rewarding scientific career for many students.'

However, despite these possibilities in TY, Hayes and her colleagues state that 'science is viewed as an integral component of the year, with a high value attached to it, but practices used within Science provision, teaching and learning, illustrate a resistance to change even when the curriculum content is fresh and different.' (ibid, p. 740). Their research 'shows that the majority of teachers are not taking this opportunity to widen their students' view of Science but are instead teaching predominantly from the Leaving Certificate Science curricula' (ibid, p. 742).

The researchers suggest that an ambiguity in the *Guidelines* sends 'mixed messages' to schools about Science in TY. They contrast the statement that 'the Transition Year is 'NOT' a part of the Leaving Certificate programme, and teachers' should not teach Leaving Certificate material' (DE, 1993, p. 5) with the statement that 'the Transition Year does not need to exclude Leaving Certificate material, but that the Leaving Certificate material should be chosen to augment the Leaving Certificate experience, laying a solid foundation for Leaving Certificate studies.' (ibid p. 5). This has led to a situation where, for 66 per cent of teachers, 'It has become the "norm" to teach aspects of the Leaving Certificate in the Transition Year' (Hayes et al., p. 741). They conclude, 'Teachers are also wary of departing from familiar practices and express concern about having to teach "outside the box", without the security of routine practices and a familiar syllabus to rely on.'

Hayes et al (2013, p. 742) state that, 'The findings ... reinforced earlier anecdotal findings that Science teachers struggled to find suitable material to teach in the Transition Year and were dissatisfied with the way Science was taught but were ill-equipped, in the main, to design their own courses and materials.' There was clearly a need to produce suitable materials to help teachers use the Transition Year more effectively to bridge the gap between junior and senior cycles.

Their findings led the Limerick researchers to develop a 'TY science project'. So far, more than a dozen modules have been published. Importantly, all followed the following criteria:

1. Builds on the Junior Science Course
2. Relates Science to everyday life
3. Develops communication skills
4. Develops ICT skills
5. Develops practical skills
6. Develops inquiry and investigative skills
7. Fosters group work
8. Develops scientific literacy
9. Encourages an interdisciplinary perspective, bringing in all the main Sciences, depending on the topic.

More about these modules is available at the website of the National Centre for Excellence in Mathematics and Science Teaching and Learning (NCE-MSTL).

Guidelines

Before moving on to individual teacher perspectives, it is worth visiting the 1993 DE *Guidelines*. They favour using TY to broaden students' experience of science activities. Astronomy, the chemical industry and food and agriculture are suggested as examples. Consistent with the underlying thrust of the TY programme, the *Guidelines* state: 'Teaching/learning methods should stress pupil activity. Practical work should be more investigatory than is usually the case for Leaving Certificate courses'. The opportunity for seeing the applications of science as well as science in social contexts is emphasised.

> In addition to providing a basis for further study in Science, a Transition Year Science module should explore the links between science and society. An example of this would be a module centered around the concept of energy – its sources, conservation, environmental effects, comparative costs, etc. Such a module could lead to interdisciplinary studies involving a range of other subjects (DE, 1993, p. 27).

The nine criteria developed by Hayes and colleagues can be seen as an imaginative development of these guidelines.

Science as thinking

'I see teaching science as a way of getting young people to ask and answer questions in particular ways', says Terry Mulcahy, a teacher of Physics, Science, Maths and SPHE at Coláiste Ráithín, Bré, Co Chill Mhantáin. He likes the freedom TY offers teachers to exercise professional judgement. For more than a quarter of a century, Terry has been engaged in developing different aspects of TY and has been a science co-ordinator and year-head as well as teacher.

'The TY module in science that I currently teach offers a different perspective to the "we are all scientists now, let's do an experiment", approach to science education. There are four distinct but interrelated modules. Firstly, students are offered opportunities to experience different domains of problem-solving and to appreciate their diversity', he explains. Some students find this challenging, 'as they would often rather be busy than be thinking hard about ideas'.

Aware of this, Terry has imaginatively injected humour, particularly with cartoons and YouTube clips, into the module. 'I think the students appreciate that in this module they get to think about thinking, about how they think and about how they learn.'

The second main strand involves 'communicating science'. Students read and study many pieces from sciences magazines or from scientific or factual books, and then choose one to make a presentation.' continues Terry He recognises that even those who embrace the module enthusiastically find making presentations scary. 'However, you can see them grow in confidence through the process and afterwards.' He adds, 'In my experience, many enjoy the breadth and variety of what we are doing, the non-schooly feel to it. Some are not too comfortable with the move away from assessment by terminal exam. I have been especially struck how this approach allows those who are particularly strong to produce some excellent work and to take pride in their TY achievements.'

The third component of Terry Mulcahy's TY science programme is a taught course on Big Science with the Big Bang Theory at its centre. The final strand is an innovative example of integrating career guidance into specific subjects. 'Each student has to tell their career story as 27-year-old adults, explaining how they got there and why,' says Terry. 'I think this module prompts them to consider what career attracts. They develop information-gathering skills. They gain insights into making informed decisions that impact on careers,' he adds.

Students develop and maintain a TY science portfolio which he assesses. Students' overall grade for TY science is based on the portfolio, the PowerPoint presentation, the career project as well as attendance and participation.

Through evaluations, Terry has noticed that some students who would have rejected science in Junior Cycle develop a more positive attitude in TY. 'The students in Coláiste Ráithín all take one science subject at LC, what we do in TY leads some to consider doing Physics and Chemistry and not opting for Biology only,' he says. 'They also get to try out new things,' he remarks. 'They are exposed to material they wouldn't encounter otherwise. They learn a little about thinking and learning. They learn the practicalities of preparing and making presentations within deadlines,' he adds.

His pedagogical approach illustrates neatly the observation by Hargreaves, Earl and Ryan (1996) that programmes for adolescents need to be relevant, imaginative and challenging. 'Yes, there is active learning. I emphasise critical thinking. Group work and discussion are central to the approach. I mix direct instruction with collaborative learning. ICT use is integrated at all stages. Students also experience project-based learning. As mentioned earlier, problem-solving, both with open and closed problems, is a thread running through everything I do. When it comes to assessment, variety is also key. I include open topic exploration, structured reading, open reading, portfolios, oral presentations as well as attendance and participation,' says Terry.

Reflective practice

Terry is a good example of what Stephen Brookfield (1995) calls a 'critically reflective teacher'. Brookfield sees excellent teachers as those who continually hone an individualised 'authentic voice'. A benefit of ongoing critical reflection is, according to Brookfield, inspirational self-assuredness, regular achievement of teaching goals and motivated, critically reflective students. Brookfield suggests that teachers need to increase their awareness of their teaching from as many perspectives as possible. In particular, he highlights four particular lenses for critical reflection. Firstly, there is the autobiographical lens or self-reflection. This is foundational, building on one's own previous experience as a learner as well as reflecting on the assumptions employed when teaching. The second lens is that of students' eyes. This involves consulting students about the quality of one's teaching. The student lens can confirm or challenge assumptions about teaching approaches as well as power relations within classrooms. Brookfield's third lens is that of colleagues, who can act as mentors and advisors. Professional conversations with colleagues can include open sharing of practices and constructive feedback. The fourth lens involves reading relevant literature, deepening one's appreciation of the wider contexts of classroom teaching.

Terry Mulcahy fits Brookfield's profile of the critically reflective practitioner more accurately than many, although he modestly dismisses such an assessment. But his conversation moves effortlessly through Brookfield's four lenses, from his reflections on his own learning, his references to student evaluations, professional conversations and widespread reading. He talks about the value of postgraduate courses at diploma and masters level as opening perspectives and challenging his assumptions and practices. He also values a more casual professional development of 'one or two night events' that give opportunities to hear what others are doing and where useful tricks and skills can be picked up. Terry reads avidly and, as a science teacher, is a keen enthusiast for factual books that place evidence-based thinking and decision-making at the centre of their argument. He cites *Thinking Fast and Slow* by Kahneman, *The Spirit Level* by Wilkinson and Pickett, *Freakonomics* by Levitt and Dubner, *Psychobabble* by Briers, *The Two Cultures* by Snow and *How the Mind Works* by Pinker as informing the content and tenor of the taught modules, and has encouraged students to read and discuss aspects of them. Within the education sphere, reflecting his individualised voice, he mentions that recent reading has included *Bad Education* by Adey and Dillon, Christodoulou's *Seven Myths about Education* and insights from the ROSE (Relevance of Science Education) project.

Discovery-based learning

Science and Maths teacher Aileen Tennant in St. Mary's Academy CBS, Carlow teaches a Sustainable Living module in TY. This is timetabled in a weekly two-hour time block. 'It is built around a number of key concerns,' Aileen explains, 'especially, sustainability. So, we focus on growing food as a basic life-skill. We explore our carbon footprints and how they can be reduced. Energy consumption at home is measured and analysed. Climate change is studied both as a scientific topic and as a human rights issue.' In Aileen's experience, many TY students engage well with the notion of global citizenship, particularly responsibilities towards the environment.

Asked about methodologies, Aileen's response is quick and detailed. 'As a science teacher I was always keen on discovery-based learning. Through TY in particular I have broadened my repertoire to include other active methodologies. The students engage in poster-making, walking debates, field trips, film reviews and guest speakers are invited to conduct workshops, assessment being both project- and presentation-based,' she says.

Aileen continues, 'I use the Virtual Learning Environment "Edmodo" to assign students projects, assignments and assessments. She remarks that it is 'an effective tool to communicate with students and to provide meaningful feedback on their work'.

Science, according to Aileen, is very suited to project work in TY. She appreciates the structure, focus and motivation that can come from students taking part in project work that has a context beyond the individual school. Over the past decade, Aileen has taught Science and Engineering, Science for Development, Environmental Science, Development Education, IT and Maths modules in TY. She has also mentored students for Young Scientist projects, Young Environmentalist projects and Scifest projects. 'Getting young people to work together in small groups on project work can involve powerful learning at many levels,' she remarks.

A particular interest in environmental issues, combined with imaginative colleagues and a willingness to explore new opportunities, led Aileen to a rich experience in curriculum development. 'I got involved in the continued development, piloting and editing of the 'Development Issues – A Course for Transition Year'. This course had been developed by Joe Clowry, St. Mary's Academy, Carlow, Katrina Foley, St. Mary's CBS, Portlaoise and Patsy Toland, Self Help Africa. Teaching this has changed how I see my role in TY: I am more of a facilitator of learning than someone imparting knowledge. I am more focused on the skills I want the students to develop,' she says. Building on their experiences teaching this course, Aileen and Joe worked on updating the course content and methodologies in 2015 in line with trends in global development. 'Discovery-based learning has become the norm in our classrooms. My own repertoire of methodologies has widened and this has enriched my teaching in Maths and Science from first to sixth year,' she adds. Influenced by these developments, the school has moved to hour-long classes. 'An hour gives more time for active methodologies and allows us dig further into content,' Aileen says. 'It also provides the necessary time for discussion and feedback, which is so important for critical reflection and learning.'

'In TY,' Aileen continues, 'we try to structure the programme around activities that are informed by the students' own interests and experiences. I love the way some of them become researchers, exploring topics they feel passionate about. TY gives young people breathing space to be themselves, to be creative, to develop confidence and a sense of their place in the world. Also, in terms of choosing science subjects for the Leaving Certificate, TY gives them a good platform.'

Aileen Tennant also believes that TY is very good for teachers. 'It gives us opportunities to share specialised knowledge as well as to pursue new areas of interest. We have the flexibility to cultivate a more student-centred learning environment. You see the benefits of this as young people become more self-directed as learners. I also think that, in TY, the rapport with students is strengthened and better student-teacher relationships are developed.' Aileen notes that working on science project with students – which in her case has included immersion trips to sub-Saharan Africa with the winners of the BT Young Scientist 'Science for Development' Award – builds very strong student-teacher bonds.

Aileen's most recent project has been as a co-founder of the Climate Justice Schools Programme (CJSP), which is an international environmental programme between Ireland and the Tanzania Secondary Schools Network (ITSSN). This involves Aileen and her students engaging with global development issues in workshops with her co-founding school, Coláiste Bhríde Carnew and two other schools in Carlow. The programme also involves annual reciprocal visits between Irish and Tanzanian teachers which enrich the level of engagement on the impact of climate change and the knock-on effect on human rights. Young Scientists Tanzania has been integral in linking together the Ireland and Tanzania Secondary Schools Network and provides on the ground support. 'This is a very exciting educational development and an indicator that you are never quite sure where TY projects lead to,' she remarks enthusiastically.

Argument

Majella Dempsey, a lecturer at Maynooth University and leader of MU's Science Education programmes, is enthusiastic about TY's possibilities. 'TY can give students the space to act as real scientists investigating real world problems and arriving at conclusions through discussion, debate and argument,' she says. Majella adds, 'A very relevant quote which I like states: "Observation and experiment are not the bedrock upon which science is built; rather they are handmaidens to the rational activity of constituting knowledge claims through argument" (Newton, Driver and Osborne, 2010, p. 555).'

She continues, 'If we want young people to make sense of the environment they live in, they need to be in it; they need to know where the artefacts they use on a daily basis come from and how they are produced. They need to question the sustainability, in global terms, of the continuity of supply of our consumer goods and recognize the impact this is having locally and globally. TY also opens up space for project work on these topics through Green schools, Young Scientist, Young Social Innovators and Development Education,' she says.

In the best TY classes Majella has observed, students 'explore what it means to be a real scientist, to be part of the process of constructing their own knowledge, to work in groups on addressing problems and engaging in whole class discussions. When you see them defending their viewpoints using data they have generated through investigation, you sense deep learning is taking place,' she adds.

Innovation

Finally, what advice might experienced teachers of TY science offer those starting out? Aileen Tennant puts it like this, 'Be innovative. Keep the material relevant to the modern lives of teenagers and developments in Science, the environment, technology or your particular subject and interest area. Develop clear and realistic aims and objectives for your course. Be realistic with the time-frames. Where possible, allow students to direct their own learning and assessments to enable students to feel responsible for their success. Remember that 'one hat does not fit all.' TY Science classes usually have a mix of abilities and interests so try to respond to them. Provide students with a variety of assessment strategies such as oral presentation skills, electronic presentation skills, time management skills, research techniques. Give the students the criteria for success when setting the assessment i.e. assign marks for time management, communication skills, presentation skills and research skills etc. Avoid eating into the Leaving Certificate programme!'

Terry Mulcahy echoes many of these themes. He says, 'Have a clear, well planned, interesting, challenging programme that allows students at all skill levels and abilities to participate. Have a sense of humour. Find opportunities outside the classroom. Encourage the students to read/access good quality materials within the study field. TY can be a slow burn, it might be years before the benefit of what you are doing becomes apparent, so don't be disheartened if the outcomes you anticipated are not immediately evident. Make mistakes!'

22

CONNECTING WITH STUDENTS

'I love teaching Transition Year,' says Seán Dingle. Seán speaks from the experience of teaching French in TY for 15 years, a module on psychology for 10 and a module on ornithology for one year. He teaches at Gonzaga College, an all boys, fee-charging Jesuit school in Ranelagh, Dublin. 'In essence, TY offers students freedom to explore a wide range of opportunities. We present them with academic challenges. We also present them with other challenges such as those found through exposure to workplaces and our social outreach programme. Most of all, TY allows them mature as human beings,' says Seán.

'As a teacher, I love the way I can explore a range of teaching strategies in TY. Being freed from tight time pressures, exam preparation and curricular restrictions can be very liberating. You connect with students in TY in a different, more human way and this relationship continues through the rest of the senior cycle,' adds Seán. He recognises that some teachers view TY as 'a bit of a nuisance' but strongly believes that if teachers approach TY with 'an open mind and a willingness to embrace its possibilities' they can be surprised by students' interest, engagement and relationships with each other and with their teachers.

Gonzaga College, with an enrolment of about 550 students, offers a wide array of subjects, modules and activities in TY. These include Astronomy, Greek, Rhetoric, Archery, Sailing, Self-defence, Golf, Photography, Horticulture, Cookery, Gaisce and much more. 'Everyone in TY has three periods of French a week,' explains Seán, ' and this is taught through four different modules of six to seven weeks each. The module I teach focuses on music in the Francophone world. This exposes the students to French as a world language and allows us to explore language and culture in Francophone countries away from exam pressure. The flexibility allows teachers to respond creatively to students' interests. Hence, with rotation I teach the same module to four different groups of students. However, each module is unique as we pursue students' interests.'

The rotating, modular timetable also applies to psychology. 'It's a basic introduction to psychology and students show a lot of interest in it', says Seán . Again, he loves the flexibility that allows students to choose topics such as neuropsychology, social psychology and abnormal psychology. 'Social psychology is especially popular', he adds.

The ornithology module is offered on a slightly different basis. 'This module is a mixture of theory, practice and fields trips', he says. It is offered as an option in a two-hour block each week from September to Christmas and again from January to June. 'Being able to share my passion for birdwatching with the students is a privilege. Through ornithology, they learn observation skills, patience, and can link the ordinary and the everyday with big global issues like climate change. Some marvel at the sheer beauty of nature and, I suspect, especially when we are in places like the Bull Island, see their teacher in a different light', he says. 'I also think that we sometimes undervalue the power of studying a topic in which a student has little or no previous experience. Watching the unfolding learning has taught me a lot about the value of presenting students with unpredictable, semi-structured challenges where they have to rely more on their own resources rather than on a spoon-feeding teacher, where learning is sometimes more natural and organic', adds Seán.

Consolidation

Sarah O'Grady also teaches French to TY students in a different part of Dublin. In the school where she works, St. Vincent's Castleknock College, TY is compulsory. There are usually four class groups, with two French classes. There have been four timetable rotations during the year, with Sarah teaching two modules to each group. However, she explains, as a sign of the ever-changing nature of TY, that, following evaluations, is due to change with each teacher having one group until December and then switching groups after Christmas. 'In TY we put a lot of emphasis on oral skills, on pupils' abilities to express themselves in French. It's also a cultural experience, where they learn about the way of life in France,' says Sarah. 'As the TY *Guidelines* propose under 'Other languages,' we also consolidate the pupils' reading and writing skills,' she adds.

In her experience, Sarah has seen how TY can facilitate more independent learning. She also likes the way young people can explore ideas, develop and express their own opinions. 'There's time to reflect on issues beyond the walls of the classroom. You can see the personal and social growth that takes pace, especially when they take part in school exchanges, go on cultural trips, volunteer for charity work and take part in Gaisce,' she says.

From a teaching perspective, Sarah, is also very positive about TY's flexibility. She says: 'As a language teacher I use a lot of pair work, group talk, project work, oral presentations and role plays. TY helps me to reflect on my teaching methodologies. I am constantly looking to find new ways to improve my teaching and my students' learning. Following a course with the NCTE I now use more ICT in the classroom. I also value a course I did on Group Talk in my local education centre. Sometimes, I find that I need to step back and let the students do more of the work, that is, become more of a facilitator. This can be difficult to do at times, perhaps because we are conditioned by the type of exam we have at LC.' Sarah also makes an important point about evaluation. 'Earlier I mentioned rotating teachers. Following evaluations, we plan to have just two rotations in future. So, I will have one group between August and December. In January we will swop groups for the remainder of the year.'

Asked what advice she might offer those starting to teach TY, Sarah quips, 'Plan, plan, plan.' She adds, 'Having said that, you also need to be flexible. As a TY teacher you have to be inventive. For example, there might be 25 students registered but on particular day, because of involvement in other worthwhile aspects of TY, they might not be in your class. The challenge is to make the class meaningful and interesting for those who are present, no matter how few.'

Facilitator

'In the TY context, I feel much more of a facilitator – seeking out students' knowledge, examining understanding and learning about learning together; you could describe me as a learned learner in the TY arena,' says Clodagh Ward. She teaches at St Wolstan's Community School in Celbridge, County Kildare, where enrolment exceeds 700 girls. 'On various occasions over the past fifteen years, I have taught English, Drama, Information Technology and History to TY students. I have also been TY co-ordinator,' she adds.

Clodagh continues: 'In TY a student-centred approach is practical and realisable because we can, to some extent, escape from the back-wash effect of exam focus. I have found methodologies associated with assessment for learning (AFL) really beneficial for student development, academic progress and personal growth. In TY the relationship between students and teachers is far more democratic and holistic. I really like that.'

She points out that the English classroom and the IT one are quite different. 'In English,' she says, 'we use lot of class and group discussion, dialogic questioning. This facilitates an openness among the girls to the insights and interpretations of their classmates. In such an atmosphere of trust, I have seen individuals grow in self-confidence and self-awareness.'

'In the IT classroom, the goal is to support the development of skills through blogs, web design and programming. We focus a lot here on reflective journaling and managing the self. Again, you see great personal and social growth,' says Clodagh. 'In IT, there is great opportunity for student-led learning – the negotiation and collective design of the learning framework means that students recognise the target outcomes and concomitant skills. Their understanding of assessment criteria is keen and they are very invested in the learning.'

As a teacher, Clodagh points to many benefits, 'I think that teaching TY has enhanced and focused my awareness of the social nature of teaching and learning. I love working alongside the students to unravel the learning. On reflection, I now realise I am instinctively disposed to informal teaching in my classroom. I think TY has made me a much more versatile teacher,' she says.

Finally, asked how teachers might best engage with TY, Clodagh offers three suggestions: 'Firstly, I'd say focus on the wider learning opportunities at such a crucial transition period in young people's lives, rather than narrowly on subject content. Secondly, negotiate the learning and assessment with the students and factor in quality feedback and opportunities for dialogue. Thirdly, be flexible and open.'

Tellingly, Clodagh, who some years ago undertook research on the impact of TY on teachers, looking at its effects on classroom practice, collegiality and professional self-concept, wishes to add a further comment. 'There is so much rich growth and learning possible during TY, I think it is important that school management, and more importantly the DES, consider optimising the pupil-teacher ratio so that these opportunities are maximised,' she concludes.

Connectedness

The experiences of Seán, Sarah and Clodagh illustrate, in different ways and different contexts, the centrality of teachers connecting with their students. They echo much of the thinking evident in the work of Parker J. Palmer.

'Good teachers possess a capacity for connectedness,' writes Palmer in *The Courage to Teach*, which carries as a subtitle, *Exploring the Inner Landscape of a Teacher's Life*. He continues:

> They are able to weave a complex web of connections among themselves, their subjects, and their students so that students can learn to weave a world for themselves. The method used by these weavers vary widely: lectures, Socratic dialogue, laboratory experiments, collaborative problem solving, creative chaos. The connections made by good teachers are held not in their methods but in their

hearts – meaning *heart* in its ancient sense, as the place where intellect and emotion and spirit and will converge in the human self (Palmer, 1998, p.11).

Palmer then attempts to weigh up some of the pros and cons of this emphasis on human connectedness. He writes:

> If teaching cannot be reduced to technique, it is both good news and bad. The good news is that we no longer need to suffer the boredom many of us feel when teaching is approached as a question of 'how to do it'. We rarely talk with each other about teaching at any depth – and why should we when we have nothing more than 'tips, tricks, and techniques' to discuss? That kind of talk fails to touch the heart of teachers' experience.

> The good news gets even better. If teaching cannot be reduced to technique, I no longer need suffer the pain of having my peculiar gift as a teacher crammed into the Procrustean bed of someone else's method and the standards prescribed by it. That pain is felt throughout education as we glorify the method *du jour*, leaving people who teach differently feeling devalued, forcing them to measure to norms not their own (ibid. p. 11).

23

Practical Skills and Technology

All schools grapple with subject choices. How wide a range should we offer? Should everyone get a 'taste' of optional subjects? What about the practical realities of playing to the strengths of the teachers we have? If we give a 'taster' in TY can we follow it up at LC level? If, especially in single-sex schools, you break from traditional patterns, will there be sufficient uptake? How small can a class group be for the subject to be 'viable' on a timetable? For example, what are sufficient numbers for a LC Higher Maths class? Might it be the same number as for a class in LC Music, or in JC Technical Graphics? All these questions involve difficult educational decisions.

St Leo's College in Carlow, an all-girls school, employed its first teacher of technology in the early 1990s. 'I was recently qualified, enthusiastic and keen on a ground-breaking challenge,' says Fergal Murphy. 'Technology is now very much part of the St Leo's programme. There's a strong LC class for the subject.' Fergal explains that TY plays a vital role in this. 'If I take the current group of 20 LC students, eight of them did not study technology in Junior Cycle. They discovered the subject in TY,' he says. The 140 girls in TY sample technology in a weekly two hour class for five weeks. 'Yes, it is relatively short amount of time,' says Fergal. 'So, my goals are to enable them to achieve something tangible, to make specific objects, to experience some success. Most of all, I want them to experience design – taking an idea, planning a course of action and then executing the plan. Along the way they get to work with wood, metal and plastic. The workshop is well equipped: bandsaw, pillar drill, scroll saw, lathe, vinyl cutter, strip heater, soldering iron, c and c router. They not only experience machinery like this and Computer Aided Design (CAD) but learn about health and safety issues,' he says.

Over time a wide collection of student projects builds up. 'I show the students examples from previous classes and ask them to come up with their own, original, designs. Simple projects like phone stands, picture frames, clocks, window signs work well. The students often say they learn a lot from the mistakes they make,' says Fergal. 'I'm also very conscious of the value of active methodologies, of experiential learning. So, through discussions, co-operative teams, making presentations, preparing for and participating in exhibitions, the students learn and practice social competence,' he adds. 'A sense of achievement in those areas may be less obvious than a neatly finished product but is also very important. TY is a great space for these students to discover new aspects of their personalities; engaging with technology enhances these opportunities,' he says.

Practical studies

There is a strong thread of advocacy for cross-curricular links throughout the *Gudielines,* but it is also clear that schools – for many understandable reasons to do with inherited traditions, teacher identity, school architecture and timetable construction – have not yet realised the potential of interdisciplinary work.

Under the heading 'Practical studies', the *Guidelines* state: ·

> Appreciation of simple design and the wider everyday life aspects of technology, applied science and arts subjects such as engineering, construction studies, technical graphics, home economics, agricultural science, art and music are invaluable in interdisciplinary contexts such as mini-companies and other project-related activities.

The *Guidelines* continue with a number of suggestions of activities which might be considered and which some schools have embraced, often shaping specific modules around these activities.

- Furniture-making and restoration; interior design and furnishings

- Know your car; routine maintenance

- Various crafts such as model-making, jewellery-making, pottery

- Home and garden maintenance

- Food studies and practical cookery

- Photography and video production

- Textile crafts such as soft toys, weaving, fabric printing, etc.

Given the increasing role of technology in our lives, the *Guidelines*' exhortations may seem too understated but need to be read in the context of the invitational nature of the TY curriculum. The principle that 'curriculum content is a matter for selection and adaptation by the individual school' is central to TY. The 'Practical Studies' section of the *Guidelines* concludes with:

> Pupils could be given the opportunity to sample subjects, to which they did not have access in the junior cycle, with a view to the development of a broader perspective on senior cycle options. It is important that pupils should develop a practical understanding of the role of technology in today's world.

Since the *Guidelines* were written, developments in information and communications technology have been dramatic. It is, therefore, worth pointing out that the section prior to 'Practical skills' is headed 'Information Technology' and includes the crucial sentence, 'Information technology should permeate the entire curriculum'. The *Guidelines* continue, cautiously inserting the telling phrases, 'Within available resources...' and later in the same paragraph, 'Depending on the resource available within the school/community' to propose extensive use of IT equipment and applications.

24

STORIES ADD UP –
THE CHALLENGE OF MATHEMATICS

The tensions between Transition Year and the established Leaving Certificate often surface most dramatically in the teaching of mathematics. The *Guidelines* and numerous inspections and evaluations emphasise TY as a distinct space that should enable young people to 'learn, mature and develop in the absence of examination pressure.' (DE, 1993, p.5). The message seems clear:

> The school should ensure therefore that, in all areas studied, there is a clear distinction between the Transition Year programme and the corresponding Leaving Certificate syllabus. A Transition Year programme is NOT part of the Leaving Certificate programme, and should NOT be seen as an opportunity for spending three years rather than two studying Leaving Certificate material (ibid, p. 5).

In case anyone might think TY involves 'dumbing down', the *Guidelines* assert:

> This is not to say that Transition Year programmes should lack intellectual content; it is essential that they offer a challenge to pupils in all areas of their development. Pupils entering the Leaving Certificate programme on completion of a Transition Year should be better equipped and more disposed to study than their counterparts who did not have the benefit of this year. Those who enter the world of work after the Transition Year should do so as well developed and reflective young adults (ibid, p. 5).

Then, in a passage open to many interpretations, the *Guidelines* continue:

> The programme content for Transition Year, while not absolutely excluding Leaving Certificate material, should be chosen largely with a view to augmenting the Leaving Certificate experience, laying a solid foundation for Leaving Certificate studies, giving an orientation to the world of work and, in particular, catering for the pupils' personal and social awareness/development. Where Leaving Certificate material is chosen for study it should be done so on the clear understanding that it is to be explored in an original and stimulating way that is significantly different from the way in which it would have been treated in the two years to Leaving Certificate (*ibid*, p. 5).

Later, the *Guidelines* state that the approach taken to mathematics:

> should seek to stimulate the interest and enthusiasm of the pupils in identifying problems through practical activities and investigating appropriate ways of solving them (*ibid*, p. 12).

They also suggest that teaching of mathematics in TY should be more student-directed than teacher-directed and should relate the application of mathematical skills to real-life situations. Suggestions for teaching mathematics in TY, which are outlined in the *Guidelines*, include problem-solving aspects of the LCA syllabus and developing different approaches to teaching known areas of weakness in the LC, such as using anecdotal history of Greek geometers to provide a greater understanding of geometrical theorems.

Resources

Aware of how challenging TY mathematics can be, the DES issued *A Resource for Transition Year Mathematics Teachers* in 2006 and sent two copies to each school. The DES has not commissioned and published a resource like this for other subjects. 'We feel it is just as important for teachers to be stimulated, challenged and entertained as it is for students, write authors, NUI Maynooth lecturers Fiacre Ó Cairbre and Richard Watson, along with TY teacher John McKeon, in the introduction. This imaginative resource book has 42 chapters which embrace a wide variety of topics, most not covered on the LC syllabus. Many present the 'big picture' of mathematics. There is a strong emphasis on the history of mathematics. Tricks, games, puzzles, paradoxes, fallacies, counterintuitive facts, cross-curricular activities, posters and other strategies, engage and inspire.

From his office on the top floor of the appropriately named Logic House in the south campus of Maynooth University, Fiacre Ó Cairbre gives a flavour of the approach to the subject when he refers to the introduction to *A Resource for Transition Year Mathematics Teachers*. It states:

> Mathematics comprises an abundance of ideas. Many of these ideas contain beauty or exceptional practical power or both. Mathematics is so much more than numbers, techniques and formulas. Techniques on their own are usually devoid of stimulation and beauty.

Fiacre pauses. He picks up a page of sheet music. 'The musical notations are one thing,' he says, 'the music itself something very different. Imagine if you never heard the music? Maths is similar. When students "hear" the music of maths – connect with the ideas, rather than just see notations on a page - a whole new world opens up,' he says enthusiastically.

The introduction continues:

> Intellectual curiosity, the quest for beauty and the need to understand and solve important practical problems are some of the motivating elements for doing mathematics. These three features are often intertwined. For example, practical power in mathematics is frequently the offspring of pure intellectual curiosity or the search for beauty in mathematics. The art of doing mathematics may involve any of the following: creativity, imagination, inspiration, ingenuity, surprise, mystery, beauty, intuition, insights,

subtlety, fun, a wild thought, wonder, symmetry, harmony, aesthetic pleasure, originality, a great sense of achievement, a profound idea, a simple yet powerful idea, deep concentration and hard work. In the physical world mathematics can do much more than analyse and solve problems; it can offer deeper insights and also create and explore new ideas (Ó Cairbre, McKeon, Watson, 2006).

A major thrust of this 145 page hardback resource is the stories – stimulating, informative and entertaining – it contains. Fiacre remarks: 'From my experience interacting with teachers of TY mathematics, teaching the subject at third-level and promoting mathematics at second-level and with the general public, I have seen the power of stories. On many occasions I have witnessed how short stories from the history of mathematics change students' perception of mathematics for the better.'

One might imagine that *A Resource for Transition Year Mathematics Teachers* would be widely used. However, recent research (Moran et al., 2013) found that only one in nine TY maths teachers was using it. This surprising figure points, perhaps, to a problem that can arise when a 'free' resource arrives into a school; because of the absence of collaborative cultures, individual teachers, perhaps unintentionally, see the resources as individual rather than communal property. Chances are high that many teachers have never seen this book (or many other TY resources) though copies may be resting in individual lockers in the staffroom.

PISA-related research

The 2013 research, mentioned above, sheds valuable light on the content of mathematics in TY as well as on teachers' views on the purposes of TY maths. Based on data from the 2012 PISA (Programme for International Student Assessment) study, one stark observation is that:

> 46.2 per cent of schools expected teachers to use Transition Year to begin covering Leaving Certificate mathematics material. This finding may be of concern in light of previous findings that Transition Year may be used as a lead-in

to the Leaving Certificate in some schools, in opposition to
DES guidelines (Moran et al., 2013, p. 33).

The researchers, Gráinne Moran, Rachel Perkins, Jude Cos-
grove and Gerry Shiel, from the Educational Research Centre in
Drumcondra, based their report on the findings of a survey of a
nationally representative sample of mathematics teachers and
mathematics school co-ordinators.

These researchers note that 'there is very little information on
the content of mathematics programmes for Transition Year being
implemented in schools' (*ibid*, 2013, p. 12). They also contextulise
the study with reference to the PISA 2012 definition of mathematical literacy (mathematics) as

> ... an individual's capacity to formulate, employ, and inter-
> pret mathematics in a variety of contexts. It includes rea-
> soning mathematically and using mathematical concepts,
> procedures, facts, and tools to describe, explain, and pre-
> dict phenomena. It assists individuals to recognise the role
> that mathematics plays in the world and to make the well-
> founded judgements and decisions needed by constructive,
> engaged and reflective citizens (*ibid*, p. 7).

The researchers present TY maths teachers as having a profile broadly similar to maths teachers generally. Thus, two-thirds
were female: around three-tenths (30.6 per cent) had been teaching for at least 21 years, a further 27.3 per cent had been teaching
for between 11 and 20 years, around one-fifth (20.1 per cent) for
between six and 10 years, 14.4 per cent for three to five years, and
7.6 per cent for two years or less; two-thirds were in permanent
positions.

Perhaps not surprisingly, given the nature of the programme,
teachers spent fewer hours on average teaching mathematics to
TY students than to students at any other year level. Overall, an
average of 83.1 hours of mathematics teaching was timetabled for
TY, and 70.1 hours, on average, were taught, though there was
considerable variation in responses.

Some specific data paint a more precise picture: 13.6 per cent
of schools in the study used ability grouping for base classes in TY;

this increased to 43.5 per cent when it came to Mathematics. According to the researchers, this was low compared to practices in third, fifth and sixth years (90 per cent). In the majority of schools, mathematics in TY had the following features: a specified mathematics programme for TY teachers to follow, regular homework, and an end-of-year test. It was much less common for schools to specify a textbook(s) for mathematics in TY (34.2 per cent).

The study offers a nuanced picture of teachers' views of the purposes of maths in TY which is captured in the table below.

Table: *Percentages of Transition Year mathematics teachers by level of agreement with various statements concerning the purposes of mathematics in Transition Year*

The purpose of Transition Year mathematics is to ...	Strongly Disagree	Disagree	Agree	Strongly Agree
Allow students to experience mathematics differently	0.5	5.6	66.5	27.3
Prepare students for Leaving Certificate mathematics	1.6	14.1	71.3	13.0
Enable students to apply mathematics in their own lives	0.8	7.3	72.2	19.6
Develop students' ability to model situations mathematically	0.6	10.4	72.1	16.9
Enable students to solve complex problems set in real-life contexts	0.7	15.1	66.3	18.0
Further develop mathematics skills acquired in the junior cycle	0.0	1.9	67.4	30.7
Familiarise students with the history of mathematics	8.5	30.5	51.2	9.9

Increase students' confidence in their mathematics ability	0.5	2.9	60.0	36.7
Improve students' confidence in their problem-solving ability	0.0	3.4	65.2	31.4
Maintain mathematics skills learned during the junior cycle	0.0	1.8	65.5	32.7
Expose students to more concrete mathematics materials	0.7	10.3	66.3	22.8
Encourage greater interest in mathematics	0.1	3.9	62.2	33.9
Introduce students to careers in mathematics	3.5	17.9	57.4	21.2

(From Moran at al, 2013, p. 35).

The researchers suggest that the reluctance to express strong agreement may indicate a lack of clarity about the purposes of Mathematics in TY.

When it came to resources, *Project Mathematics* material topped the list of reported usage. The researchers suggest that 'These findings may imply a dearth of appropriate resources for mathematics in TY prior to the introduction of *Project Mathematics*, or of teachers' knowledge of such resources, or ability to access or utilise them.' The plight of *A Resource for Transition Year Mathematics Teachers* may be a case in point.

A majority of teachers reported extensive use of end-of-year tests. The commentary observes:

> Differences in the assessment practices between initial Project Mathematics schools and others suggest that Project Mathematics may be providing teachers with the resources to implement more innovative methods of assessment that are more suited to the active approach to

213

learning that characterises Transition Year, such as group project work (*ibid*, p. 43).

The report continues:

> The topics that were most frequently taught in mathematics class in Transition Year included statistics (covered by 84.9 per cent of teachers), probability (83.3 per cent), algebra (79.1 per cent), and real-life problems (70.2 per cent). Statistics and probability now receive greater emphasis than in the old mathematics syllabi, and were included in the first phase of the introduction of Project Mathematics. Just four in ten teachers covered the history of mathematics, even though this is encouraged in the Transition Year guidelines, and resource materials are available. These findings suggest that teachers may need to be encouraged to draw on a range of content areas in mathematics in Transition Year, though individual content areas do not need to be presented in isolation, but can, instead, be combined into integrated modules or lesson plans (ibid, p. 43).

Finally, the uneasy relationships between Junior Cycle, TY and the established LC is underscored in the following telling observation in the report:

> Junior Certificate examination results were the most important factor for schools in assigning Transition Year students to Leaving Certificate mathematics programmes (73.2 per cent of schools reported that this factor was assigned a high level of importance), while very little emphasis was placed on either standardised test results (15.7 per cent), or an end of Transition Year test in mathematics (17.2 per cent).

The evidence suggests that mathematics in TY continues to present students, teachers, schools, support services and policy makers with some of the most urgent challenges.

The power of story

As mentioned earlier, one illuminating pathway for TY maths lies in telling stories from the evolution of mathematical understanding. A study by Carter and Ó Cairbre (2011) offers further promising evidence. They report on the implementation of 20 TY lesson plans of the history of mathematics. An immediate positive change in the perception of mathematics in all students after the first lesson was noted. Furthermore, the authors observe that this positive change was sustained after completion of the twenty lessons. One student in that study remarked:

> I do enjoy maths now because I realised that it's okay if you don't understand something the first time it's explained to you because it took mathematicians thousands of years to understand some things that we know today (ibid, p. 100).

Another stated:

> It's just an idea someone had but they turned it into a proof so now we study it. There's this amazing history behind maths that I never knew about. There's so many people behind maths. It's not just a boring textbook anymore (ibid, p. 100).

It seems that stories can add up!

25

RELIGIOUS EDUCATION

Some years ago, a teacher posted the following message on a Irish website. 'Hi, I'm teaching religion to TY, fifth and sixth years as a non-exam subject. They don't have a religion book. Does anyone have any tips on topics to cover?' Depending on your viewpoint, you might read that as typical of a random looseness that can arise when school programmes, like Transition Year, are not prescriptive. Alternatively, you might read this as an open-minded teacher, reaching out to learn from colleagues, engaging in some forward-planning. A third viewpoint might question the use of terms like 'tips on topics to cover' and ask about 'process'. A fourth might enquire about rationale, and so on.

Under 'Religion', the 1993 TY *Guidelines* offer broad signposts rather than specific directions. They state:

> The wishes of parents and their children will be vitally important with regard to the process and methodology to be used to develop Religion within the programme. While a simple subject approach could be used, a thematic format might be considered to blend more appropriately with the programme as a whole. In addition, relevant learning environments and real-life work or work-related situations might be found as a way of giving practical realisation to the study of selected areas or topics (DE, 1993, p. 18).

Areas for consideration in the programme might include:

self-awareness and self-assessment; relationships with others and with God; prayer, both community and personal;

vocation and ways of living it out; respect and dignity of the human person; human rights, justice and peace; principles of morality; Third World issues.

Some of the responses to the website request from the puzzled teacher reveal varied practice. Suggestions ranged from asking the students what they would like to study to an exploration of religious imagery in *Lord of the Rings* and touched on organising a trip to a synagogue and a mosque, eco-ethics, capital punishment, abortion/IVF-type issues, the search for meaning through music, involvement with local charities, Buddhism and Shintoism. Movies, TV programmes and the occasional book were also mentioned: *The Simpsons, The Matrix, Hotel Rwanda, Shooting Dogs, The Boy in the Striped Pyjamas, Schindler's List, Mean Creek, The Book of Eli*, Richard Dawkins' *The God Delusion*. Other comments included, 'cults is a great one'; 'I do debates etc in class on popular issues but to be honest it's a hard slog'; 'you must have a plan cos if you have an inspection you are in BIG Trouble'; and 'it's not just about showing an episode or a movie for a laugh, it is a good way of introducing a topic or a theme in a way they can relate to and then having really good discussions about it'.

Framework

Unfortunately, some of the responses – and maybe even the question – imply filling timetabled slots rather than offering a well-thought out RE programme. One useful template for framing an RE programme that provides both structure and freedom can be found on the website of the Le Chéile Trust (www.lecheiletrust. ie). It proposes clear statements about the school's character and ethos, e.g., 'As a Catholic school we are committed to the provision of a holistic education based on the unique dignity of every human being as a person made in the image and likeness of God', and is also respectfully sensitive to the beliefs of the diversity of learners encountered in the RE classrooms.

The Le Chéile framework proposes three overarching goals for a school's RE programme:

- To foster the growth of faith at a personal and communal level, especially through understanding of and participation in prayer and liturgy

- To teach students to think, research, reason, reflect and act in the light of Gospel values

- To provide an intellectual framework for reflecting on life decisions and to encourage students to give witness to the integration of faith and life.

The framework also offers a practical set of headings for shaping an RE programme. These include context, staffing, curriculum, children with special educational needs, child protection guidelines, resources, liturgical celebrations, retreats, outreach programmes, parental involvement, inclusion of students of other faiths.

A varied programme

Lori Fields is a trained catechist who has been teaching Religious Education for the past twenty years. Her school, Manor House, is an all girls school with an enrolment of over 800. It occupies a complex of red-brick buildings on the road from North Bull Island to Raheny village on Dublin's northside. 'In Transition Year, each class group is timetabled for three periods each week,' explains Lori. 'As a team of catechists we work together to develop the students' personal skills, evolve their technological skills and raise expectations of themselves and others.' This translates into specific aims and a yearly plan for the five-person team. 'We aim to explore the search for meaning which finds expression in religion. We identify how understandings of God, religious traditions, in particular the Christian tradition, have contributed to the culture in which we live and have an impact on personal lifestyle,' says Lori. 'We encourage our students to explore the richness of religious traditions and in so doing this it contributes to their spiritual and moral development,' she adds.

Surely teaching religious education in twenty-first century Ireland is especially challenging, not least because of the many church-related scandals revealed during the lifetime of current TY students? 'Yes, challenging but also rewarding,' responds Lori. 'As I see it, underneath the exterior of a teenager lies a kind, empathic and congruent person who really wants to bring about a change in society and make the world a better place. Unlike adults, most teenagers are not cynical, so for me they are and will always be a breath of fresh air,' she says.

Like many other teachers encountered throughout this book, it is the relationship with young people, the ability to be energised by them, that appears to nurture Lori's commitment. She continues: 'Teenagers see justice and injustice around them every day. They speak openly and honestly about a just world where everyone has the right to water, a roof over their head, food and an education. They are passionate about inequality in our world where the rich are very rich and the true poor are very poor.'

What about resources? Lori says: 'We don't use a set textbook but share resources with each other including excerpts from *Searching, Kindle a Fire* and *A Question of Faith*. In 2014/2015 we tried some new teaching methodologies that we believed worked well with our groups. Think, Pair, Share worked really well as no student was put on the spot to answer a question and real learning took place within their small groups. Co-operation, collaboration and clear communication amongst the students in their working groups was key to their learning.'

The team notices that one of the spinoffs of small group work in TY is new friendships among students. 'In TY students can be in new groups, knowing only a few students from their junior year base classes,' says Lori. 'Co-operative learning methods helps the new groups gel together,' she adds.

Lori admits that for an experienced teacher, embracing co-operative methodologies brings challenges. 'Take the year just gone when we experimented with the Jigsaw method. The students were in small groups teaching each other new concepts while we facilitated the process. Now, I found this quite difficult because I saw it as letting go of what I believed was valuable teaching time. This approach allows the student to be the teacher. I was more a facilitator. It was really interesting to see the very real learning that occurred among the groups.'

Lori and her colleagues in Manor House presented their TY students with a project to be completed over a four-week period. This was an individual activity with students choosing 'an inspirational person in their lives' and presenting their projects to their peers. 'I think this worked very well,' says Lori. 'I was so surprised with the number of students that chose a family member that had inspired them or inspires them daily. I expected them to choose a musician or artist but family won out. Both my classes did an exceptional job in presenting and although some students were nervous others made sure that they were a captive audience,' she says.

The TY RE programme in Manor House blends class discussion, group work, teacher input, YouTube clips, a reflective journal, brainstorming, artwork, visualisation, bible reading, carol services, charity collections, DVDs, songs, simulations and role-plays. A glance through the resources used illustrates an imaginative mix: *Desiderata* alongside the film *The Best Exotic Marigold Hotel*; Harold Kushner's *When Bad Things Happen to Good People* alongside the *Book of Amos*; Mother Teresa, Mandela and Gandhi alongside Donal Walsh and Joanne O Riordáin.

Neither does the programme confine itself to the classroom. 'This year, we brought all TY students to County Longford to see St Mel's' Cathedral,' says Lori. 'A number of students had watched the TV documentary about the fire which had damaged the cathedral a few years previously. A discussion arose about the amount of money that had been spent on the rebuild. One theme to emerge was, considering the state of the economy in Ireland, why was this money not being put to another, possibly better use? This enabled some discussion about one's own value system,' she says.

'The upshot of the discussion was a decision to visit the cathedral and see for ourselves. We saw how important this cathedral was, not only as a building but as a place of worship and a place steeped in history. We learned a lot from our discussions before the visit and the actual visit there,' remarks Lori.

Imagination and flexibility

Such imaginative responses to students' questioning is easier in TY than in any other year. TY's flexibility also informs the annual Knock Youth Gathering (KYG), started in 2013. The purpose of KYG is to bring transition years and first year A-level students to Knock on the feast of the Holy Rosary so that they can experience faith and spirituality among their peers. Imagination and flexibility are also evidenced in some of the many TY RE courses that schools have posted in their own school websites.

Finally, any discussion of religious education in today's Ireland cannot run away from issues of ethos, patronage and choice. TY religious education classes offer a space where these issues can be explored. One starting prompt might be the following extract from the Church of Ireland Archbishop of Dublin, Michael Jackson. He was speaking in 2012 at an event marking 150 years of Coláiste Iognáid, the Jesuit School, in Galway. Archbishop Jackson said:

> ... much of the contemporary debate in both educational and media circles luxuriates in kicking a tired institutionalized Christianity when it is lying on the floor. It does not take cognizance of the wider reality that religious belonging and expression worldwide is increasing and changing and is *not* ceasing to exist. It is not necessarily religion as we have come to know it through our own experiences of religion in our own lives (Jackson, 2012).

26

Personal Identity and Creativity

Art teacher Nicola Lee loves the space and freedom students have in TY to explore visual work without the constraints of a formal syllabus. 'For those who didn't do art in junior cycle, it opens up new possibilities, for those with some foundation, they can dig deeper into bigger projects', she explains. Nicola's TY art programme in De La Salle College, Waterford, focuses on personal identity and creativity. 'The module runs from September to January for one group of boys, from January to May for the second group. Classes are timetabled for three periods of forty minutes, one double and a single. According to the feedback from the students, they like the emphasis on the journey, the exploration, rather than on having to produce specific artefacts or meet deadlines', she adds.

Nicola encourages students to take part in large projects in which they can immerse themselves. Nicola cites Junk Kouture and Milk It as examples. The former challenges teenagers to create wearable fashion from everyday junk that might normally find its way into the bin. According to the project's website, 'Junk Kouture aims to inspire and ignite passion in these teenagers while at the same time subtly educating them about the importance of recycling and reusing waste.' For example, Junk Kouture national winners from Elphin Community School, County Roscommon (2015), Our Lady's Bower, Athlone, County Westmeath (2014) and Coláiste Ioseaf, County Limerick (2013) all produced wonderfully imaginative creations.

Milk It invites students to form an advertising agency with up to six team members and to create a campaign based on a brief and guidelines. The initiators intended Milk It to be a fun and engaging way for teenagers to learn about the nutritional benefits of the 'milk, yogurt and cheese' food group, whilst offering cross curricular applications for both teachers and students. It was developed against a background of research from a national survey showing that 42 per cent of Irish teenage girls and 23 per cent of Irish teenage boys have insufficient calcium intakes.

Meanwhile, back in her beautifully refurbished art room in the distinguished nineteenth century De La Salle building, Nicola is enthusiastic about how art in TY can both build students' confidence as well as strengthen the foundations for those who aspire to taking the subject at Leaving Certificate and, perhaps, pursue arts based careers. 'Firstly, as mentioned, those who didn't do art as a Junior Cycle subject often have a low opinion of their ability. It's wonderful to see, once they master some basic techniques, how they gain confidence, not just in their work, but in themselves as people,' she explains.

The TY onion

Nicola's focus here is important. In the 1990s, 'the onion' became a frequently used metaphor for imagining TY programmes. This consisted of four 'layers'. The first is an inner core of continuity subjects such as English and Maths, usually offered for the full year. Secondly, there is subject sampling, where students 'taste' Leaving Cert subjects with a view to making informed choices (these tasters are usually , though not always, a function of optional subjects offered in fifth year). 'Tasters' are sometimes offered as modules that run for half or a third of the year and, of course, should have an educational value in their own right. Thirdly, what might be called the TY-specific layer, consists of subjects and modules that are 'stand-alone', with little direct connections with Junior Cycle or Leaving Cert subjects. These often engage students' interests and imaginations and relate explicitly to TY's overall vision (e.g. mini-company, self-defence, community service, personal development, coding, Japanese and many more). Finally, the fourth, outer, and often most visible layer, includes 'once off' activities such as trips, visiting speakers, exhibition of work, plays, concerts etc.

Aesthetic activities can be encountered in different guises, especially at levels two, three and four. To see art or music solely at the sampling level is educationally narrow and restrictive.

The approaches that Nicola has found to work well in TY include sampling work done by previous TY students as this raises expectations and widens possibilities. Particularly effective is what she calls 'before and after' work. 'This highlights how much improvement can be achieved when techniques demonstrated in class are applied,' she explains. Nicola also uses visual mind maps creating a grid of quick doodles which are selectively combined to create a unique image. 'I also let the students encounter the work of a big cross-section of artists, animators and graphic designers,' she adds. 'And, of course, when I can get guests to come in, they are usually very popular.'

While now very positive about having students in class who had not attended art classes in junior cycle, Nicola admits it wasn't always like that. 'Initially I struggled to make the subject interesting,' she admits. 'Many would conceal their insecurities about their art by being dismissive about their work, giving up quickly, acting up in class. I realised lessons needed to be more appealing/engaging. Partly by trial and error, I found that they responded well to cartooning, to gaming and to creating with Lego. I integrated all these into my modules. The result was a lot of excitement, attention and engagement from almost all students,' she adds.

Nicola explains that the response to creating cartoon figures has been especially effective. 'As part of the identity project, students first study well-known cartoons depicting a boy figure such as Adventure Time's Finn or Dennis the Menace. We then explore how the plain outline is also recognizable as the character, as is a silhouette of a De La Salle student. This leads on to the fact that even though their 'templates' are similar, they are all different individuals. Pupils then proceed to fill in a large Lego template of themselves including their uniform but putting in their own individual characteristics. Next, they turn the templates into actual Lego characters, similar in build and uniform but each one very different. The students love this project. At the TY graduation, they are presented with their mini-figures. The boys openly express their delight and you can see how proud they are of their creations – regardless of their initial creative ability,' she says.

Asked for her advice to other art teachers, Nicola's response is relevant to all teachers in TY. She states: 'Teachers need to be a lot more malleable and adaptable. They also need to be more engaging when teaching TY. Without the sight of a state exam looming in the short term, pupils tend to glide along unless interest is ignited. I also think it's important to ensure that pupils have a sense of achievement in what they are trying to achieve in class. By keeping project modules short and making sure that all produce something tangible which they can be proud of and value has worked well for me. Once all that happens, teaching TY can be professionally very fulfilling.'

TY as an open space

One of the great strengths of Transition Year, as the *Guidelines* state, is that it opens up a space where creativity and innovation can be nurtured, where students and teachers can express themselves in new ways. Ken Robinson, an internationally known critic of the factory-model of schooling, contends that schools are increasingly about conformity and standardisation. 'We need to go in the opposite direction,' he argues in a witty YouTube talk that has been viewed more than 12 million times. He sees divergent thinking as an essential capacity for creativity. Robinson highlights the need for aesthetic experience, 'where your senses are operating at their peak, when you are present in the current moment, when you are resonating with this "thing" you are experiencing, when you are fully alive.' These ideas resonate with the work of Hungarian positive psychologist Mihaly Csikszentmihalyi, who writes persuasively about the idea of 'flow'. Flow is characterised by a feeling of great absorption, engagement, fulfilment and skills during which temporal concerns – time, food, ego-self etc – are typically ignored. Ken Robinson fears that much schooling has an anaesthetic effect, shutting off the senses. Such an analysis results in locating aesthetic education as central to schooling.

A year of possibilities

In the busy, creative, intense atmosphere of the National College of Art and Design in the former Power's distillery in Dublin's Thomas Street, Fiona King, based in the NCAD School of Education, is well positioned to comment on TY. In her capacity as a classroom practice supervisor, she regularly visits schools and sees art in TY up close. 'I see it as a year of possibilities,' she says. 'Most art teachers like the opportunity for risk taking, for pushing the boundaries of what art can be,' notes Fiona. 'There is no doubt that many embrace the opportunity to be open and explorative. Becoming writers of their own TY programme is very empowering. I have seen teachers who worked closely with living artists, who engaged in a wide range of collaborative projects with people inside and outside the school, who explored human rights issues, who engage imaginatively with galleries and living artists. In the classroom you can see how they capture students' interest and curiosity.'

Fiona King's reference to collaborative projects is neatly illustrated by an example from Ashbourne Community School, County Meath. There, teachers Margaret Maher and David O'Connell worked together to enable students to produce stylized cats, Artykats. The coming together of subjects such as art and construction studies brought a new focus on practical, creative, artistic and entrepreneurial skills. Details of Artykats Transition Unit can be accessed on the NCCA website (www.ncca.ie).

Similar to Nicola Lee in Waterford, Fiona King also observes how TY facilitates a creative space to capture the interest and curiosity of those pupils who did not elect to take art in the junior cycle. Through the Artist Mentoring Programme, co-ordinated by Finola Mc Tiernan and delivered by Fiona King in the School of Education in NCAD, student teachers work with TY and senior cycle students to give them the opportunity to engage in imaginative art process that bridge the gap between second level and third level visual art pedagogical approaches.

Nicola's two project examples are noteworthy at a few levels. Firstly, they provide structured, flexible frameworks for students and teachers to engage with creativity and innovation. They are also cross-curricular. While not exclusively aimed at Transition Year, the uptake by TY students is significant. These schemes also feature national recognition events in the final school term. For the schools involved, such events can be intense celebratory experiences and can attract positive publicity to the relevant school.

Finally, as evident also in other chapters, Transition Year seems to attract such sponsored projects more than any other school programme. Advertisers invariably find the innocence, beauty and honesty of teenage endeavour incredibly attractive. At one level, support from business and other agencies for a grossly under-funded schooling system can be welcome. However, the responsibility of TY co-ordinators, teachers and school principals to protect young people extends in many directions; weighing up the educational value of engaging with outside agencies is always a central concern.

27

Local Links, Arts, Culture and Social Awareness

In many schools, Transition Year has not only seen schools harness resources on their doorsteps, but has enabled them to build closer links with local communities. When young people engage in practical community projects they often see their surroundings differently. At best, such engagement brings young citizens closer to the phrase of the TY mission statement of becoming 'autonomous, participative, and responsible members of society'.

Larkin Community College in Dublin's city centre takes the notion of school-community links so seriously that it has appointed its own 'Partnerships Coordinator'. 'We devise and develop a range of partnerships projects with Junior Cycle students,' explains Máire O'Higgins, 'so by the time they reach TY, students not only continue their engagement but also act as mentors.' She mentions an impressive string of projects and visiting speakers that Larkin Community College has encouraged since its foundation in 1999.

One project, called Moving Statues, led the TY students to design and construct six giant puppets, six metres high, inspired by familiar statues on nearby O'Connell Street. There were multiple collaborations in this project: with student-teachers from the National College of Art and Design who acted as mentors, the education team at the National Museum, theatre director Mikel Murfi, Pete Casby of Macnas and Helen Lane, an independent artist. Next, the group made a seventh giant puppet based on life drawings of one of the older people from the Lourdes Day Care Centre from further down Seán McDermott Street. Then Mikel Murfi devised a script and a performance which culminated in the Larkin students and the older people conversing over time in a giant puppet show for the public in Collins Barracks. Fifty first-year Larkin students, as part of a service to their local elderly community, then brought older adults from Cross Care Dublin and clients from Lourdes Day Care Centre for the Elderly, to see the performance in Collins Barracks.

Even that brief outline of the project draws attention to its inherent multiple learning possibilities – in art, in construction, in drama, in history, in geography, in civic, social and political education, in intergenerational learning and more.

Not only do students interact with older people, they have also done projects with homeless people and children with special needs. Máire and her colleagues have also built strong relations with arts and cultural institutions, philanthropic partners and non-governmental organisations. 'It's very much about developing active citizens,' she emphasises, 'so the students are centrally involved in making decisions about projects and programmes and then in delivering them. They get to write the press release. They meet the media,' she adds.

Máire's experience convinces her that, for some students, involvement in these projects has been life-altering. She mentions a human rights project with Amnesty, performance projects with the Abbey Theatre and the Localise, Caring in the Community project.

According to the *Guidelines* for TY, a key feature of every school's programme should be the use of a wide range of teaching/learning methodologies. Many of the examples cited in the *Guidelines* are evident in Larkin Community College's partnership projects. These include negotiated learning, activity-based learning, personal responsibility in learning, integration of appropriate areas of learning, project work and research, group work, team teaching, study visits and field trips, work experience, work simulation, community service and visiting speaker and seminars.

When it comes to visiting speakers, Máire reels off a stunning list of recent visitors who have met with the students of Larkin Community College. They include Barack and Michelle Obama, Hilary Clinton as well as Chris Balderston, John Hennesey-Niland and Stuart Dwyer and the US Embassy staff, suggesting that their link with the embassy has been especially fruitful. She continues with Barry McCall, Doug Baxter, Victoria Smurfitt, Malala Yousafzai, Harry Belafonte, Yoko Ono, Roddy Doyle, Eoin Colfer, Peter Sheridan, Diarmuid Gavin, Brendan Gleeson, Senator David Norris, Simon Harris TD, Bertie Ahern TD, Sile de Valera TD, President Michael D. Higgins, Joe Costello TD, Frances Fitzgerald TD, Senator Fiach Mac Conghail, Senator Katherine Zappone, Ruairi Quinn TD and Jimmy Deenihan TD.

This experience resonates with a similar story from the UK. In her page-turning account of her time as principal of St Georges, a challenging school in London, Marie Stubbs makes some relevant points about their Distinguished Visitors Programme. In *Ahead of the Class* (Stubbs, 2003) she recounts how the young people in the school began to see visitors from a cross-section of society as role models and living examples of positive achievement. It is also evident that these visits lifted the collective self-esteem of students and staff.

Máire O'Higgins is keen to emphasise that the list is not intended to 'show off'. 'Perhaps because our students live in an area of socio-economic disadvantage, they engage well with stories of "success". Many are motivated as a result of the encounter with people they would not normally meet in their community. We want to show them that barriers can be overcome, that there should not be limits to their ambition. So, when they meet someone working for the UN or the Director of Amnesty International or the first black President of the United States, they don't forget. What we have also learned is that these same people want to be role models for our students.'

Máire recounts how John Hennessey Niland, the previous Chargé d'Affaires at the United States Embassy, spent ten weeks at a time over three years 'giving back' to Larkin Community College students. 'He invited students to sit around the then US Ambassador to Ireland Dan Rooney's dining table in the Phoenix Park, to plan a party for athletes from Special Olympics Ireland who were travelling to the World Games in Athens, Greece,' recalls Máire.

'John did this work as part of his commitment to service for the national service learning Localise Caring in the Community schools programme which began in the College in 2008. The school's partnership with the US Embassy had continued through John's successor, Stuart Dwyer. Recently, for example, our students were invited to the Embassy to assist with a Christmas Gift Appeal for the homeless.'

As she recounts her experience with some of the visitors, Máire remarks that 'my own teaching life has been transformed by these generous people. They have taught our students the importance of giving back to the community. They have also given us all memories to treasure forever.' She then recounts how John Hennessey Niland arranged for the Obamas to meet Larkin students to thank them for building a Garden of Hope for the Simon residents in Seán McDermott Street. She continues: 'John also arranged for students to meet Hilary Clinton and her Global Affairs coordinator Chris Balderston. Chris came to the College and discussed US Foreign policy with students in the Library. One of the TY students interviewed him!'

Maire's unique role with Junior Cycle students is cross-curricular, extra-curricular and whole school. 'TY students who opt to engage with TY programmes have usually had a taste of these kinds of programmes in Junior Cycle. Some are self-motivated. We try to catch their interests. The role of Partnerships Coordinator is very much that of a facilitator. The intention is to guide students to complete tasks associated with different stages of a project and to draw out reflections and evaluations. A lot of this reflective practice is done through oral presentations. These could be meetings, speeches, interviews where students discuss and debate projects. Some of the work is done away from the school building. I firmly believe that we should not limit learning to within four walls.'

Máire's feelings for learning beyond conventional classrooms are strong. 'All schools should be doing this kind of work,' she asserts. 'One issue is that teachers are not given enough time to prepare innovative action-based projects and programme within their working day. I don't think the Department of Education and Skills knows how, or has to date, with the Department of Finance, chosen to invest sufficient funding into programmes to train teachers to be able to do such work and to talk to each other about their work as part of their working day. I do accept that in the current climate in schools, some teachers lack the confidence to do this kind of work. Some are uneasy about the different facilitative skills that they will need to develop, away from the desk at the top of the classroom, in order to do this kind of work. Others still fear the power they would be passing on to the young person who finds a voice through this experiential holistic way of working. Appropriate and relevant training will help teachers to develop the necessary skills to be the best they can be.'

One imagines that if the renowned American educator, John Dewey, who died in 1952, were to visit Larkin Community College he would be enthusiastic. Dewey saw education as a social process, as growth, not as a preparation for life, but life itself. He regarded art as the most effective mode of communication that exists. He was critical of schooling that was predominantly static in subject matter and authoritarian in methods. Dewey contended that too many educators' imaginations were limited because they didn't pay enough attention to young people's experiences. Like Máire O'Higgins, Dewey knew that contact with ordinary community life provides significant learning experiences.

What advice would Máire give to teachers starting to teach a TY module or programme? Her reply is clear, nuanced, practical and wise: 'Make the programme challenging and fun. Try to engage with people from the "real world" that is, the world of work. Students need as much exposure as possible to what they will experience once they leave school. Include a strong self-directed learning component. Include an active task component where students have to "do" something practical as art. Test the programme on yourself by completing the assignments before you test them on students. That way you will work out the timing and find out how good and how engaging a module/programme is. Keep a reflective diary and read it! Keep good balance in your own personal and professional life as it is not what you teach but who you are as you teach. Finally, trust students. Ask them what they think of the work they are doing. Listen to their responses. Change what is not working for them and for you. Become a facilitator of their learning.'

28

RESPONDING TO A SCHOOL'S CONTEXT

The importance of 'school context' is a recurring theme in the conclusions of much educational research. Increasingly, national policies recognise the need to be sensitive to local circumstances; one size does not fit all. While all students in a school need to feel safe, to experience a sense of belonging and to have their learning needs addressed, how these goals are realised varies depending on context. A key principle of the Transition Year *Guidelines* is to give schools great freedom to shape their own TY programmes. For example:

> Curriculum content is a matter for selection and adaptation by the individual school having regard to these guidelines, the requirements of pupils and the views of parents. In establishing its curriculum, the school should also take into consideration the possibilities offered by employers and other work-providing agencies and the wider interests in the local community (DE, 1993, p. 5).

History and geography are strong factors in determining the school context of St Eunan's College, Letterkenny, County Donegal. Its Transition Year programme reflects the school's unique situation, tradition, culture and ethos. 'Our Transition Year has two distinct options: PE (Physical Education) or ICT (Information and Communications Technology),' explains Principal Chris Darby. 'It is unique in that the boys take GCSE in one of these subjects at the end of the year. It is intensive – 10 class periods per week in PE or ICT.[1] That's what grounds our Transition Year, he says. Normally a GCSE course runs over two years but St Eunan's successfully negotiated a one-year deal with the nearby Northern Ireland authorities.

When the school first introduced Transition Year, it was 'not an altogether happy experience'. 'It is an all-boys school and they weren't into the singing and dancing,' laughs Chris. He says that parents needed to be convinced that they were doing something worthwhile. 'Now every student who does TY comes out the far end with a GCSE qualification,' he explains. 'A lot of the credit for setting up the GCSE link has to go to Eddie Harvey, a teacher who was very innovative around using computers in schools. He set up the ICT strand in TY as a GCSE subject. It immediately improved TY's profile locally. Later we developed the PE strand along similar lines. My experience in this school is that the boys respond very well to anything to do with sport. It doesn't really matter whether it's football, soccer, golf, swimming or anything else. They really go for it. So, if you come to this school you know in advance you will benefit from an intense programme in either ICT or PE in TY,' he continues. Currently there are two TY class groups following ICT and two pursuing the PE strand.

Previously, Chris had worked in schools in the VEC (now ETB) and Community and Comprehensive sectors. 'I am struck by many things, one of which is how much these boys love being in school,' he says. 'There is a warm, easy-going atmosphere around the school – happy and secure, at ease, good relationships between teachers and students. The lads are at ease here, well-mentored. That really drives so much.'

The school building also shapes the context. It is an imposing three-storey structure with turreted round towers that date from 1906. It is known locally as 'the castle on the hill'. Pictures on the walls tell many stories. St Eunan's began as a minor seminary, a feeder school for the national seminary in Maynooth. 'In the early days, boys from all over County Donegal and beyond won schol-

---

[1] GCSE refers to the General Certificate in Secondary Education, the qualification achieved by young people following the Northern Ireland curriculum.

arships to attend here. Many went on to be priests. That's part of the tradition,' explains Chris. Sport is another strong tradition with significant recent achievements in Gaelic football, soccer, basketball, athletics, golf and swimming. More than half the 2012 All Ireland winning Donegal team are former St Eunan's students. So is international cyclist Philip Deignan. 'Sport is the lifeblood of this school,' adds Chris. Hence, the PE option in TY is very popular.

Chris Darby is sensitive to the school's history and tradition. 'Yes,' he says, 'in many ways it is quite a traditional school, like many former diocesan colleges. There would be a lot of chalk and talk in classes. But the boys seem happy with this. You could try something quite "flowery" in TY, and they wouldn't like it.' The shape of St Eunan's TY programme is visibly different to that of many other schools. 'We explain to the parents how the GCSE takes up an enormous amount of time and therefore there is less going out and about or having people coming in to classes compared to other schools. It probably makes our TY more academic,' says Chris, adding, 'that seems to suit this school.' Sitting the formal GCSE exam in either PE or ICT at the end of the TY year underlines this further.

Like many schools with a distinguished past, a visit to St Eunan's brings to mind Stephen Ball's observation:

> Schools are complex, contradictory, sometimes incoherent organisations, like many others. They are assembled over time to form a bricolage of memories, commitments, routines, bright ideas and policy effects. They are changed, influenced and interfered with regularly, and increasingly. They drift, decay, regenerate. (Ball, 1997, p. 317).

How has the Inspectorate reacted to St Eunan's novel approach to TY? 'There was a Whole School Evaluation (WSE) in 2009 and they thought it was very good,' responds Chris. He explains that initially admission to the school's TY programme was quite strict. 'You applied. Your behaviour record was looked at. The list was sent to the staff. The staff said "yes" or "no" to people. So, you had to be quite good to get into TY. We have loosened that, a bit, opening it up more and numbers doing TY have jumped,' he says.

ICT

Lisa Gallagher has been teaching on the GCSE ICT module in St. Eunan's for eight years. 'Yes,' she acknowledges, 'ten periods each week is intense and demanding. Eight sessions focus on practical assignments and two deal with theory. In effect everything has to be wrapped up by Easter, completing assessments and sending the marks away. Students and teacher know from the outset how much work has to be done so there is little time for distractions or for misbehaviour,' explains Lisa. 'They develop skills of independent learning and working to deadlines, especially time management,' she adds.

With two class groups of approximately 25 students, Lisa shares the teaching with her colleague Pauric O'Donnell 'So, each of us works with the two groups which I think is a good idea,' says Lisa. Pauric picks up the point about students being focused. 'There's always another deadline around the corner,' he says. 'As the year unfolds from September onwards you can see them develop. We don't hold their hands. They have to do assignments, figure things out for themselves. Let me give you an example. At the start they usually don't read instructions. They want the teacher to tell them, step by step, how to do something; they don't seem to be able to interpret instructions for themselves. The assignments force them to figure things out. We see this very clearly with HTML tasks,' continues Pauric. He adds that he thinks students develop their research skills very well through this module. As a former student of St Eunan's, Pauric has a unique perspective on this as he did this module when he was a TY student himself. Lisa add that she sees the structure of the module as 'a very relevant preparation for third-level education'.

Pauric continues: 'About ten years ago a lot of the fascination was with the question, how do things work? – the internet, smart phones and so on. Now, students are very familiar with how to use ipads and often show little interest in how they work.' Lisa recalls that when she began more students were interested in creating their own websites, less so now. 'Nowadays they are more likely to want to create games,' she comments.

Beyond the Leaving Cert

Guidance counsellor Joe Gallagher provides a further perspective on St Eunan's specific context. 'Last year, we had nearly 60 students applying for higher education through the UCAS system.[2] That involves a lot of work for us teachers.[3] Students write a personal statement and we have to be in tune with that. The GCSE modules carry weight. There are a lot of sports-related courses available: PE, sports management, physiotherapy, sports psychology, sports nutrition.'

Donegal's long-standing links with Scotland, combined with the absence of fees, makes Scottish universities especially popular. 'Also,' adds Joe, 'you can fly from Derry to Glasgow in just over half an hour for a little more than £20.' He is well positioned to know this as he himself is pursuing doctoral studies in Glasgow. Of course, Northern Ireland universities, Queen's in Belfast and the University of Ulster at Coleraine and Jordanstown, are also popular destinations. A few years ago, some students were attracted to English universities to follow courses such as medicine and physiotherapy. 'But now that's more of less out of the question because of the fees,' remarks Joe. 'The GCSE ICT strand in St Eunan's TY provides a valuable platform for many third-level courses, especially in Coleraine, Magee College in Derry and Letterkenny Institute of Technology (LYIT),' explains Joe. He adds that the latter, on the school's doorstep, is a 'great resource for us.'

To sharpen TY students' focus, Joe Gallagher addresses the TY students at the start of each year. One of the items he explains is how the UCAS system works, in particular, the personal statement. He points out how an appropriate work experience place-

---

[2] University and College Admissions Service coordinates entry to about 37,000 courses offered by about 300 providers in Northern Ireland, Scotland, Wales and England.

[3] The UCAS system requires 'an education professional' to write a reference about the suitability, academic ability, interests and skills for a particular course. Referees also comment on applicant's personal statements and provide relevant information of the school context. In some cases the reference can be the difference between being offered a place and not.

ment can add weight to a personal statement. 'To take an obvious example, if someone is applying for a course in veterinary medicine, stating you like animals in the personal statement may help but it seems a lot more real when you can say you spent a work experience placement in a vet's clinic,' he says, adding, 'as we know this is not counted in a CAO application.' Joe also links the PE and ICT modules with UCAS applications. 'If you can say on your personal statement (for UCAS) that you have the top grade, an A star, this cuts a lot of ice with colleges,' he adds.

From a guidance and counselling perspective, Joe Gallagher is highly conscious of tensions associated with supporting large numbers of students who will apply through both the CAO and UCAS system. 'I think a big fault of the CAO system is that you can generate points in many subjects that don't relate to the course you apply for. For example, a person might get in to study engineering with 'A's in subjects such as Spanish, Art and Home Economics. The UK colleges don't just want the points; they often want particular grades in relevant subjects, for example Maths and Science for engineering. They also favour particular kinds of work experience,' he explains. 'So, from the very start of TY, we help the students clarify which higher education courses they wish to apply for. If they lean towards a UCAS application, then subject choice for Leaving Cert is critically important.' Joe says this presents dilemmas for many students. He cites the example of someone interested in architecture. If going the UCAS route, then Technical Graphics and Art are obvious subject choices, but if trying to maximise points, the student might say, 'but I have a better chance of getting an A in Geography.'

Other features

In the St Eunan's timetable, Tuesday is work experience day. 'Local employers are very co-operative,' says Chris Darby. Each student does two placements, one prior to Christmas and another one afterwards. The principal knows that, from a school organisation viewpoint, having the boys on placement every Tuesday means TY teacher resources have only to be deployed on four rather than five days. Employers seem happy with this model, remarks Chris, noting that the nearby Loreto College also adopts this approach. Are there disadvantages to a one-day a week policy on work experience? 'One disadvantage is that if someone wants to go further afield, for example RTÉ in Dublin, that's not possible. Occasionally, individuals have been facilitated in getting a week's placement outside of Donegal, but that's rare enough, exceptional.'

A knock-on effect of the need to focus on the GCSE strands is to reduce the flexibility to complement the TY timetable with once-off events like visiting speakers and trips away. 'So, we have a busy cluster of modules on a Friday afternoon,' says Chris. 'Some are school-based, some community-based. These include music production, car maintenance, driver awareness, first aid, chess, ceramics, food safety, computer aided design, and cooking for college,' he adds.

The right formula?

As the optional modules suggest, St Eunan's is particularly sensitive to its context as an all-boys school. This is very evident in the 'Formula One' or 'F1' module. Here the core activity is students, working in small groups, designing, building and racing miniature compressed gas-powered balsa cars. 'Initially, we offered this as an extra-curricular activity. It proved so popular we decided in 2013 to include it on the timetable, a double period each week,' explains Chris Darby.

Teacher Seán McGinley is enthusiastic about this module. 'I like teaching it because it's so broad – it's business, it's science, it's physics, it's maths, it's sponsorship, it's finance, it involves so much,' he says. Cars are designed and built on a scale of one-twentieth of a Formula One car. These are raced competitively along a 20 metre track. Seán shows an example of a race recorded on his iphone. It lasts no more than a few seconds! Teams can involve up to six students. In a class context, comparing and contrasting processes and products facilitates learning, he adds. 'Everyone has a defined role with the teacher very much acting as a mentor,' continues Seán. He brings in one of the previous year's participants, appropriately named Ayrton, who clearly loved being involved in this project. Ayrton recounts how his team took part in the regional finals and how they added a cross-border dimension by testing their vehicle on a track in Omagh, County Tyrone. 'The competition is not just based on the speed of the car,' Ayrton explains. Five assessment criteria are used at these events: the car itself; the race; the portfolio recording the project's progress; sponsorship and marketing and oral presentation of the work. Success at the regional event led Ayrton and his classmates to the national finals which was a very memorable event, he says, remarking on how their wheel design might have been improved and the advantages of involving singer Daniel O'Donnell in their marketing which extended to Australia, Singapore, New York and London. It is clear that this project sent ripples way beyond TY, first through the school itself and then further afield.

As a teacher of woodwork, construction studies and technical graphics, Seán relishes the interdisciplinary aspects of the F1 project, dipping into aerodynamics, marketing and the wider STEM (Science, Technology, Engineering and Mathematics) agenda. 'For me as a relatively new teacher, there is great learning in a project like this. It's a form of professional development,' he says

If there is a downside, it can be that one double class per week for the module seems insufficient. And so, like many TY projects, activities can spill out beyond the usual school day, placing additional demands on teachers and students. According to the website:

> The competition inspires students to use IT to learn about physics, aerodynamics, design, manufacture, branding, graphics, sponsorship, marketing, leadership, teamwork, media skills and financial strategy, and apply them in a practical, imaginative, competitive and exciting way. (http://www.f1inschools.ie/resources/F1_in_Schools_Brochure_2014-15.pdf)

Lingering questions

Leaving St Eunan's College and, indeed, some other all boys schools, one of the lingering questions is: nationally, has the TY programme been developed in ways that are more appealing to girls than boys? In their assessment of TY, Smyth, Byrne and Hannan (2004, p. 159) noted that 'principals in boys' secondary, vocational and small and/or designated disadvantaged schools were somewhat less likely to view the programme as successful as were those with a compulsory Transition Year.' A further question is: do many popular TY modules and activities run more smoothly in co-educational and all-girls' schools than in all-boys' ones? Behind Chris Darby's remark about 'singing and dancing' lie serious educational questions. Do schools need to be more inventive in devising learning activities, especially in TY, to engage teenage boys?[4]

---

[4] An important indicator of the ongoing evolutionary nature of TY programmes is illustrated by this chapter. The school was visited initially in May 2014. When a draft chapter was sent back to the school for comments prior to publication, Chris Darby noted that the school has co-operated with Loreto College, Letterkenny in staging a joint musical over five nights in March 2105, each one sold out. He also noted that three class groups had grown to five with a view to accommodating everyone who wanted to do TY.

29

THE GREAT OUTDOORS

Transition Year students from St. Joseph's Mercy Secondary School, Navan, County Meath are enthusiastic about the benefits of outdoor pursuits. They had just returned from Carlingford Adventure Centre in County Louth. They immediately mentioned bonding, teamwork, facing new challenges, becoming more independent and learning new skills. TY is optional in the school, 55 students are drawn from five different third year classes. 'An overnight trip away with lots of stimulating activities in the adventure centre is a great start to Transition Year,' explains Co-ordinator Mary Doherty. 'It brings them together in a way that begins to build the group identity that is special to TY,' she adds. 'The students state that one of their fears at the start of TY related to being in class with a lot of people they didn't know previously. I could see how as they tackled rock climbing, kayaking, canoeing, even being together on the bus broke down barriers quickly,' says Mary. 'Skywalking, where the challenge is to overcome fear of heights, was especially popular.'

As a TY Co-ordinator, Mary Doherty sees tremendous value in an outdoor pursuits trip at the start of the year. 'It brings together in practice so many ideas that are key to TY,' she says. 'For example, the fact that the learning is away from conventional classrooms, that it is learning by doing, that it involves teamwork where without the co-operation of others you will fail, where you have to face your own fears, where strong personal bonds are built.' Mary adds that a further bonus of trips to adventure centres is the mixing with students from other schools.

In St Joseph's all TY students are encouraged to take part in the Gaisce Bronze Medal Award. This adds extra purpose to the Carlingford trip. The award, which takes at least 26 weeks to achieve, involves undertaking challenges in four distinct areas. As well as engaging in an adventure journey, young people have to get involved in a community activity, develop a personal skill and take part in physical recreation.

'Gaining a Gaisce award can be a powerful confidence builder. When a group of TY students take part together, morale is boosted. The award scheme can build a valuable bridge between activities in TY and in fifth and sixth year, especially when recipients of bronze awards decide to advance to silver and gold levels. Many TY co-ordinators talk readily of the resonances between TY's goals and the Gaisce scheme,' agrees Mary Doherty.

Gaisce

The President's Award is a self-development programme for young people which enhances confidence and wellbeing through participation in personal, physical and community challenges. Gaisce is a direct challenge from the President of Ireland to young people aged 15-25 to dream big and realise their potential. The challenge dates from 1985, the International Youth Year. Gaisce's mission resonates well with the mission and purposes of TY:

> Provide opportunities for young people to realise their potential through personal challenges, facilitating the transition from young person to young adult and enhancing their potential and contribution as active participants in society.

Over 22,000 young people take part in Gaisce each year,' says Yvonne McKenna, Chief Executive of Gaisce. 'Last year we saw over 12,000 young people across Ireland complete the Gaisce Award programme, a 10 per cent increase on 2013 levels.' Those figures translate into an impressive legacy: over 300,000 young people across Ireland have been involved with Gaisce since its inauguration.

On the Gaisce website, President Michael D. Higgins, puts the awards scheme in a wider context. He says:

At my inauguration I spoke of the importance of all citizens, of all ages offering their own imaginative and practical contribution to the shaping of our shared future. The engagement of our young people as active and reflective members of society is critical if we are to work together to build an active, inclusive citizenship based on equality, respect for all and the flowering of true creativity. The ability to make a commitment beyond the self and to sustain that commitment over time by taking part in the collective endeavours of local groups or associations, is, I believe, one of the building blocks of a strong and genuine republic. The President's Awards or Gaisce Awards are a form of recogniton of the efforts of many young citizens of this country who are prepared to challenge themselves and to transform ideas into action as they constantly strive to reach their full potential. Time and again we have witnessed the great wealth of talent and innovation that our young citizens have to offer society. I've also seen the determination, self-discipline and strength of mind that is essential to the attainment of a Gaisce Award, awards which are not earned without great effort or achieved easily...

There are three types of award, Bronze, Silver and Gold. In order to merit an award participants set goals for themselves in different types of activity: community involvement, personal skills, physical recreation and an adventure journey.

The award is non-competitive in that once the four goals are reached the participant automatically gains the award. The award itself comprises a medal, a certificate signed by the President of Ireland and a lapel badge. The Bronze Awards are presented in the local community, the Silver is presented by celebrities in the four provinces and the Gold is presented by the President in Dublin Castle.

Participants are mentored by voluntary adults who are trained by Gaisce. These are known as President's Award Leaders or PALs. There are approximately 1,100 PALs nationwide. The work of PALs is essential to the success of Gaisce and they contribute over 100,000 voluntary hours each year.

Yvonne McKenna provides a wide range of examples of community involvement 'supporting older people such as providing meals on wheels, entertaining, and teaching them about computers and smart phones is popular,' she says. 'So is volunteering with young people in youth clubs, summer camps and with organisations like the Scouts, Foróige, Macra na Feirme and so on. There are thousands of ways for young people to volunteer and connect with their community.' Yvonne continues with other examples such as community groups like credit unions, the defence forces, first aid groups, life-saving activities, tidy towns, local libraries. 'Of course, Gaisce participants are also involved with a wide range of sporting organisations like the GAA, FAI and IRFU. Indeed, the list is endless, you could add in charity shops, the Society of St Vincent de Paul, Amnesty, supporting homeless people and much more,' she says.

To mark 30 years of Gaisce, the organistion commissioned research on the award's impact. This research, involving 647 participants, was published in 2015. The findings indicate that taking part in the Bronze Award improves significantly participants' levels of hope (pathways), self-efficacy, self-esteem, happiness and psychological well-being. There is also evidence that those with the greatest psychological needs are among those who benefit most from taking part in Gaisce. The research found that participation also enhanced positive relationships, promoted empathy and altruism. There is evidence that engagement with Gaisce increases resilience. In addition, more positive thought, greater fitness and increased positive emotions were measured outcomes. An important conclusion from the research is that:

> More widespread participation in programmes such as Gaisce would have positive implications for the psychological health of young people in Ireland.

Further opportunities

Sporting organisations have also seen the opportunities TY offers young people and have devised a number of programmes that enhance practical skills. Four brief examples illustrate some of the activities. Munster Rugby ran a TY Rugby programme in Christian Brothers College, Cork: 33 TY students learned how to plan and deliver a rugby coaching session for 120 primary school pupils. Loreto College, Foxrock, Dublin includes a GAA Ladies Gaelic Football TY Programme as part of TY. In May 2015, students from Davis College in Mallow, County Cork received GAA Foundation Level Coaching Certificates. FAI coaching courses feature in TY programmes in many schools, including St Laurence's College, Loughlinstown, Dublin and Coláiste Mhuire, Buttevant, County Cork. In 2014, students from Borris Vocational School, County Carlow were among the first participants in the 'Get Rowing with TY' pilot programme run by Rowing Ireland. The Irish Hockey Association has a specialised TY programme. The Irish Volleyball Association runs a SpikeBall Leaders Award Programme aimed specifically at girls in TY.

Finally, the network of outdoor pursuits centres provides great resources for TY programmes. Indeed, for many former TY students, mention of locations like Cappinalea (County Kerry), Gartan (County Donegal), Carlingford (County Louth), Delphi (County Galway) and Shielbaggan (County Wexford) conjure up memories of lack of sleep, mud and exhaustation; they also reverberate with excitement, friendship, challenges faced and conquered.

30

MORE TEACHER VOICES

'It's a time of opportunity, Transition Year,' says Bridie Corkery. 'Opportunity for personal and social development, to learn more about current affairs, to broaden the learning experience inside and outside the school, to make mistakes in a supportive environment, to reflect on one's direction in life.' Bridie has worked as a TY co-ordinator, as a year head and was a member of the first national support team that spearheaded the mainstreaming of the programme in the mid-1990s,

'One of the biggest changes TY brought to my own teaching was that it helped me to take a step back, to allow students to take responsibility for their own learning. It also brought a greater realisation of the emotional aspects of teaching as well as the importance of affirmation. When teaching English, I saw, in particular, how students' confidence grew through taking part in debates and public speaking as they honed their communication and analytical skills. I also used the opportunity in TY to open up literature from different cultures. As a teacher of French I thought TY provided a welcome space where students could really develop their aural and oral skills while maintaining their reading and writing competence in another language. In terms of developing autonomous learners, as the *Guidelines* state, my experience tells me that research by students themselves, peer support, assessment for learning and well thought out experiential learning strategies are very effective,' she says.

Reflecting on more than two decades of involvement with TY, Bridie believes the programme has had a very profound effect on

Irish society, on developing self-confidence. 'You can see this in particular among the number of young women emerging in politics, the media and elsewhere who will say that TY gave them the to confidence to express themselves in public,' says Bridie. From a teaching point of view, Bridie emphasises planning and collegiality. She says: 'Plan the module well. Involve the students at every opportunity. Engage with agencies outside the school. Talk about the programme with colleagues.'

Aligning TY and a school's ethos and values

'Transition Year is education as it should be. While based on what young people need to learn, it is not exam-driven. Assessment is continuous, often project-based. We have deliberately developed TY as an expression of the philosophy of the school,' says Liam Wegimont, Principal of Mount Temple Comprehensive School, Dublin.

'From our first encounters with parents of incoming students, we are clear about how TY relates to the school's learning policy, to our ethos, to what we are about,' he says.

'We spent a lot of time developing a learning policy. Schools are constantly being told what our obligations are, the need to have this policy and that policy. Ten years ago we found it strange that we were being encouraged to develop a CCTV policy, but the core business of the school – learning – was absent from policy-making. So, over a two-year period, we worked together – staff, students and parents – to come up with what is really important: a learning policy. Essentially it's about relating our ethos to everything that happens in the school in terms of learning, sorting out our values. I think TY is probably the best expression of our values and ethos. Unfortunately, the Junior Cycle has become an exam-focused programme, with the push for exams starting in second year. Leaving Cert has a stranglehold on learning with its high-stakes exam focus. TY is a space for freedom; it allows teachers to design courses based on what students need. Here we constantly tweak things to make sure they are right,' he contends.

This principal is extremely forthright about weaknesses within current provision. He says, 'At our board meetings we have healthy debate in regard to whether the LC may be a necessary evil, or whether it is just evil. Increasingly, I hold the latter position. We are very clear with parents, while we strive to enable students to get better results in the LC, we don't lie to them or our students about the limitations of the LC. I believe the system should have been dismantled twenty-five years ago. We tell them we long for the day when LC works more like TY. The LC should be abolished. It should have been abolished a long time ago. If what schools are about is care and learning, then the LC diminishes the ability to care and disrupts the ability to teach and learn. So for us, TY is about designing the way learning should be, by putting learning first.'

For principals, a good co-ordinator is crucial for TY's success. In Mount Temple, co-ordinator Barry Kearns leads a very energetic group of teachers who are, in Barry's words, 'up for doing innovative things in TY'. Liam adds, 'One thing I would like to emphasise is how important it is to have a co-ordinator who, like Barry, is very calming, very reassuring but can also look critically at the programme and adjust it each year in ways that make sense to student learning. I'd go further. It's absolutely crucial. I think these qualities have been developed through listening carefully to feedback, feedback from teachers, students and parents.

What is distinctive about the school's TY programme? Barry replies, 'The community work and the volunteering work, the European Youth Parliament, the musical, the Gaeltacht trip are examples of novel features. That Gaeltacht trip has always been seen as the big trip of the year. It's Coláiste Uisce, a week of Irish studies mixed in with water sports. Now, obviously, there are issues associated with a week's residential trip. Not everybody is able to make it. For those who can't go, there will be an alternative activity week.'

Barry continues, 'A distinctive feature of the TY programme here in Mount Temple is the idea of a number of activity weeks, that is, where there is no "regular" schooling. For example, with the musical in January, we have a week in December devoted exclusively to preparation for the musical. There are also 40 students who are not doing the musical; they will be engaged in sporting activities when everybody else is singing and dancing. Specifically, they have the option of trying a new sport, water-polo, or doing a certified first-aid course,' says Barry. Liam adds, 'Activity week would also have things like action-track, which involves writing, designing and performing a play from start to finish; musical technology; cookery; craft work.'

Does the idea of suspending the regular timetable for action weeks not meet resistance, especially from teachers of continuity subjects? Liam responds, 'Don't get me wrong! We use the core subjects to maintain academic progress, especially in Maths, English and Irish. That's got stronger over the last while. But activity weeks are also about learning, sometimes in ways that last a lifetime.'

Barry adds, 'Of course, in TY we have to remind the students that, after it, they will be back in the academic heat. It's about balance. In the year there are four weeks of work experience. There are two activity weeks. Most of the rest of time they are on the premises. As I say, it's about balance, maintaining continuity while still taking all the opportunities to do what's possible in TY. I should add that we also have a French exchange and we have lots of small groups who do distinctive things. There is a Maths group that were out in the Science Gallery in Trinity College. As we speak, about 40 TY students are in the city doing a bucket collection in support of an NGO that works against child trafficking.'

What's also distinctive about Mount Temple's TY is that every Tuesday afternoon students are required to go out on community service. Barry says, 'We make the point to the students and to their parents that up to now the students have always been at the centre of attention, receiving care, attention and love from parents, family and teachers. As they grow from dependence to independence they need to start looking outward a little bit. Hence, we ask students 'what can you give back?' In March of third year, we ask future TY students to find a place for September where they can volunteer to give two hours of their time back to the community, ideally on Tuesday afternoon. Sometimes it doesn't work out like that as it might be training younger children playing football on a Saturday morning. It has to be recorded. They have a space in their journal, a log book section, where they reflect on this.

Liam Wegimont returns to a favourite theme, that of values in education: 'We built the values together. Schools don't exist in a vacuum. I'm highly sceptical of the notion that it's a highly charismatic principal that builds a school. Here we inherit values that are based on the Protestant tradition, independent thinking. It's about protest. It's about quietly being critical, against the status quo, being non-majoritarian. So, those values clearly have implications for learning. TY, for example, is not compulsory because we try to avoid making things compulsory. At the same time, more than 95 per cent of students opt for TY. Now, while I wouldn't like to pretend we're a school independent of the system – there's enough history of failed attempts by schools to go it alone – we are very clear about what our values are in relation to learning and teaching. All that forms the basis for the TY work and we clearly relate what we do in TY to the rest of school life,' says Liam.

DEIS contexts

Josephine McGrath, a TY co-ordinator in a DEIS school, completed research in Maynooth University in 2014. 'Some of what I found surprised me and forced me and my colleagues to look at our underlying assumptions. I found that some newcomer children tend to avoid TY. Then, tracking their LC performance, I found that they actually achieved higher grades than their native counterparts who did TY. When I analysed the results further, I could see significant differences in the family backgrounds,' she says.

Josephine explains the variations as follows. 'Many parents of newcomer children are educated people who had a high socio-economic standing in their countries of origin. However, in Ireland they don't necessarily work in the jobs they were trained for. Sometimes they are working in service jobs or unskilled positions. They often have very high expectations of their children. Many of the newcomer pupils I interviewed and work with tend to be very motivated and hardworking. Within such families, the central focus is on securing a place in third level with a view to particular careers. A year that offers 'increased maturity', 'vocational preparation' and taking greater responsibility for their own learning is often seen as unnecessary, even a waste of time so they tend to avoid TY', says Josephine.

'Then,' she continues, 'when I looked at the experience of the native students, it is clear that TY gives many opportunities that would not be otherwise available to them. For example, work experience is enormously relevant for those who come from households in which no one is in active employment. It opens up thoughts, ideas and pathways that might not be considered otherwise.'

'Importantly, and this was my biggest finding about TY generally, the programme's impact on relationships, between students and between students and their teachers, is very strong. This builds a platform for friendships but also for peer support in fifth and sixth year,' she says.

Based on her findings, Jospehine expresses concern about those who opt for a five-year cycle. She says, 'I think they miss a lot when they don't have that relationship-building year in their lives. As for the newcomer children, when they do engage with TY it is very clear that their integration with their classmates is strengthened and, arguably, their integration into Irish society is deepened,' she says.

While keenly aware of the opportunities TY can offer young people in disadvantaged contexts, Josephine is also very conscious of the financial burden it can impose. 'I think that in schools located in areas where people are on low incomes, the challenge is to run a good low-cost TY. You don't want to put extra burdens on people but you don't want the students to miss out on trips and other enriching activities. Josphine cites an example of a school that introduces a payment plan for the €250 for TY activities that starts in third year. 'In many cases the students are fully paid up by the start of TY and this removes a lot of the attention on money and keeps the focus on good educational experiences,' she says.

Support service worker

Before returning to school in September 2015, Cornelius Young spent eight years seconded from school working with the Professional Development Service for Teachers (PDST). 'I always remember seeing Michael O'Leary addressing the school staff in 2002. There was some apprehension, nervousness and we took a bit of convincing. But he listened to teachers. I think that's very important in support work. I've always remembered that,' he adds.

Cornelius says that a staff's apprehension about introducing TY is sometimes because of a concern, even a fear, for their students. 'They worry about whether they will stick a six-year course. They don't want anyone to drop out. Staffs need time to prepare, to come around to the view that TY is manageable, that the capacity is there within the staff team.' He also makes the point that preparing for TY can be a great time for staff development. 'You see younger or newly appointed staff contributing new ideas, bringing freshness, creativity and confidence. More experienced teachers are often energised by this and see TY as an opportunity to re-charge their batteries, to build on their experience, to break new ground. This can be a lifeline for a school as it's easy – especially if the school faces a lot of challenges – for teachers to get into a rut. We all need to renew ourselves every so often,' he says, smilingly.

Cornelius continues: 'Especially in disadvantaged contexts, you can't take anything for granted. You continually need to be flexible, imaginative. You need innovative teachers with a "can-do" attitude. TY gave us the opportunity to push the boat out, to apply a bigger vision, to use more engaging, active methodologies.'

As he reflects on his time supporting schools in areas like information and communications technology, in active learning methodologies, Cornelius also expresses concern about keeping TY 'fresh'. 'You also have to keep the people fresh,' he says. 'There have been occasions I wondered about how well people grasped the vision of TY. On a bad day I'd even ask myself: Did they ever have the vision? Did they have it once and does "system thinking" take over?'

He links his support work in PDST with his days as a student. 'One of things I learned as a student teacher in the University of Limerick is the importance of "big picture" thinking. That is so important in teaching. I was fortunate in Limerick having Jim Gleeson as a lecturer. A passion for education just oozed out of him. He showed us how to do big picture thinking, how to see the multiple mechanisms that inform curriculum. That stood to me a lot during the support work, when you could get bogged down in technical details,' he says.

He continues: 'From my experience of being in and out of a lot of schools, I think, for teachers on the ground, TY is very attractive. There is freedom to play around, to try things out, to make, break and re-make something. You try something this year and you can tweak it the following year. There can be fun and creativity. There's also a lack of fear in TY about experimenting. You measure yourself against yourself rather than against the results of some paper test.'

From seeing the inner workings of many schools while doing support work, what strong messages emerge? Cornelius says: 'I am struck by the difference between schools in their TY programmes. You see very different dynamics at work in different schools.' He believes that TY enables schools to develop their own values, adding, 'though a lot depends on the capacity of the teachers'. As he sees it, 'I think the system would like to be able to judge everyone by the same yardstick. But different cultures, different leadership and different staff capacities lead to very different results. I like cultures that give scope for imagination and creativity. I see tensions between a "one-size fits all" perspective and the TY focus on individual teacher creativity.'

Cornelius continues: 'You hear stories of WSE and SSE where the attention seems to be on learner outcomes that can be put down on paper; what is tangible is valued. TY is more intangible. When TY is dynamic and sustainable it is usually across the spectrum in a school through a wide variety of experiences. In such schools all students get something out of it that meets their needs. That's not easy to measure.'

But, in an exam-dominated system, is TY not a little out of sync? 'Understandably, teachers are attracted to tangible results. So, for some, a TY that is part of a three-year LC can appear to give more structure, uniformity and certainty. It is perhaps because some teachers have a lack of faith in the process of TY. When TY works well it can be truly transformative. But this is only likely to happen when people keep the big picture in mind: what should be the overall purpose of school? What are we trying to achieve for the students in TY? What is the educational purpose of particular activities – the musical, fundraising, trips abroad and so on? These are important questions to ask,' he says, with feeling.

Cornelius concludes: 'In summary, I think TY works well when it is seen as a space where teachers can apply co-operative and creative active methodologies to enrich young people's learning. I would like to see the leaders in the system showing more aware-ness of the dynamics needed to create school cultures that make this possible. Teachers need a lot more time to talk to each other about their practices.'

31

Lights, Camera, Action –
Media and Film Studies

In Scoil Chaitríona, a co-educational voluntary secondary Gael-scoil in Glasnevin on Dublin's northside, film studies is a compulsory module in Transition Year. Teacher Trish Wall has been teaching the nine-week module, timetabled for a double period each week, for the past few years. 'The students respond enthusiastically,' she says. 'They are highly motivated when it comes to digital media. All students find some area they are particularly interested in, whether it be writing analytically or working behind the camera. They have always engaged with whatever text has been chosen, no matter how alternative it may have seemed to begin with. They enjoy offering their opinions and the course provides for significant group discussion and team work,' says Trish.

Like all media studies teachers, Trish has selected a personal range of films to explore with TY students. She groups *Stand by Me*, *Mean Creek* and *Mean Girls* together, and one can see rich seams and themes of adolescent identity, bullying and friendship. Another group of films that Trish uses investigates aspects of the western genre and screen portrayals of violence: *A Fistful of Dollars*, *The Unforgiven* and *There Will Be Blood.* She notes that the middle title in that series is the 1960 film with Burt Lancaster rather than the 1992 one with Morgan Freeman and Clint Eastwood. A third cluster of films includes *The Hurt Locker*, the documentary *Restrepo* and the computer game *Modern Warfare.* This combination enables Trish and her students to explore aspects of recent wars in Iraq and Afghanistan in creative ways.

According to Trish, 'there are numerous goals when working with the students on film. It's a medium with which they are very familiar and I want to deepen their digital literacy. So, I use short clips and have devised worksheets to illustrate shots, angles and other filmic terminology. Film is an art form and I want them to see that too. Film offers a great platform for developing skills such as acting, writing screenplays and storyboards. Using digital cameras the students also learn filming and editing skills. We are also strengthening a foundation for studying film in the Leaving Certificate, learning to read films as literary texts,' she says.

Depending on time and other opportunities throughout the year, Trish also occasionally organises short film-making competitions, invites in actors and directors as part of a school-wide film festival and arranges TY outings to the cinema. In passing, Trish mentions that, a few years ago, she and her students grasped TY's opportunity to create other original learning opportunities and published a book of stories, *Lost in Translation.*

Trish Wall remarks that, despite young people's comfort with the medium of film, every year she is struck by how the majority of the class will have a very limited knowledge of the films that are out there, and how they are made. When she evaluates the module, these two areas are commented on by the students as being the most intriguing parts of the course. 'Personally, I feel that without this film module, the students are not fully alert to the world of film and continue to interpret film as individuals or with small groups of friends. Within the classroom setting, the students develop whatever knowledge they have previously acquired and build on it,' she says.

Trish adds that she sees the learning from the module very clearly evident when she is teaching LC English. 'It works well as an introduction and it stimulates an awareness of this media. For this reason alone, I feel it is worth the investment,' she says.

Other options

Another possibility for media studies – indeed for any TY module – is to develop Transition Units (TUs). The NCCA developed a useful framework for TUs. The framework and examples of TUs can be accessed on the NCCA website. The broad structure of a 45 hour TU is as follows:

1. Title of unit

2. Area of study

3. Overview

4. Links

5. Summary outline of unit

6. Breakdown of unit

7. Aims

8. Learning outcomes

9. Key skills

10. Methodologies

11. Assessment approaches

12. Evaluation

13. Resources.

Teachers responded with some imaginative examples and these can be accessed on the NCCA website (www.ncca.ie). For example, Moving Image, developed by the Irish Film Institute, is a superb example of a comprehensive Transition Unit. Norma Murray of Glanmire Community School developed a unit Soap Operas and Popular Culture that focused on the analysis of contemporary themes from modern culture as conveyed through soaps and aspects of cinematography.

Multiple activities

Pippa Brady teaches at St Mary's College Dundalk, a co-educational voluntary Catholic secondary school under Marist trusteeship. She echoes many of the insights voiced by Trish Wall. 'In my experience over twenty years, I have found that the TY students engage really well with Media Studies,' she says. 'Making their own advertisements is a great way to understand how persuasive techniques work,' Pippa explains. 'The students engage in the whole process from pitching for an ad, designing storyboards, actually filming, then editing and presenting. With camera phones nowadays so much is possible.' This work in St Mary's is backed up by studying particular films. Classroom time is limited so the teachers often show clips and find that the students themselves often then go and view the full film. 'We have an exciting new development here in Dundalk where the local Táin Theatre will screen films for groups as small as 50 students at minimal costs. This will be a huge boost to media studies,' she adds.

St Mary's, like many other schools, sees TY as a space where young people can be introduced to the rich heritage of Irish cinema. 'There are always strong reactions to films like *The Quiet Man, My Left Foot, Into the West*, and *Adam and Paul*,' she says, adding, 'you need a good sound-proofed roof for that last one.' Pippa belives that the inclusion of films in Leaving Cert English has been a valuable development and a good foundation can be built in TY. 'You can look at classics that are not on the LC syllabus for a particular year. Over the years, I recall good responses to *Strictly Ballroom, Rebel Without a Cause, Edward Scissorhands*,' she says.

Pippa makes the point that many students come to TY with very little experience of European films. 'I know that language teachers find films such as *Amelie, I'm Not Scared* and *Run, Lola, Run* work well in their classes. And, of course, everyone loves *Cinema Paradiso*, an excellent film to study,' she adds.

Teachers in St Mary's have also found 'stop-go' animation very effective. 'For example, we made an animation based on a nightmare. It was great fun as well as rich in learning opportunities about storyboarding, music, editing, presentation and so on,' says Pippa.

Like Trish Wall, Pippa Brady is also an enthusiastic believer in the rich learning involved when TY students work together on a publication. 'They bring great enthusiasm, dedication and hard work to a project like this,' she says. 'This' is a colourful, 64-page school yearbook packed with reports, reviews, opinion pieces, short stories, graphic stories, photographs, artwork and advertisements. Pippa adds that she has found the Write-a-Book project also very productive.

The bigger picture

Alicia McGivern, Head of Education with the Irish Film Institute (IFI), makes an eloquent and convincing case for greater study of film in schools. She has seen the IFI's extensive film education pro-gramme grow to a point where it now reaches over 15,000 young people throughout the school year. Through film screenings and related events, IFI takes a number of different approaches to film in the classroom. 'One of our main aims in IFI Education is to support teachers in their subjects, but also to promote film as an artform in itself and to provide access to a wide range of film,' says Alicia.

'The place of film in curricula has changed dramatically over the years and IFI's activities in the field have expanded as a result,' she continues. 'During the early days of our programme in the mid-1990s, film was tied into a broader concept of media studies, which included study of TV and newsprint. Where other curricula such as in the UK offered film as a subject in its own right, in Ire-land film was regarded as something often utilised to encourage learning among weaker students or filmmaking projects cropped up as a typical youth group activity,' she explains. 'Increasingly, however, as teachers recognised how young people of all abili-ties were motivated by film, they drew on it in different ways to enhance their teaching. TY offered a space where many teachers began to use film in the classroom for the first time.'

Alicia is pleased with the introduction of film to the revised English Leaving Certificate as the first significant move to include film as a 'text' for study in its own right, 'although it has limita-tions in that a focus is often on narrative or extracting key scenes to compare with written texts,' she remarks. The new Junior Cycle Framework for English also offers an extensive film list, and film has a significant presence across Irish, Art, Modern Languages at LC, while it also has a place on LCA courses and LCVP.

Alicia is very aware that, nowadays, film and media are the lan-guage through which young people communicate. 'I believe that, as with written literacy, media literacy should be recognised as a right for all citizens. Media literate consumers will be active, informed and critical. As has been seen across the world, they can also contribute to public debate, campaigning and democratic movements,' she says.

But, are there not downsides to the media's role in modern life? 'Although a common perception remains that media consumption is a passive activity,' responds Alicia, 'media users are actively interpreting, making selections, discarding information, creating and following narratives. Undoubtedly there are valid concerns regarding cyberbullying, access to pornography, trolling and other negative aspects of media usage. Calls for responsibility from service providers seem like a little too late, it is more imperative that young people are educated in critical media literacy skills so that they can make informed and educated choices rather than relying on "industry" to safeguard our societies,' she says.

Recent research by the IFI has confirmed that young people and their teachers are highly motivated and engaged by film and media-based projects and they want to learn more. Alicia refers to two studies in particular, Film Focus (http://www.ifi.ie/filmfocus) and The 12-13 Project (http://www.ifi.ie/12to13project) to support her case.

She explains that, 'Building on these action-research projects, IFI has gone on to develop a Short Course in Film for Junior Cycle which will be available to schools through the IFI website. This is in partnership with FIS Film Project and Fresh Film Festival and comprises strands in Watching, Making and Showing. IFI continues to support teachers through the schools programme which now tours to over 25 venues around the country.' She also mentions a range of other educational services which can be seen on the IFI website and, of course, refers back to the Transition Unit, Moving Image.

Alicia concludes: 'Despite the availability of downloads, box sets, multi-channel and multi-platform options, we continue to promote the idea of cinema as the optimum venue for viewing film, promoting as it does the shared viewing experience, the film as the director intended it to be seen. Yet we are aware that for young people, content is the thing – whether watching on TV or on mobile device or in cinema. Media and film literacy can raise their awareness of what the difference is – including issues of copyright – and also encourage them to be informed, creative and critical users. We hope through our schools programme and other activities to be able to contribute to this. TY offers great opportunities for developing such media and film literacy.'

Nurturing citizenship

Many of Alicia's points resonate with Anthony Malone. 'In my experience, observing TY lessons over the years, I am always struck by the appetite students and teachers have to critically engage with the various digital and print media,' says Anthony, a lecturer in education at Maynooth University. He says: 'In a technology-driven, globalized world, mass media plays a significant part in our lives and has brought about decisive changes in how we communicate with one another. It is now more important than ever before that students are provided with meaningful opportunities to capably engage and critically negotiate their way through a fluid and changing world. Media Studies challenges students to understand the constructed nature of media representations and how these work to shape and influence our views and those of others.'

Anthony, who has worked in schools as a teacher of English and as a deputy principal, emphasises that a persistent task within lessons is to engage students in a critical and creative questioning of their world so as to better understand the parts they play. He adds: 'The accounts by Trish and Pippa ring true with my experience and provide strong evidence of how Media Studies in TY can actively build students' personal, social and communication skills.' He continues: 'Whether that is through active participation in discussions and debates – sharing and listening but also through using multimodal media for purposes of democratic self-expression, there is no shortage of opportunities. For some it might be the opportunity to take up various roles associated with film, radio and print media production; planning zoom events such as film festivals; or organising in-school or local civic campaigns. These activities not only afford students the opportunity to develop higher order skills but also, and perhaps more importantly, the opportunity to work together in collaborative, purposeful ways with others. In doing so students are offered very significant life chances to exercise leadership and forge an identity around what are often new and demanding roles. Such opportunities are crucial for the development of an active citizenship within a thriving democracy. TY offers the ideal space in which to build these capabilities.'

32

LEARNING BEYOND THE CLASSROOM

In the final week of January 2015, on two different occasions, I found myself walking through large slices of Dublin city, coming and going to interview people for this book. The icy, biting wind was memorable and so was the sight of numerous clusters of uniformed school children. On enquiry, it invariably emerged that they were Transition Year students, sometimes whole class groups. Each day I noticed at least ten groups. They were engaged on out-of-class learning activities, going to the National Library, the National Gallery, the offices of the European Commission in Ireland, Dáil Eireann, the Writers Museum, the Museum at Collins Barracks, Kilmainham Gaol, cinemas and elsewhere.

The sight of so many TY students, not only in Dublin but up and down the country, could be seen as a vibrant sign of the realisation of TY's goal to broaden young people's learning, to assist them to engage with the wider community, to develop active, participative citizens. But that might be naive. As evident in the chapters on community care, work experience and mini-companies, experiential learning is richest when teachers put in the work of preparation, monitoring and de-briefing. Learning outside the classroom makes different demands on teachers than classroom-based experiences.

'Trips' of some sort seem to feature in almost every school's TY programme. Some sound inspired, magical, stimulating, adventurous. The range of destinations and activities can be breathtaking. For example, students from Millstreet Community School visited a synagogue and a mosque in Cork to discover more about Islam and Judaism. Boys from St Mary's College Rathmines, Dublin walked 60 kilometres from Longwood, County Meath to Dublin, along the way raising funds for Spirasi, an organisation for victims of torture, asylum seekers and refugees. Students from Scoil Mhuire, Longford brought their football coaching skills to the children from nearby St Joseph's National School. A group from Scoil Dara, Kilcock, County Kildare, like many others, made the trip to Dáil Éireann. There were paintballing trips, karting outings, walks along the Wicklow Way, the Kerry Way, the Wild Atlantic Way. Trips to museums, art galleries, factories, farms, seashores and higher education institutions feature in many TY programmes. Students from Mount Sion in Waterford went on a fishing trip. The boys from Clonkeen College, Dublin went to Hook Head on a coasteering adventure.

Trips often feature among people's most distinct memories of their schooldays. In evaluations, overnight trips, especially when combined with adventure sports and outdoor pursuits, are often cited among the highlights of TY. Days in adventure centres can be especially formative as bonding with classmates often builds lifelong ties. Frequently, when TY students reflect on TY and adventure centres such as Delphi, Carlingford, Cappanalea, Gartan and Shielbaggan are mentioned, eyes light up.

Going abroad

Many schools include a trip abroad, usually optional, as part of their TY programme. Experiencing another culture, even if at a superficial level, during mid-adolesence can be eye-opening in ways that fit well with TY's aim to give young people a broad education. Evidence from newspapers, school websites and social media gives some idea of the range of destinations schools choose, including Belgium, China, Ecuador, France, Germany, Ghana India, Italy, Japan, Lesotho, Mexico, South Africa, Spain, Sweden, Thailand, Switzerland, Uganda, United Kingdom, United States and Zambia.

Some trips have a specific language learning focus and may be for an extended period, involving small groups or individual students. A number are skiing trips. Occasionally, political education is a central purpose as, for example, visits by students from St

Dominic's, Ballyfermot, Dublin, St Paul's Secondary School, Monastereven, County Kildare and others to the European Parliament.

Some trips are components of exchange programmes. For example, at Easter 2015, Coláiste Bríde in Clondalkin, County Dublin hosted students and teachers from Presentation Delhi in India.

TY students' visits abroad may be through an NGO, such as the Hope Foundation, or a university programme like UCC's link with Shanghai University. In 2015, TY students from more than 30 schools travelled to India with the Hope Foundation. These included: Castletroy College, Limerick; Loreto College, Wexford; Newtown School, Waterford; St Angela's College, Cork; Gaelcholáiste Luimnigh; St Declan's, Kilmacthomas, County Waterford; Davis College, Mallow, County Cork; Rockwell College, County Tipperary; Glanmire Community College, County Cork; and Alexandra College, Dublin. TY students attending many Christian Brothers schools, for example in Thurles, County Tipperary; Portlaoise, County Laois, Tralee, County Kerry; Fairview in Dublin went on an immersion visit to Zambia. Students from St Andrews College in Booterstown, Dublin travel to Uganda. Boys from St Mary's, Rathmines go to Ghana. Immersion projects tend to combine exposure to a different culture, practical action – often including some teaching – and the cultivation of new friendships.

One example

Every year since 2002, Transition Year students from John Scottus School in Dublin have travelled to Kolkata, India. In collaboration with Loreto Sealdah school in Kolkata,[1] the Irish TY students have assisted in the building of over 30 village schools in West Bengal. More than 20,000 educationally disadvantaged young people there have gained school places as a result. 'Quite simply, the project has proved to be a transformative experience for our TY students with immeasurable benefits for thousands of young West Bengalis,' says teacher John Alexander. The project also funds a monthly training programme for teachers in the Jharkhali Village School and

---

[1] www.loretosealdah.org.

10 other schools on the island of Basanti in the Sunderbans. 'The programme is approved by the Indian Government,' adds John.

The images of TY students from Dublin working alongside their counterparts from the Loreto school as well as local village children are powerful illustrations of global solidarity. The TY students also engage in a joint English language teaching programme. 'Part of our interpretation of the TY mission is that we aim to enable students to take a stand in order to create in the world around them a better place for everyone to live,' explains John. He continues: 'The trip to India is a key focus of this but it's also there in the way we introduce and develop many topics, ideas, and activities that we consider to be very good for the development of the human being and which do not get sufficient time in the normal curriculum of the secondary school. Our TY is a year of active learning, of maturing physically emotionally and spiritually. We see the results in TY giving students spiritual knowledge, expanded vision and new learning skills. It equips them to know their inner potential better.'

How does a project like this get funded? 'Personal travel costs have to be met by each pupil,' says John. Including airfare, vaccinations and visa costs, internal travel, accommodation and insurance, this amounts to about €1,800 per student. 'Then there is a separate fund raising programme on evenings and weekends run by students and parents and this seeks to reduce the individual contribution to €1,500,' adds John.

The relevance of immersion projects and development education activities outlined in Chapter 2 as features of 'a broad education' are put into sharp relief by some sobering statistics from the annual report of Credit Suisse. *The Irish Times* reported on 21 October 2014 that:

> Taken together, the bottom half of the global population own less than 1 per cent of total wealth. In sharp contrast, the richest decile hold 87 per cent of the world's wealth, and the top percentile alone account for 48.2 per cent of global assets.

CONCLUSION

Having viewed facets of Transition Year from multiple perspectives, the reader will have preferences as to which stories appeal and which challenge, which resonate with experience and which seem to be contrary. Depending on the lens the reader brings to the book, particular themes may stand out. There will also be, one hopes, questions raised – about TY, about young people, about teachers, about schools, about the education system and about society.

The foregoing chapters provide evidence of how some teachers have grasped the TY ideal in a particular subject area or activity and realised its promise with spectacular learning for their students. Forty years on from its introduction and twenty years after its mainstreaming, TY has led to significant changes in how schools engage with young people and with local communities. Many schools have 'domesticated' the programme, shaping it to fit the school's ethos and traditions, playing to strengths and pushing innovation but also, in cases, avoiding or diluting some of the more challenging features of the TY vision.

Young people

There is growing evidence that young people mature through the TY experience, that their confidence is boosted, that career and life aspirations are clarified, that voices are discovered, that personal identity is enriched, that engagement with the world beyond the school is increased, that personal agency and capacity for action as citizens increases. Bonding among students in TY – and between students and their teachers – also appears to nurture valuable strengths and resilience for the challenges ahead, particularly in fifth and sixth year. Indeed, incidental and anecdotal evidence suggests that many friendships formed in TY endure long into adulthood. The strong emphasis in TY programmes on personal and social development can also be effective in providing a more inclusive and more positive learning environment for young people whose experience in Junior Cycle was not good. Building relationships with peers in TY can be especially valuable for children whose families are new to Ireland.

Teachers

If some TY programmes can be transformative for young people, the evidence also points to some teachers being enriched professionally, enjoying the freedom to shape a module and create learning situations not easily implemented within the constraints of an examination-led programme. TY's innovator, Richard Burke, TD, was very clear about the programme's potential for teacher development. 'So in a sense it (TY) was a kind of Normandy landing to secure a bridgehead for proper education; although the teachers were idealistic they were almost inhibited from giving of their best because of the pressures of the treadmill, of the grind system, of the points system,' he said in 2001 of his 1974 initiative. He added, 'If you ask me for a word that sums up the Transition Year, it was to give the individual teacher who was well motivated an opportunity to influence the character and formation of the person in front of him (sic) in a more interpersonal and less restrictive and less hostile environment.'

Greater teacher professionalism enables TY to flourish as a dynamic form of curriculum development. Throughout TY programmes, there is convincing evidence of teachers working out in imaginative practice the ethical values that underpin the Code of Professional Conduct (Teaching Council, 2012): Respect, Care, Integrity and Trust. When teaching we continually battle to overcome barriers of predictability, of boredom, of resistance, of preconceived notions about learning, of our own mediocrity. TY's mission and aims point to the persistent need for educational imagination, for practitioners to reflect and to re-think.

Whole school

One of the most telling lines in the 1993 *Guidelines* is a short, simple sentence: 'The aims and philosophy of Transition Year should permeate the entire school.' This was also clearly part of Burke's original vision. He said in 2001, 'It (TY) was the freedom from the treadmill which one hoped then would continue in the latter years of second-level education, both from the teachers and the pupils who would not easily go back to the *status quo* because they had been changed mentally and otherwise by this programme. It was subversive.' While some report TY having a very positive impact on the culture of schools, there is little evidence of 'the treadmill' diminishing in size or velocity. Indeed, the persistence of stories related to competitive individualism, rote learning, teaching to the test, student stress and self-harm arising from the points system of admission to higher education suggests that the problems in 'the latter years of second-level education' are, if anything, under-challenged, under-analysed and under-reported. That said, if the robust adherence to the *status quo* evident in resistance to proposed changes in junior cycle education are an indicator, reforms of the established Leaving Certificate will require more sophisticated and courageous discussion between all stakeholders. There is ample evidence that TY's envigorating approach to teaching and learning can infuse other programmes. As Denise Kelly (2014) has suggested, TY has shown us how curriculum reform can work. Reform at junior and senior cycle needs to build on TY's combination of top down/bottom up initiatives and recognise how trusting schools and teachers enhances capacity.

Indeed, a disturbing feature of much debate related to Junior Cycle reform over the past decade is how little consciousness there seemed to be of TY. Many of the 24 statements of learning (DES 2012) resonate with TY's aims and achievements. TY stories told on previous pages demonstrate how, in practice, the six key skills proposed for junior cycle[1] can be realised. One can also see in accounts of schools connecting with local communities, especially

---

[1] Managing Myself, Staying Well, Communicating, Being Creative, Working with Others, Managing Information and Thinking

through community care, work experience and visiting speakers, how the final two years of schooling might be enriched further. TY also abounds with stories of teacher inventiveness, of teacher collaboration, of varied forms of assessment, and, possibly most significantly of all, of active engagement by students in their own learning.

A fear is that, despite claims of TY being 'embedded' (DES, 2004) in the system, it remains a sort of parallel universe, its own bubble, cut off from the harsher realities of the competitive individualism associated with LC grades and 'points', admission to higher education and schools' rankings on so-called 'league tables'.

Structure

The availability on the internet of TY-related resources makes planning, evaluation and re-freshing TY, more manageable. The 1993 *Transition Year Programmes Guidelines for Schools* remains pivotal. Individual school websites frequently include rich examples of good practice. Reports from the Inspectorate on individual school programmes illustrate strengths to aspire to and pitfalls to avoid. While often couched in cautious language, these reports nonetheless leave the reader in little doubt about approval or disapproval. For example, it's encouraging when a report notes: 'There is a whole-school approach to the planning, development and promotion of TY within the school and this is strongly supported by senior management.' 'The curriculum offers a variety of subjects, modules and activities and is broad and balanced in line with Department guidelines.' 'The core team meets formally on a monthly basis and weekly on an informal basis. Monthly meetings are minuted, filed and made available to school management.'

On the other hand, one can imagine varied reactions when a Board of Management meets or during a staff meeting to statements such as: 'It is recommended that the school should restructure its timetable to ensure that each TY student receives their minimum entitlement to twenty-eight hours of instruction time.' 'It is recommended that a career-guidance plan be drawn up for the whole school, Transition Year included.' 'Should the number of TY groups increase, as is planned, it is recommended that a parent-teacher meeting be introduced for TY and it is suggested that the students may be present at this meeting.' 'It is recommended that an end-of-year portfolio assessment be introduced.' One might go further and wonder how disappointing must a TY programme be to evoke recommendations such as: 'Group work should be introduced to some lessons to enhance student participation.' 'Targeted questioning should be used wherever possible in all lessons and higher-order and lower-order questions should be used to challenge students to achieve their potential.' 'Teachers should develop strategies to make it possible for all students, and especially EAL students, to participate as fully as possible in lessons.' 'Whole staff CPD for TY should be organised to support planning for TY at programme and subject level.'

Co-ordination

The centrality of imaginative and effective co-ordination emerges strongly as a key pillar of every school's TY programme. The challenge to keep TY 'fresh' rests heavily on the shoulders of co-ordinators and co-ordination teams. Cutbacks in recent years have, in some schools, weakened the programme. It's also clear that TY thrives when school principals and deputy principals understand and value TY's goals and are prepared to lead in ways that nurture innovation. Many co-ordinators who pioneered TY in their schools indentify local and regional workshops where they could share ideas with colleagues as especially helpful in implementing change. These workshops were part of a wider structure of support, facilitated by a group of seconded-teachers. In 2004, Doreen McMorris, an assistant chief inspector in the DES, told a joint Oireachtas Committee meeting[2] that TY's mainsteaming was greatly assisted by modest financial support to schools, new *Guidelines* (in 1993), and a national programme of in-service for teachers that included on-site visits to schools. A new dedicated team of experienced teachers, and perhaps a revision of the *Guide-*

---

[2] 25 March 2004, Joint Committee on Education and Science Debate. http:debates.oireachtas,

lines for schools, could give this unique programme the sustenance it deserves.

Inequalities

In a school system riven with inequalities, a critical question to be asked of any innovation is whether it extends, re-inforces, challenges or diminishes existing disparities. TY's difficulties in this regard arise from its optional nature and from a grossly under-funded system generally. The evidence points to higher participation rates in a six-year cycle by children of well-resourced parents compared to those from poorer families. The rights and needs of those who don't avail of a six-year cycle hangs uncomfortably in debates about second-level schooling.

While many DEIS schools provide imaginative TY programmes, they often struggle, particularly with out-of-school activities, to offer the range of learning experiences available elsewhere. Low participation patterns among teenage boys, especially from families with limited experience of formal schooling, is a particularly worrying indicator. The challenge to make TY programmes more attractive to this group of learners is clear.

Selection

Inevitably, the question arises: how typical are the stories told in these chapters? Is it a question of cherry-picking, of finding exceptional practitioners and letting their voices be heard? There are dozens of schools and teachers who are exemplars of creative practice who are not written about in this book. A completely different set of informants could have been selected and their stories would have been enlightening, perhaps even as imaginative and as inspirational as what's included. Indeed, I expect to be admonished by numerous principals, co-ordinators and teachers who will say, 'You know the good work we are doing, how come you didn't write about us?' Such questions will confirm the rude health of TY in certain schools. There will, I suspect, be others who will marvel at some of the stories told here and wonder could such practice flourish in the schools where they work. With TY posited on the idea of individual schools' freedom to devise their own programme and now with each of more than 600 schools throughout the country offering its own unique TY, unevenness of aspiration, provision and practice is almost inevitable. The wish is that the accounts in these chapters will inspire greater realisation of excellent TY programmes.

Freedom

As Irish society seeks renewal in these times of centenaries by revisiting previous episodes and individuals, the educational perspective of Padraic Pearse in *The Murder Machine* has a curious resonance with TY. Pearse wrote:

> The first thing I plead for, therefore, is freedom: freedom for each school to shape its own programme in conformity with the circumstances of the school as to place, size, personnel, and so on; freedom again for the individual teacher to impart something of his (*sic*) own personality to his work, to bring his own peculiar gifts to the services of his pupils, to be, in short, a teacher, a master, one having an intimate and permanent relationship with his pupils, and not a mere part of the educational machine, a mere cog in the wheel; freedom finally for the individual pupil and scope for his development within the school and within the system. And I would promote this idea of freedom by the very organisation of the school itself, giving a certain autonomy not only to the school, but to the particular parts of the school: to the staff, of course, but also to the pupils, and, in a large school, to the various sub-divisions of the pupils. I do not plead for anarchy. I plead for freedom within the law, for liberty, not licence, for that true freedom which can exist only where there is discipline, which exists in fact because each, valuing his own freedom, respects also the freedom of others (p. 35).

Cross-cultural learning

The final lens in this overview of TY is Korean. When, in 2013, Park Geun-hye took up elected office as President of the Republic of Korea, educators there knew change was on the cards. In her election manifesto, Mrs Park had signalled her intentions for school reform, particularly by introducing a 'free learning semester' (FLS). 'In FLS the focus is on "happy education", helping middle school students realise their talents and dreams,' explains Lee Ji-Jeon of the Korean Research Institute for Vocational Education and Training (KRIVET). Specifically, the FLS aims to activate career exploration and to stimulate the development of personality and creativity. Despite high ratings in PISA tests, the President and many Korean educators were concerned that the price being paid for a grind-type schooling culture was too much. Statistics for self-harm and suicide disturbed.

Researchers from KRIVET looked to the Irish TY and found much that appealed and inspired. Since then, students, teachers and policymakers, for example from Yonsei University, from Changnam Education Service and from KRIVET, have visited schools in Ireland to inform their planning. Prior to their visits, the Koreans typically read everything available about TY. They arrive with focused questions. For example, to what extent is TY a bottom-up development or a top-down one? They liked the idea of school-based curriculum development but wanted to know more about consistency across schools. How well did TY reduce stress in young people, maximise their happiness? How effective were monitoring and feedback mechanisms? How motivated were teachers to promote the active learning advocated in the *Guidelines*, especially giving greater 'voice' to students? When engaging with parents and community interests, how best to convince them of an unproven programme? How are 'life skills', communication skills, ability to relate to others, indeed any learning outside the conventional classroom, best assessed?

Following their visits to schools they often have incisive observations and further questions. In February 2015, twelve visitors from eastern Korea remarked on how well TY seemed to be tailored as creative responses to the obvious intercultural profile of the student population in two schools they visited. In another school, they observed that many students came from families that faced severe financial challenges and were impressed by this school's pastoral concern as well as their links with community organisations. They commented on how impressed they were with how another two schools had seized the opportunity of the Korean visitors to construct a rich cross-cultural learning experience, including language, music and art.

The visitors marvelled at the network of contacts another school had built with nearby employers, particularly for work experience. They recognised, almost instinctively, how work experiences placements might reinforce existing inequalities. They commented on TY being compulsory in some schools and optional in others, and explored some of the consequences of this flexibility. They remarked on how sensitively one of the schools catered for children with special educational needs.

The visitors liked some design features, such as the school that had extensive IT facilities and flexible classroom spaces. They commented on the teaching methods they had observed, including team teaching, mind-mapping, group work. The visitors posed questions about the balance between academic rigour and personal and social development activities in TY. They noticed varied leadership styles and remarked, in particular, how un-hierarchical some principals were. Perhaps most telling of all, as they stood back and sifted through what they had seen of TY in the schools they visited and tried to apply what is relevant to their situation in Korea, one remarked, 'Our focus is on young people's happiness. In each school these TY students seemed happier than schoolchildren in Korea.'

BIBLIOGRAPHY

Association of Secondary Teachers, Ireland (1994), *Transition Year Option, A Teacher Handbook*, Dublin: ASTI.

Association of Secondary Teachers, Ireland (2002), *Provision of Transition Year Education in Second-Level Schools, A Survey,* Dublin: ASTI.

Ball, S. (1997) 'Good School/Bad School: paradox and fabrication', *in British Journal of Sociology of Education*, Vol. 18. pp. 317–336.

Barth, R. (1990) *Improving School Plans from Within: Teachers, Parents and Principals Can Make the Difference*, San Francisco: Jossey-Bass.

Black, P. and William, D. (1998) 'Inside the Black Box, Raising Standards Through Classroom Assessment', *The Phi Delta Kappan*, Vol 80, No 2 (October 1998), pp. 139-148.

Black, P. and William, D. (2010), 'Kappan Classic: A Pleasant Surprise', *The Phi Delta Kappan* Vol. 92, No. 1 (September 2010), pp. 47-48

Briers, S. (2012) *Psychobabble, Exploding the Myths of the Self-Help Generation*, New York: Pearson.

Brookfield, S. (1995) *Becoming a Critical Reflective Teacher,* San Francisco: Jossey-Bass.

Byran, A. and Bracken M. (2011) *Learning to Read the World, Teaching, Teaching and Learning about Global Citizenship and International Development in Post-Primary Schools,* Drumcondra, Dublin: Centre for Human Development, St Patrick's College.

Burke, R. (1974) Address to the Regional Meeting of the Dublin Education Council for Secondary Schools, in Synge Street CBS, 2 December 1974.

Burke, R. (2001) *Interview with the author,* 16 November 2001.

Carter, S. and O'Cairbre, F. (2011). A study of the benefits of using the history of mathematics in Transition Year. In T. Dooley, D. Corcoran and M. Ryan (Eds.), *Proceedings of the Fourth National Conference on Research in Mathematics Education*, MEI 4, St Patrick's College, Drumcondra, Dublin, pp. 93-103.

Clerkin, A. (2012). Personal development in secondary education: The Irish Transition Year. *Education Policy Analysis Archives, 20 (38)*. Retrieved 3 December 2012 from http://epaa.asu.edu/ojs/article/view/1061.

Clowry, J. and Tennant, A. (2015) *Development Issues, A Course for Transition* , 2nd edition, Available at developmenteducation.ie.

Cohen, L. Manion, L. and Morrison K. (2000) *Research Methods in Education, 5th edition*, London and New York, Routledge Falmer.

Coláiste Bhride Carnew and St Peter's College, Dunboyne (2009) *Twenty Fifteen - Thoughts and reflections on the first Millennium Development Goal to eradicate poverty and hunger.* Carnew and Dunboyne: Colásite Bhríde and St Peter's College.

Coolahan, J. (2003) *Attracting, Developing and Retaining Effective Teachers – Country Background Report for Ireland* Paris: OECD:

Covey, Sean (1998) *The 7 Habits of Highly Effective Teens: The Ultimate Teenage Success* Guide, New York, Fireside Books.

Csikzentmihalyi, M. (1990) *Flow: The Problem of Optimal Experience*, New York: Harper Collins.

CEB (Curriculum and Examinations Board) (1986*) Transition Year Option, Guidelines for Schools,* Dublin: CEB.

Deane, P. (1997) The Transition Year: A case study in the implementation of curriculum change, Unpublished MEd thesis, NUI Maynooth.

Day, C., Stobart, G., Sammons, P., Kington, A. and Qing, G. (2007) *Teachers Matter: Connecting Lives, Work and Effectiveness,* Buckingham: Open University Press.

Dempsey, M. (2001) The Student Voice in the Transition Year Programme A school based case study, Unpublished MEd dissertation, NUI Maynooth.

DE (Department of Education) (1976), *Rules and Programmes for Secondary Schools,* Dublin: Stationery Office.

DE (1980) *White Paper on Educational Development*, Dublin: DoE.

DE (Department of Education) (1985), Circular Letter M85/85.

DE (Department of Education) (1993), *Transition Year Programme, Guidelines for Schools*, Dublin: Department of Education.

DE (Department of Education) (1993a), Circular Letter M31/93.

DE (Department of Education) (1993b), Circular Letter M47/93.

DE (Department of Education) (1994), Circular Letter M36/94.

DE (Department of Education) (1996), *Transition Year Programme 1994-95: An Evaluation by the Inspectorate of the Department of Education*, Dublin: Department of Education.

DES (Department of Education and Science) (1999a), *School Development Planning, An Introduction for Second Level Schools*, Dublin: Department of Education.

DES (Department of Education and Science) (1999b*) Commission on the Points System, Final Report and Recommendations*, Dublin, Stationery Office.

DES (Department of Education and Science) (2000a), Circular Letter M1/00.

DES (Department of Education and Science) (2000b), website *'A Brief Description of the Irish Education System'* http://www.irlgov.ie/educ/pdfs/education_system.pdf.

DES (Department of Education and Science) (2000c) *Report on the National Evaluation of the Leaving Certificate Applied*, Dublin: Department of Education.

DES (Department of Education and Science) (2001) Strategic Plan.

DES (2004) *A Brief Description of the Irish Education System*, Dublin: DES.

DES (2006) Resource for Transition Year Mathematics, Circular letter, 0060/2006.

Dewey, J (1915) *The School and Society and The Child and the Curriculum*, reprinted 2001, New York,: Dover Publications.

Doyle, E (1986) 'Transition Year Programmes: The Challenge' in *Journal of Institute of Guidance Counsellors*, Dublin: IGC.

Doyle, E. (1990) 'The Transition Year' in *Aspiration and Achievement: Curricular Initiatives in Irish Post-Primary Schools in the 1980s* edited by G. McNamara, K. Williams and D. Herron. Drumcondra: Teachers' Centre.

Doyle, E., Halton, M.A., Jeffers, G., Keane, M., Quish, D. (1994) *Transition Year Programme Resource Material,* Dublin: Department of Education.

Education Times (1974a) Martyn Turner Cartoon, June 7.

Education Times (1974b) 16 September 1974.

Egan, O. and O'Reilly, J. (1979) *The Transition Year Project,* in *Oideas 20,* Spring, Department of Education.

Egan, O. and O'Reilly, J. (1980) *The Transition Year Project* 1974-1979, An evaluation, Dublin: St. Patrick's College.

Eisner, E. (2002). 'The Arts and the Creation of Mind', In Chapter 4, What the Arts Teach and How It Shows. (pp. 70-92). Yale University Press. - See more at: http://www.arteducators.org/advocacy/10-lessons-the-arts-teach#sthash.dJ2OfU3G.dpuf.

Eisner, E. (1998) *The Kind of Schools We Need,* Portsmouth NH: Heinemann.

Elliott, I. (2000) *Creating Healthy Citizens: A Report of and recommendations from the Transition Year Student Health Fora in the Eastern Region,* Dublin: Health Promotion Department for the Area Health Boards of the Eastern Region.

Evans, R. (1996) *The Human Side of School Change: Reform, Resistance, and the Real-Life Problems of Innovation,* San Francisco: Jossey-Bass.

Fullan, M. and Hargreaves, A. (1992) *What's Worth Fighting for in Headship,* Buckingham: Open University Press.

Fullan, M. (1991) *The New Meaning of Educational Change,* 2nd edition, London: Cassel.

Fullan, M. (1993) *Change Forces,* London: Falmer Press.

Fullan, M. (1999) *Change Forces, The Sequel,* London: Falmer Press.

Fullan, M. (2001) *The New Meaning of Educational Change,* 3rd edition, London: RoutledgeFalmer.

Fullan, M. (2005) Education in Motion, *Leading in a Culture of Change,* UK and Ireland Workshop Tour, May 2005, www.michaelfullan.ca.

Gardner, H. (1984) *Frames of Mind: The Theory of Multiple Intelligences,* New York: Basic Books.

Gardner, H. (1993) *Multiple Intelligences: The Theory in Practice,* New York: Basic Books.

Bibliography

Gleeson, J., King, P., O'Driscoll, S. and Tormey, R. (2007) *Development Education in Irish Post-primary schools, Knowledge, Attitudes and Activism* Shannon and Limerick: Shannon Curriculum Devleopment Centre and Curriculum Evaluation and Policy Research Unit, University of Limerick.

Gleeson J. (2000) 'Sectoral interest versus the common good? Legitimation, Fragmentation and Contestation in Irish Post-Primary Curriculum Policy and Practice' in *Irish Educational Studies*, Spring 2000 Vol. 19.

Gleeson, J. (2004) 'Cultural and Political Contexts of Irish Post-Primary Curriculum: Influences, Interests and Issues' in C. Sugrue (editor) *Curriculum and Ideology: Irish Experiences, International Perspectives*, Dublin: The Liffey Press.

Gleeson, J. Conboy, P. Walsh, A. (2004) *The Piloting of Exploring Masculinities Context, Implementation and Issues arising, Report of External Evaluation*, Dublin: Department of Education and Science.

Gleeson, J. (2010) *Curriculum in context: Praxis, partnership and power.* Oxford: Peter Lang

Goodson, I. (1994) *Studying Curriculum*, Milton Keynes, The Open University.

Government of Ireland (1992) *Education for a Changing World, Green Paper*, Dublin: Stationery Office.

Government of Ireland (1995) *Charting Our Education Future, White Paper*, Dublin: Stationery Office.

Granville, Gary (2006), *Cultivating Professional Growth: An Emergent Approach to Teacher Development. Final Evaluation Report on the Experience and Impact of the Second Level Support Service* Dublin: SLSS

Greene, M. (1995) *Releasing the Imagination: Essays on Education, the Arts and Social Change*, New York: Wiley.

Greene, M. (2013) 'The Turning of the Leaves: Expanding Our Vision for the Arts in Education,' *Harvard Educational Review* Vol. 83, No. 1 Spring 2013, pp. 251-252.

Halton, M.A. and Jeffers, G. (1996) *In Search of Europe, Resource Pack* Dublin: Department of Education and European Commission Representation in Ireland.

Hanafin, M. (2005) Press release on the occasion of the launch of *The Transition Year Programme: An Assessment*, 5 January, Dublin: Department of Education and Science.

Hargreaves, A. Earl, L Ryan, J (1996) *Schooling for Change, Reinventing Education for Early Adolescents*, London: Falmer Press.

Hayes, S., Childs, P. and O'Dwyer, A. (2013). Science in the Irish transition year: an opportunity to change the way science is taught. In T. Plomp, and N. Nieveen (Eds.), *Educational design research – Part B: Illustrative cases* (pp. 733-755). Enschede, the Netherlands: SLO.

Humphreys, E. (1996b) 'Transition Year: Its contribution to Whole School Development' in Hogan P (editor) *Issues in Education, Vol. 1*, Dublin ASTI.

Humphreys, E. (1998) 'Transition Year - An opportunity for creative assessment', in A. Hyland (Editor) *Innovations in Assessment in Irish Education, Multiple Intelligences, Curriculum and Assessment project*, Education Department, University College, Cork.

Irish Aid (2013) *One World, One Future, Ireland's Policy for International Development*, Dublin: Department of Foreign Affairs.

Irish Independent (2000) 11 January

Irish Independent (2008) 17 September

Irish Independent (2009) 4 June.

Irish Times, (1996) 'Department tells 10% of secondary schools to improve their transition year programmes', 14 February.

Irish Times (2005) 1 July.

Irish Times (2013) 'President warns of 'danger' of disregarding creativity' 16 May.

Irish Second Level Students Union (ISSU) (2014) *Transition Year Exploring the Student Experience*, Dublin ISSU.

Jackson, M. (2012) 'Ethos Both a Habitat and a Way of Life" in Schools – Archbishop Tells Conference' at http://dublin.anglican.org/news/2012/11/Ethos-Both-a-Habitat-and-a-Way-of-Life-in-Schools--Archbishop-Tells-Conference.php.

Jeffers, G. (2002) 'Transition Year Programme and Educational Disadvantage', in *Irish Educational Studies*, Vol. 21, No. 2.

Jeffers, G. (2003a) 'The Senior Cycle and the Guidance Counsellor' in *Guideline, Newsletter of the Institute of Guidance Counsellors*, October 2003, Dublin: Institute of Guidance Counsellors.

Jeffers, G. (2003b) 'Work Experience Can be the University of Life' in *Business and Finance*, 6 November 2003 Dublin: Moranna.

Jeffers, G. (2006a) 'Talking about teaching in non-crisis situations: learning from a teacher support project' in *Irish Educational Studies,* Vol 25, No. 2.

Jeffers, G. (2006b), 'School guidance counsellors leaning through work experience placements' in *Reflective Practice,* Vol 7, No 3, August.

Jeffers, G. (2006c) 'Conversation on Teaching and Learning: A Challenge for School Leadership', in *Oideas* 52.

Jeffers, G. (2007) *Attitudes to Transition Year, Summary of a Report to the Department of Education and Science,* Maynooth: Education Department, NUIM.

Jeffers G. (2008a) 'Innovation and Resistance in Irish Education, The Case of Transition Year' PhD thesis, University of Limerick. Available at http://eprints.maynoothuniversity.ie/1227/1/JeffersPhD.pdf.

Jeffers, G. (2008b) 'Parents want more dialogue about Transition Year' in *Irish Independent* 17 September http://www.independent.ie/life/family/learning/in-my-opinion-parents-want-more-dialogue-about-transition-year-26477561.html.

Jeffers, G. (2011) 'The Transition Year programme in Ireland. Embracing and resisting a curriculum innovation', in *Curriculum Journal,* Vol 22: No 1, 61–76.

Jeffers, G. (2012). *Work experience placements in school programmes: stretching horizons.* Paper presented at the Educational Studies Association of Ireland annual conference, Cork, March 30.

Joint Oireatchtas Committee on Education and Science (2004), Proceedings, 25 March 2004, Vol 32.

Kamp, A. and Black, D. (2014) *3 PLY Exploring the Limits and Possibilities for Transformative Workplace Learning in Irish Schools, Proceedings, European Conference on Education Research,* Porto, 2-5 September 2014. Available at http://doras.dcu.ie/20270/1/KAMP%26BLACK_3_PLY_ECER2014.pdf

Kahneman, D. (2013) *Thinking, Fast and Slow* New York: Farrar, Strauss and Giroux.

Kellaghan, T. and Lewis, M. (1991). *Transition education in Irish schools.* Dublin: Educational Company of Ireland.

Kelly, D. (2014) 'The New Junior Cycle: Learning from an Innovation in Transition' in *Pathways to Innovation and Development in Education, A Collection of Invited Essays,* edited by Rose Dolan. Maynooth University, *eprints.maynoothuniversity.ie/5788/*

Kolb, D. (1983) *Experiential Learning: Experience as the Source of Learning and Development*, New Jersey: Prentice Hall.

Leithwood, K., Louis, K.S., Anderson, S. and Wahlstrom, K. (2004) *How Leadership Influences Student Learning, Review of Research,* University of Minnesota, Ontario Institute for Studies in Education and the Wallace Foundation.

Levitt, S. and Dubner, S. (2005) *Freakonomics: A Rogue Economist Explores the Hidden Side of Everything,* New York: HarperCollins.

Lewis, M. and McMahon, L. (1996) *Evaluation of a Training of Trainers in Service Education Model: The Transition Year in-Career Development Programme,* Dublin: Educational Research Centre.

Lorenzi, F. and White, L. (2013) *Evaluation of the Fighting Words creative writing model,* Dublin: School of Education Studies, Dublin City University. Available at http://www.fightingwords.ie/publications/dcu-report-fighting-words-model.

Madaus, G. (1988) 'The distortion of teaching and testing: High-stakes testing and instruction', *Peabody Journal of Education,* Vol. 65, pp 29-46.

Mental Health Ireland (2001) *Mental Health Matters,* Dun Laoghaire, Mental Health Ireland.

Millar, D. and Kelly, D. (1999) From Junior to Leaving Certificate, A Longitudinal Study of 1994 Junior Certificate Candidates who took the Leaving Certificate Examination in 1997, Final Report, Dublin: ERC/NCCA.

Moynihan, J. (2013) *Work experience in transition year: a mixed methods study of subject and career choices*, PhD thesis. Cork: University College. Avalable at https://cora.ucc.ie/handle/10468/1259.

Murphy, I. (1999) 'Evaluation of Transition Year in 18 Second-level Schools' in *Nuachliter do Chigirí agus Síceolaithe na Roinne,* Umih 5.

NCCA (2002) *Developing Senior Cycle Education, Consultative Paper on Issues and Options,* Dublin: National Council for Curriculum and Assessment.

NCCA (2003a) *Developing Senior Cycle Education: Report on the Consultative Process – Consultative Meetings, Seminars and Submissions* Dublin: National Council for Curriculum and Assessment.

NCCA (2003b) *Developing Senior Cycle Education, Directions for Development*, Dublin: National Council for Curriculum and Assessment.

NCCA (2006) *Social, Personal and Health Education Curriculum Framework for Senior Cycle, Report on Consultation*, Dublin: National Council for Curriculum and Assessment.

Newton, P., Driver, R and Osborne, J. (2010). The place of argumentation in the pedagogy of school science. *International Journal of Science Education*, 21(5), 553-576.

Noddings, N. (2005) *The Challenge to Care in Schools, An Alternative Approach to Education*, New York: Teachers College Press.

O Cairbre, F., McKeon, J. and Watson (2006) *A Resource for Transition Year Mathematics Teachers:* Dublin: Stationery Office.

OECD (1991) *Review of National Policies for Education: IRELAND*, Paris: Organisation for Economic Co-Operation and Development.

OECD (2005) *Teachers Matter: Attracting, Developing and Retaining Effective Teachers* OECD: Paris.

Palmer, P.J. (1998) *The Courage to Teach: Exploring the Inner Landscape of a Teacher's Life*, San Francisco: Jossey-Bass.

Reichental, T (2011) *I was a Boy in Belsen*, Dublin: O'Brien Press.

RIAI (1997) *Shaping Space, Architecture in the Transition Year*, Dublin: Royal Institute of Architects of Ireland.

Rudduck, J. and Flutter, J. (2004) *How to Improve your School: Giving Pupils a Voice*, London: Continuum.

Ryan, A., Corkery, B., Cooke Harkin, C., Moran, J., Cawley, P. and Frend, L. (2004) *Transition Year Minicompany, Get Up and Go Programme Materials and for Students and Teachers*, Dublin: Second Level Support Service. Available at http://www.pdst.ie/sites/default/files/GetUpAndGoManual.pdf.

Sarason, S. (1990) *The Predictable Failure of Educational Reform*, San Francisco: Jossey-Bass.

Schein, E. (1992) *Organisational Culture and Leadership* (2nd edition), San Francisco: Jossey-Bass.

Senge, P.M. (1990) *The Fifth Discipline: The Art and Practice of the Learning Organisation*, London: Century Business.

Sergiovanni, T.J. (1994) *Building Community in Schools*, San Francisco: Jossey-Bass.

Sergiovanni, T.J. (1996) *Leadership for the Schoolhouse*, San Francisco: Jossey-Bass.

Smyth, E. (1999) *Do Schools Differ? Academic and Personal Development among Pupils in the Second Level Sector*, Dublin: Oak Tree Press.

Smyth, E., Byrne, D. and Hannan, C. (2004) *The Transition Year Programme: An Assessment*, Dublin: Economic and Social Research Institute and Liffey Press.

Snow, C.P (1959)*The Two Cultures*, Cambridge: Cambridge University Press.

Stenhouse, L. (1978) *An introduction to Curriculum Research and Development*, London: Heinemann.

Stoll, L. and Fink, D. (1995) *Changing Our Schools*, Buckingham: Open University Press.

Sugrue, C., Morgan, M., Devine, D. and Raftery, D. (2001) *Policy and Practice of Professional Development for Primary and Post-primary Teachers in Ireland: A critical analysis* (unpublished).

Teaching Council (2012) *Code of Professional Conduct for Teachers*, Maynooth: Teaching Council.

Trant, A. (2007), *Curriculum Matters in Ireland*, Dublin: Blackhall.

TYST (Transition Year Support Team) (1994-1998) *Transition News* Issues No 1–9, TYST, Blackrock Education Centre, Dún Laoghaire, Co. Dublin

TYCSS (Transition Year Curriculum Support Service) (1998-2002) *Transition News* Issues No 10–14, Transition Year Curriculum Support Service, Blackrock Education Centre, Dún Laoghaire, Co. Dublin.

TYCSS (Transition Year Curriculum Support Service) (1999a) *Writing the Transition Year Programme*, TYCSS, Blackrock Education Centre, Dún Laoghaire, Co. Dublin.

TYCSS (Transition Year Curriculum Support Service) (1999b) *Relationships between the Transition Year Programme and 'disadvantage'* A report to the Department of Education and Science, Transition Year Curriculum Support Service, Dún Laoghaire, Co. Dublin.

TYCSS (Transition Year Curriculum Support Service) (1999c) *Transition Year: Some Recent Research*, TYCSS, Blackrock Education Centre, Dún Laoghaire, Co. Dublin.

TYCSS (Transition Year Curriculum Support Service) (2000a), *Supporting Teaching and Learning: Project Work*, Blackrock Education Centre, Dún Laoghaire, Co. Dublin.

TYCSS (Transition Year Curriculum Support Service) (2000b), *Transition Year Survey on Co-ordination, Report on Findings,* Blackrock Education Centre, Dún Laoghaire, Co. Dublin.

United Nations (1989) *United Nations Convention on the Rights of the Child,* New York: UN.

Ward, C. (2004) The Impact of Transition Year on Teachers: An Investigation of the Effect of Teaching an Innovative Programme on Classroom Practice, Collegiality and Professional Self-Concept. MEd (School Leadership) Unpublished dissertation, Education Department, NUI Maynooth.

Warwick Commission (2015) *The 2015 Report by the Warwick Commission on the Future of Cultural Value,* Warwick University. http:// www2.warwick.ac.uk/research/warwickcommission/futureculture/ finalreport/

Wilkinson, R. and Pickett, K. (2011) *The Spirit Level: Why Greater Equality Makes Societies Stronger,* New York: Boomsbury

Wyn, J. (2009). 'Touching the future: Building skills for life and work.' *Australian Education Review* 55. Melbourne: Australian Council for Educational Research.

Zimmer-Gembeck, M. and Mortimer, J. (2006) 'Adolescent work, vocational development and education' in *Review of Educational Research,* Vol. 76, pp. 537-566.

INDEX

288